The Common Market's Labor Programs

THE

COMMON

MARKET'S

LABOR PROGRAMS

MARK J. FITZGERALD, C.S.C.

Professor of Economics, University of Notre Dame

UNIVERSITY OF NOTRE DAME PRESS · 1966
NOTRE DAME AND LONDON

331.094
F554

Library of Congress Catalog Card No.: 66–24922
Manufactured in the U.S.A.

PREFACE

IN THE FIFTEENTH YEAR OF THE COAL AND STEEL COMMUNITY and in the ninth year of the Economic Community and the Atomic Energy Community (Euratom), a period of transition has passed the halfway mark toward achievement of the Common Market in Europe. Despite recurring political crises, the overwhelming success that has already favored the economic program of the European Community—composed of France, Germany, Italy, Belgium, The Netherlands and Luxembourg—is widely acknowledged.

Nevertheless, the remarkable achievement in the economic phase of the Common Market agenda has tended to make almost the entire present concern of American interest in the European Community relate to the impact which that institution has on world trade and the American economy. What is overlooked is the area of notable internal changes in the social and economic structures that are envisaged for the several nations comprising the Common Market.

One of the significant internal changes specified in the treaties establishing the Communities has to do with the whole field of the worker in relation to his living and working conditions. To this end, attention will be given in the following chapters to the precedent-making programs of international research sponsored by the European Economic Community and the European Coal and Steel Community in the fields of vocational training, conditions of employment, wage standards, health and safety and social security. Note is also taken of their programs relating to research on worker housing projects, regional development and studies supported by the Communities on general trends in the area of labor-management relations. New sources of data and new forms of national and supranational associations have been utilized for this presentation. The past record of actual financing of housing projects—especially by the European Coal and Steel Community—is also given attention.

Since comparison with American experience in several of the labor programs of concern to the Common Market brings out rather sharp contrasts, some attention is given in certain chapters to the developments in this country.

At this point a brief description of the relationship between various branches and organizations of the Communities, as presently constituted, might be helpful for better understanding of their respective roles in bringing to fruition current accomplishments in the general area of labor affairs. Some modifications of their future functions, as set forth in the pending merger treaty, will also be noted.

The European Economic Community, established by the Treaty of Rome in 1957, has for its administrative board a commission consisting of nine members, each in charge of a particular activity. However, this commission is collectively answerable for its decisions. Similar to the European Coal and Steel Community, no more than two members of the executive board may come from one country of the Community. A president and two vice-presidents are appointed from within the commission. Serving as an advisory body for both the European Economic Commission and the Euratom Commission is the Economic and Social Committee.

A commission of five members serves as the executive body in charge of the European Atomic Energy Community. The commissioners are chosen for their special competence to pursue the objectives of the Euratom treaty of 1957.

The European Coal and Steel Community, established by the Treaty of Paris in 1951, has been administered by the High Authority, a board of nine members. The Consultative Committee, discussed below in conjunction with the Economic and Social Committee, functions in an advisory capacity with respect to the High Authority.

Each of the executive bodies for the three Communities is responsible to a council of six ministers representing the national governments. At times they are the six foreign ministers, but depending on the agenda for a given session, cabinet ministers in other fields may substitute for the foreign ministers.

The two treaties which established the Economic Community and the Atomic Energy Community have placed in a council of ministers the power of decision on whether a given policy proposed by the commission is to be adopted for execution by the commission. In this sense, it has been said, the council acts as the legislature for these two Communities. By contrast, the Treaty of Paris empowered the High Authority of the European Coal and Steel Community to draft policies, adopt them and put them in effect. Accordingly, the control of the Council over the Coal and Steel Community has been less rigid than that over the other two Communities.

The European Parliamentary Assembly, now consisting of 142 members who are elected from their own ranks by the six national parliaments, serves as a reviewing body for the European Coal and Steel Community as well as for the other two Communities. It is not actually a law-making assembly, but each Community must submit annual reports to the European Parliament as well as explain and defend policies and programs. The European Parliament has the ultimate power of sanction, including dismissal, over the High Authority and the commissions.

In recent years the European Parliament has been very active in using the committee approach to analyze and evaluate the work being done by the three executive bodies of the Communities. It endeavors to keep in close communication with the executive boards and the councils of ministers. As a strong proponent of the European Community, it does not hesitate to offer criticism and recommendations when it regards a particular policy or program as deficient.

For all three Communities the Court of Justice, which presides at the Hague, has been instituted to ensure adherence to law in the interpretation and execution of the separate treaties. The Court is composed of seven independent judges appointed by agreement among the member governments.

In consequence of the merger treaty of 1965, which has not yet been ratified by the member states, the executive boards of the three Communities would be fused, and the three currently separate councils of ministers would become one body empowered to decide policies for the three Communities. Within a definite time period the commission for the three Communities would consist of nine members. Initially, however, there would be 14 members on a single commission.

A common budgetary authority for the three Communities would be the commission, the European Parliament and the Council of Ministers, as set forth above.

Like its predecessors, the new commission would be responsible to the European Parliament, which would continue to have power of sanction over the executive branch.

ACKNOWLEDGMENTS

A NUMBER OF PEOPLE WERE MOST HELPFUL DURING THE WRIT-ing of this volume. Particular mention is made here of the guidance and encouragement of George N. Shuster, Thomas J. McDonagh and the sage comments of Kurt Braun, Chief of Western Europe Section, U. S. Department of Labor. Gratitude is due Louis F. Buckley and Louis J. Putz for reading the manuscript and to Mrs. Peter Papandria who typed it. Valuable source material was made available by Leonard Tennyson, Gianfranco Speranza and Stephen Freidberg of the European Community. Meyer Bernstein and George P. Delaney were most helpful in arranging research schedules in Europe. I am grateful to Stephen Kertesz as well as to Clayton P. Lewis for their interest in this project. Special thanks is due the O'Brien Foundation for a grant toward the completion of this study.

CONTENTS

1.

The Advisory Organs
of the Communities

THE EUROPEAN ECONOMIC COMMUNITY

ECONOMIC AND SOCIAL COMMITTEE

IN PART FIVE THE TREATY OF ROME STIPULATES: "THERE SHALL hereby be established an Economic and Social Committee with consultative status."[1] It is true that the Treaty does not quite consider the Committee as a Community institution in the full sense of the word; nevertheless, it gives considerable attention to setting forth the Committee's salient characteristics. Membership is drawn from such representative groups as "producers, agriculturists, transport operators, workers, merchants, artisans, the liberal professions" and the general interest areas.[2]

By Treaty requirement, in order to give some latitude in making appointments each member state at regular intervals sends to the Council of Ministers a list of twice as many names as officially allotted for membership from that state. It is the responsibility of the Council to see that the composition of the Committee duly recognizes the existing categories of economic and social life in the Community. For guidance in making its selections, the Council may seek the opinions of European organizations represented in the Economic Community.

It is evident that thus far the Council has been content to choose members for the Committee directly from the lists sent by member

1

governments, without exercising its right to consult with European economic and social organizations.

As now constituted, one-third of the Committee's membership comes from employer organizations, one-third from trade union groups, and the remaining third is made up of the liberal professions. The Committee includes lawyers, economists, consumer representatives, as well as farmers, merchants and representatives from small business.

Membership is set at the figure of 101, with Germany, France and Italy each having 24 representatives. By unanimous vote of the Council of the Community, Committee members are appointed for a term of four years, which may be renewed. Considerable significance is seen in Article 194 of the Treaty, which specifies that the members of the Committee shall be appointed on their own merits and are to be under no mandatory instructions from their respective governments. Over the five years of the Committee's existence there has been a very stable membership, with a turnover of only 10 to 15 per cent.

On specific economic areas mentioned in the Treaty, such as agriculture and transport, the Committee shall be consulted by the Council or Commission. On other matters the Committee may be consulted if the Council or Commission deem it appropriate.

ORIGIN OF THE COMMITTEE

At the time the Treaty of Rome was being drafted, there was no unanimous support for the establishment of the Economic and Social Committee. In Germany, and to some degree in Italy, the very nature of such an institution was hardly known, and to a certain extent this situation remains true in those countries even at present.

Thus little interest in the proposal was shown by the Germans, who saw no great advantage in establishing the Committee when some countries had no previous experience with this type of structure. There was fear that the mechanism of the Community would be needlessly complicated by this elaborate consultative organism, which might serve to slow up urgent action.

It was actually at the initiative of the Benelux countries and of France that the Committee became part of the Economic Community's structure. In Belgium and The Netherlands there were also in existence advisory bodies partly similar in nature and function to the Community's present Economic and Social Committee. France likewise has had a similar group of economic and social advisors for some years prior to the Treaty of Rome.

There was at the start a mild tendency among the various economic and social groups represented to align themselves on nationalistic patterns. The movement was soon discontinued, however, when it was found that the members who took an active part in Committee deliberations could not be subdivided along such lines. They were, nevertheless, inclined to observe European divisions according to the categories of employers, employees and the so-called third group. The latter designation supposedly covers representatives who are not so directly related to the other two segments in the Committee. Especially during the plenary sessions, when decisions are being made on the European aspect of problems under consideration, there is rarely a nationalistic separation of points of view, such as French, German or Dutch, but instead all approaches converge on the project as a European problem. Recently France has modified this approach.

The Committee is empowered by the Treaty to adopt its own rules of procedure, after Council approval, and to appoint its own chairman and officers for a term of two years. It is significant that one of the first efforts to revise the Committee's rules of procedure had to do with an attempt of some members to give more importance to the Committee by trying to establish a so-called right of initiative in bringing issues to the Council or Executive Commission.

Previously the language of the Treaty always had been interpreted to mean that the Council or Commission first had to request the Committee to formulate an opinion on some particular issue. Yet from the start of the Committee's activity some members have regarded this restriction as a weak point in its structure. For them it appeared that if the Committee were to have a significant role in the Community, it would have to take the initiative in studying various problems. The rules of procedure thus far remain as originally approved by the Council.

FORMULATING OF COMMITTEE OPINIONS

From Article 198 of the Treaty of Rome it would appear that an advisory rather than an active role is assigned to the Economic and Social Committee. The Article reads as follows:

> The Committee shall be consulted by the Council or by the Commission in the cases provided for in this Treaty. The Committee may be consulted by these institutions in all cases in which they deem it appropriate.

Though Article 197 of the Treaty mentions only agriculture and transport as the special concern of subcommittees, in actuality there are many other specialized sections carrying on studies in preparation for opinions, under the general competency of the Committee as a whole.

The subcommittees prepare draft opinions for the consideration of the Committee. Moreover, the Council or Commission may not bypass the Committee as a whole by requesting an opinion directly from a subcommittee or specialized section. Only after an opinion by a specialized section has been given final approval by the Committee, may it be submitted to the Council or Commission of the Community.

On matters of agriculture and transport the Committee must be consulted by the Council and Commission.[3] The Treaty also imposes on the Council or Commission the obligation to consult the Committee in regard to harmonization of legislation and policy in regard to such matters as employment, social security, working conditions, vocational training, protection against occupational hazards, laws on trade unions and collective bargaining.[4] A similar obligation is imposed on the Council of Ministers by the Treaty of Rome to consult the Economic and Social Committee on matters relating to ending restrictions on freedom of establishing an economic enterprise within the Community.[5] Another issue, which by Treaty also requires consultation with the Economic and Social Committee by the Council or Commission, relates to the European Social Fund.

According to Article 198 of the Treaty, the Council or Commission, if necessary, may set a time limit for the Committee to submit an opinion on a question presented to it. However, this time limit may not be less than 10 days. If at the end of this period, no opinion is forthcoming from the Committee, the Council or Commission may proceed without it. Though there are no published proceedings of the Committee, Article 198 of the Treaty requires that a record of the deliberations must accompany the submission of an opinion. The foregoing provisions of the Treaty have given a considerable scope of responsibility to be exercised by members of the Committee.

Though there was not much action taken in the first two years of the Committee's existence, this initial period was of great importance in resisting hostile opposition and in testing initial procedures. It was a rather formidable task to bring into concrete application the regulations the Treaty had laid down for the Committee, especially when strong support for the Committee was lacking at that time among some member states.

In the second phase of the Committee, during its third and fourth years of existence, the chairmanship was held by Ludwig Rosenberg, vice-president of DGB, the German Federation of Trade Unions. Through his great personal influence and dynamic leadership, considerable progress was made in the development of the Committee.

Rosenberg began his chairmanship with visits to the different capitals of the member states and endeavored to meet with his counterpart in the various national economic and social committees. On each visit he also met with representatives of the national governments, who, at the time or later, were members of the Council of the Community.

Rosenberg's personal influence played a large part in increasing the importance of the Committee within the Community. During his tenure as chairman, the Committee was consulted very frequently by the Council or Commission, even on problems where there was no obligation to seek consultation under the terms of the Treaty. As instances of such nonobligatory consultation the Committee was asked to submit opinions in regard to Community policy on energy and cartels.

The third chairman of the Committee was Emile Roche of France, who also exercised dynamic leadership and a determination to enhance the powers of the Committee. He was the first chairman to put stress on the need of consulting the Committee, not only on very specific, minor problems but also on broad policy questions, as had been done earlier in a few instances. Also under Roche's chairmanship a revision was begun of the regulations on procedure for the Committee, especially concerning initiative in regard to consultation. There was strong hope at the time that this revision would considerably enhance the importance of the Committee.

Though the language of the Treaty provides no legal basis for such initiative, it is believed that an arrangement could be made so members of the Committee might request to submit an opinion on a particular problem. This desire first would be made known to the Committee chairman who in turn would inform the Council or Commission, thus seeking a ruling on such a submission.

GROUPS REPRESENTED ON THE COMMITTEE

In regard to the specialized sections established by the Committee in accordance with Article 197 of the Treaty, it is possible that the authors of the Treaty had in mind highly technical subdivisions. However, the composition of the Committee is, in fact, on such a broad scope that rarely are members found who have specialized in narrow technical fields. For example, it is not possible to find nuclear energy experts in each of the member states' delegations. In practice, therefore, the specialized sections have tended to reflect the general educational and economic background of the Committee members as a whole.

Each member of the Committee is assigned a specific area of

responsibility in some economic or social sector, such as transportation, agriculture, developing countries, social problems and nuclear energy. All projects submitted to the Committee for comment are first referred to these specific technical divisions of the Committee, where working committees are formed to study each project in detail. Then reports are drafted, which are considered and discussed in plenary sessions before votes are taken and conclusions adopted for ultimate transmittal to the Council of Ministers.

Since care has been taken to have representatives of all the member states in each specialized section, opinions submitted by subcommittees to a plenary session of the Committee do not provoke anew a second study of the problem under discussion. This arrangement greatly helps to expedite procedures for authorization of opinions. It is true that one or two points of a report might be changed in the plenary session—only a minor delay compared to that caused by a new study.

As acknowledged in the Secretariat of the Committee, a common objection to the third group on the Committee is that instead of being a truly independent body of specialists and professional people, it has a rather amorphous character. For example, one Committee member in this group is associated with savings banks. He looks and acts like a banker and, therefore, may be aligned with employer interests; yet, in actuality, it cannot be said that he represents employers or industry or finance, for the funds entrusted to his savings banks belong largely to employees and small industry. Accordingly, his background, from the point of view of the Secretariat, properly entitles him to representation in the general interest group.

Another instance cited was a Belgian professor associated with various economic institutions who was also a member of Belgium's Central Council of the Economy. He was considered to be of independent stature, allied with neither employers nor workers.

A member of the Committee who was designated as a spokesman of consumer interests, and therefore in the third group, represented the Belgian flour industry and was also a vice-president of the National Union of Belgian Consumers.

True, members such as spokesmen from small industry, who tend to view issues from the aspect of the employer, can be found in the group designated as representing the general interest. In contrast with the third group in the International Labor Organization—which is made up of government representatives and which can take a middle position for most countries between workers and employers—a large segment of the third group in the Economic and Social Committee is regarded as employer orientated by union members of the Committee.

Nevertheless, the chairman of the Committee in 1963, Emile Roche, was not only a journalist and author prior to his membership on the Committee but also had a background in French political life. He was not regarded as a representative of either employer or worker groups, but one of the general interest section.

As a concrete instance, to challenge the objection that the third group tends to reflect the views of employers, one might recall that in 1960 the Committee had to issue an important opinion on a proposal of the Commission in regard to agricultural policy. The proposal of the Commission was adopted by a majority of the Committee, through the cooperation of the third group and worker representatives, in opposition to a heavy vote by employer representatives.

The issue put to a vote related to whether the Community would develop more fully its own agricultural resources or continue to be dependent in the future on food imports from countries outside the Common Market. The German point of view, largely supported by employer representatives on the Committee, stressed that there was no need for concern about greater agricultural production, since German industry was not only well equipped to export manufactured goods on a large scale, but also considerably beyond the volume which could be absorbed by the Common Market itself. The Germans, therefore, favored continued dependence on nonmember nations for agricultural supplies.

It might be noted that despite differences in points of view, the personal qualifications of the Committee membership are of high order and, on the whole, the various economic and social sectors of the Community are rather well represented. Ranking leaders from the member countries in the fields of labor and industry are members of the Committee.

POLITICAL ROLE OF THE COMMITTEE

Over the years of the Committee's existence, its potential importance has become realized within the Community. As one indication, there is now awareness that the Committee may serve as a possible channel for directing pressure groups. It is convenient today for top officials, when approached directly on some issue, to say that there is an institution at hand within the Community where expression can be given to particular views on matters being considered by the Council or the Commission. With such a forum for the meeting of pressure groups, it is believed there is less danger of any one focal center of influence exerting a disproportionate impact on policy. Instead, the various pressure areas may tend to neutralize each other.

In any event value is seen in the possibility that through the Economic and Social Committee the Commission may know in advance of a potential reaction to the application of a new ruling under consideration. If there is to be opposition, it is considered advantageous to know about it ahead of time.

The Economic and Social Committee in effect is a quasi-"European Parliament" as related to the Executive Commission of the Community. Nevertheless, the Committee has no legislative power. All instruments of authority are prepared by the Commission itself; texts of such documents are then sent to the Economic and Social Committee for comment and advice, prior to rendering of decisions by the Council of Ministers.

This procedure has important significance, since the original drafts first seen by the Council of Ministers are prepared by technical experts only. The Economic and Social Committee, representing a broader cross-section of the Community than technicians, makes possible in every conference a confrontation between the theoretical contributions of the technicians and the myriad realities as experienced by the members of the Economic and Social Committee. Before a final legislative draft is drawn, the Council of Ministers weighs the counsel offered by Committee members.

No institutional relation exists between the Economic and Social Committee and the European Parliament. However, the president of the Committee has informal, personal communications with members of the Parliament. Again, the Committee has no official channel to the Consultative body of the European Coal and Steel Community. Regret has been expressed over this situation, and there is a movement now to establish a formal relationship.

Yet there is advantage in providing a meeting place where leaders among employers and workers from the member states may express their approval of a certain Community project. It is assumed that later in their particular industry or union of the home country, they will explain to all concerned why they voted in the affirmative on a project. In case the issue on which action is to be taken, such as free movement of workers, may bring some practical difficulties in a Committee member's industry or union, he can help prepare the way for the changes. At any rate, when at home, a complete change to disapproval of a ruling or project, previously endorsed by a member at a meeting of the Economic and Social Committee, is not very likely. This auxiliary role of the Committee and its members is an additional reason why there has been a gradual gain in the importance assigned to the Committee's function by the various institutions making up the Community.

Nevertheless, it is not quite certain that all or most of the individuals who hold key positions in industry, unions or other callings in their respective countries will seek reappointment on the Committee. Instead, they may plead that excessive burdens of responsibility in their home countries make it too difficult to spend a large part of their time at Committee meetings in Brussels, in addition to days of preparation.

There has been a suggestion by some members that insofar as continued service on the Committee is concerned, a better response might be obtained from these top echelon individuals who have economic and social responsibility in their home countries if all the preparatory work for subcommittees were done by staff personnel. Committee members would then be required to come to Brussels only for the purpose of making crucial decisions. Moreover, a delegate or technical advisor might represent members during the days of preparation prior to the plenary sessions of the Committee.

Other members of the Committee would prefer to keep the present type of Committee membership, with more use of experts as advisors to the members. Though such experts do not take part in questions of policy or in plenary sessions of the Committee, they presently do participate in studies by working on specific problems. It has been proposed that each Committee member should have one of these experts as a permanent counselor. However, there exists a practical barrier to such a proposal, since even at present Committee funds do not provide for compensating the experts now available.

Further, it has been stressed that the Economic and Social Committee was not intended to be a forum for the meeting of technicians, but rather to formulate broader aspects of policy. Experts are intended to serve only as functionaries for the Community. In addition, such a change in the responsibilities and procedures for members of the Committee would require the approval of the Council. There is no certainty that this modification would be approved.

Another phase of procedure where the Secretariat might welcome revision concerns the regulation against publicity of the Committee's opinions. At present they are available only to the Council or the Commission. It is said this is a point of dissatisfaction with many members of the Economic and Social Committee. Moreover, there might be real advantage to publicity for a fully developed opinion, approved by the Committee in plenary session. Publication of such an opinion would give to the world the fruits of the long labors of the Committee. It is hoped, therefore, that eventually opinions of the Committee will be made matters of public record, with minority views attached.

There is agreement that the public should not attend the sessions of the Committee and that journalists should not be present. It is felt that the deliberative value of the Committee might be impaired if journalists had the opportunity to put emphasis on some point in the discussions of slight actual importance.

Then, too, some Committee members contend that publication of the proceedings might encourage certain individuals on the Committee to make speeches for home consumption. Such a tendency might lessen the deliberative quality of Committee sessions as now constituted, which aims to avoid nationalism and arrive at European solutions. If all discussions were open to the public, or available later in published form, certain Committee members might fear for their political interests in their home countries. As a consequence there might be less willingness to accept compromises, often necessary, on the European level.

Though merit is seen by Committee members in the practice of not publishing the proceedings of its sessions, it has been suggested, nevertheless, that in certain instances there may be a necessity for it. In any event the chairman of the Economic and Social Committee always gives a press conference, so that important issues get to journalists.

The majority opinions of the Committee have usually supported proposals made by the Commission. This positive and constructive approach may be one of the factors accounting for the continued influence growth of the Committee. Since the Commission has been experiencing some opposition to its proposals in the European Parliament, the large scale endorsement of its agenda by the Economic and Social Committee has been particularly welcome.

From 1958 to 1963 opinions and recommendations of the Committee in regard to social questions have included harmonization of social security programs for migrant workers, the operation of the European Social Fund and methods of investigating wage rates. The

Committee has also made recommendations on measures to promote the free movement of workers in the Community, industrial hygiene and a common policy for vocational training.

On such a matter as promoting vocational training, there have not been great differences in points of view between industry and union representatives on the Committee.

It is believed, nevertheless, that the final opinions presented by the Committee to the Commission of the Community are often expressive more of the divergent views held by the members than they are a consistently molded draft of the Committee's general approach to a particular problem. In the instances where unanimity may be expressed, however, such as may occur on technical phases of a question, considerably more weight is put on the Committee's action by the Commission. The entire process required to study and act on a proposal submitted to the Committee may take up to a year's time, which includes the detailed preliminary work by a specialized section.[6]

One prominent official of the Dutch Confederation of Trade Unions, a member of the Committee, has expressed regret that the Commission of the Economic Community has failed to take more ultimate consideration of the proposals put forward by the Economic and Social Committee. He has been unable to find, in official statements of the Commission and in its proposals to the Council of Ministers, a number of the recommendations coming out of the discussion of the Economic and Social Committee. This situation has given rise to some sense of dissatisfaction and has made the realization more evident that a weak point of the Committee is that it has no power, and is only advisory in nature to the Commission making recommendations to the Council. Here he noted that for the building of a united Europe on a democratic basis, treaty language directed to that end is not enough. The personal attitudes of the officials entrusted with policy implementation also will have a vital part to play in the outcome.

Concerning consultation, the members of the Commission for the Community have shown a most cooperative attitude toward the Committee. If a member of the Commission is asked to make a statement or clarify a point on an economic or social question, either the commissioner or an official of the Community in charge of the field involved will appear before the Committee to speak on the point and answer questions. Moreover, in such discussions the representatives of the Commission endeavor as far as possible to accept the opinion of the Committee members.

Concern has been expressed even so over what is considered to be lack of specific language in the Treaty's chapter on social policy, an area of vital importance to the Committee, as compared with other areas of the Treaty.[7] In effect some believe the determination of the Community to establish a common policy in the social field is not so evident as it is, for instance, in the strictly economic sphere. The rather general language of this chapter on social policy is considered the basis for such attitude, along with the resulting difficulty in discussing social questions meaningfully.

A contention also exists that even on the Economic and Social Committee there are some members who regard it as a wrong approach to aim at coordination of social policy for the six nations of the Community. Yet there are other members of the Committee who believe that a common social policy should come about, and this by direct coordination of all departments and offices responsible for implementation of social policy.

Despite these differences in views, decisive action takes place in the Committee. One Committee member has observed that a special subcommittee on social affairs, of which he was chairman, had one time issued a strong report on an action program for the "second phase" of the Community's development. The report contained statements on policy and practical suggestions for the consideration of the Commission of the European Economic Community. In formulating the report, the subcommittee had discussed the action program on social affairs as well as proposals for future development in the economic sector. A resolution to move toward a common social policy was unanimously accepted by the subcommittee.

Such an agreement on the part of this subcommittee in the view of its chairman was a welcome contrast to the situation in the Economic and Social Committee during earlier years. At that time it was not believed that such unanimity of approach would ever be possible. Over the years the members of the Committee, while still aware of their differences in points of view, nevertheless show a more tolerant understanding of the positions held by Committee members from the different countries of the Community. The adoption of the resolution in regard to the subcommittee's report served to indicate to the Committee chairman that despite varied points of view, unanimous agreement on policy can be reached. Yet a qualification was added that it was an agreement only on principle. Not much was said, for instance, by the employer representatives on practical applications.

At least it was agreed by all the members of the subcommittee that to promote the free movement of workers in the Community, adequate worker housing must be encouraged in all the six nations. To this end, it was urged that particular attention should be given to the problem of financing of home construction. The subcommittee called attention to the diversity of interest rates and other terms under which loans were obtained for worker housing among the member nations. On this question it was noted that the Commission would later submit to the Economic and Social Committee a specific proposal for consideration.

Specifically on the issue of promoting harmonization of social legislation and standards among the Six, an area where the Commission must consult the Committee, some Committee members have stressed that worker groups at the lower levels of the income scale should receive social gains in greater proportion than those in the upper income levels. However, this admonition does not necessarily mean that the more prosperous member nations or the higher income groups within a nation should hold back to wait for the less affluent member nations or groups to catch up. Here the members recalled a statement in the Preamble of the Treaty for the Economic Community that there must always be progress and social development for all people in the Community. This point officially reads as follows:

Article 2
It shall be the aim of the Community, by establishing a Common Market and progressively approximating the economic policies of Member States, to promote throughout the Community a harmonious development of economic activities, a continuous and balanced expansion, an increased stability, an accelerated raising of the standard of living and closer relations between its Member States.

A member of the Economic and Social Committee, who is president of a national federation of unions, has stated that while the primary objective of the Treaty of Rome—that of raising the standard of living of the people in the European Community—is a social goal, the means taken to attain it are economic. He believes the very reason for the establishment of the Economic and Social Committee was to make possible the regular meeting of representatives of the various economic and social forces in conjunction with political and business groups.

The Committee itself is directed by a governing body composed of a president, two vice-presidents and fourteen members. In 1963, with the chairman a member of the general interest group from France, one vice-chairman was a union representative from Germany, and the other was an employer representative from The Netherlands.

It is acknowledged that although the Committee has made studies on many important social questions, the point has not yet been reached where the Committee could contribute significantly to the social progress of the Community. At present, it was felt that the rather minimum social role of the Economic and Social Committee was concerned largely with efforts to encourage harmonization in the social legislation of the six member states.

There is evidence that considerable differences still remain in such laws. One instance is the issue of equal pay for equal work for men and women, especially in the textile industry. The point has been made that if a country pays different wages to men and women doing the same kind of work, serious distortion in standards can result which may even bring about "social dumping" by a member state against other countries in the Community. There has been mention that there is also room for harmonization in regard to annual vacations.

Again, there is need for a common policy of transportation in the Community: the intention is to encourage comparable social standards for workers on trucks, boats and trains so as to avoid a competitive advantage by any one type of transportation, based on poor working conditions. The Committee has encountered situations where employers in the transport industry have sought to lower work standards in order to charge cheaper freight rates than offered in competing forms of transportation.

The view has been stressed that the responsibility of the Committee is not to make it easier for employers in transport to make greater profits, but to see that good wages for all workers prevail in this industry, and that the public has efficient, diversified service at not too high a price. There is belief that the Committee members generally support such objectives.

Yet some Committee members hold that the cause of the divergencies does not stem from varying concepts of social justice, but from different elements of the social question in the member countries. Even on the matter of tariff, differences in policy still remain among member states of the Common Market. It is pointed out that some countries claim they are entitled to higher price levels in certain areas because their wages are above average or their social security benefits are greater.

The primary task of the Committee in any event is not to seek for uniformity in the social legislation of the Six, but rather for greater harmonization so as to make comparable the social costs of production. In no case is it expected that the Committee should make suggestions for modification of standards that would lead to the diminution of social benefits in any member country.

The pervasiveness of the social role for the Committee becomes evident by observing that even in technical discussions social aspects must be given attention. Here it can be noted that social considerations do not stop merely at wage levels, but rather take into account the general aim of the Treaty of Rome, namely, "improvement of the living and working conditions of labour so as to permit the equalisation of such conditions in an upward direction."[8]

After this first phase has been achieved, namely, social harmonization, the next task for the Committee would be to push actively for general social progress.

THE EUROPEAN COAL AND STEEL COMMUNITY

THE CONSULTATIVE COMMITTEE

In the European Coal and Steel Community, senior to the Common Market by six years, there exists the Consultative Committee to the High Authority situated in Luxembourg. This body was actually the prototype for the European Economic and Social Committee.

Under Article 18 of the Treaty of Paris, which established the Coal and Steel Community, it is stated that the Consultative Committee "shall consist of not less than thirty and not more than fifty-one members. . . ."[9] The representation by Treaty provision arranges for an equal number of producers, workers, consumers and dealers. In actuality the Consultative Committee has two divisions, one for coal mining and one for the steel industry.

A significant variation in the manner of appointment for the Economic and Social Committee, as compared with the Consultative Committee, is in the source from which lists of candidates are selected. By Article 18 of the Treaty of Paris, the Council of Ministers shall select representative organizations to draw up lists with twice the number of names as the number of seats allocated to each organization. The Council makes appointments from these lists.

In contrast, the Treaty of Rome in Article 195 stipulates that the lists of candidates from which appointments are to be selected shall come directly from the member states, rather than from representative organizations. The same Article declares that the Council in making appointments to the Economic and Social Committee should consult the Commission. The Council may obtain the opinion of representative European organizations, but it has not done so.

This less democratic method on the part of the European Community in selecting members for the Economic and Social Committee is one of the indications of the changed political atmosphere among the member states in 1957, as compared to 1951. The term of appointment for the Consultative Committee is two years, as compared to four years for the Economic and Social Committee.

From Article 19 of the Treaty of Paris it is obvious that a closer relationship was intended between the High Authority and the Consultative Committee than is the case between the Executive Commission and the Economic and Social Committee. In Article 19 of the Treaty of Paris it is made obligatory for the High Authority to "submit to the Consultative Committee the general objectives and programmes established under the terms of Article 46 and shall keep the Committee informed of the broad lines of its action under the terms of Articles 54, 65 and 66." No such directive is laid down for the Commission in the Treaty of Rome establishing the European Community. Instead the Commission and the Council of Ministers have only the obligation to consult the Economic and Social Committee in areas stated in the Treaty, but may extend the range of consultation when deemed appropriate.

The Consultative Committee, or members of it, are free to ask for a discussion with the High Authority on any problem that arises. A date for the session is readily set and both parties express their views on the subject. An immediate achievement of a satisfactory policy may not result, however, since the Treaty for the Coal and Steel Community does not give direct power to the High Authority on social questions.

As an instance of the initiative taken by members of the Consultative Committee, in 1958 a proposed European statute on working conditions for coal miners was drafted to be used as a standard in the Community. It is true that no action has followed from this proposal. Opposition from France may be a cause, since in that country coal mines are under government ownership and operation; there, governmental resistance to change in methods of operation is considered to be formidable. Further, differences in point of view on matters of working conditions also persist among other producers in the Community.

In general, labor representation on the Consultative Committee for the Coal and Steel Community finds much more satisfaction with results obtained than is the case with labor representation on the Economic and Social Committee of the European Community. Not only are labor groups represented on all technical, social and economic committees for coal and steel, but they are closer to all the activities of the High Authority. This is not so in Brussels with the Executive Commission in the European Community.

Matters in the domain of collective bargaining as such are outside the jurisdiction of the High Authority. However, the High Authority can institute studies on these issues and publish the findings. Moreover, it can arrange for meetings between employers and worker representatives. In any event there are remaining areas outside collective bargaining where the Consultative Committee can work closely with the High Authority and obtain tangible results.

Nevertheless, there is also, as in Brussels, a certain dissatisfaction among labor members with the composition of the third group in the Consultative Committee, which includes consumers. It is contended that workers are also consumers, just as are fabricators who use steel parts, but this role of the worker is not given recognition in the third group.

THE ADVISORY ROLE IN THE UNITED STATES

Though in the institutional framework of government there is no organization either in Britain or the United States similar to the Economic and Social Committee of the European Community, a comparison might well be made between it and the Business Advisory Council set up originally in the 1930's as a consultative group to the Department of Commerce. The Council membership includes top officials of the dominant corporations and appoints its own replacements. Due recognition is given by such appointments to the relative economic position held in the various industries by the leading corporations.

Though the group ostensibly was established to serve the Department of Commerce, in practice there have been regular meetings with the BAC and government officials in more strategic areas than the Department of Commerce. Like the Economic and Social Committee, the BAC publishes no records of its proceedings. Unlike the Committee, however, there is no official requirement that a record of the BAC's deliberations be forwarded to any government agency. In effect, the BAC has met in closed sessions with high public officials in Washington and elsewhere, with no record of the discussions available to Congress, the President or the Cabinet.

This situation was criticized by Secretary of Commerce Luther Hodges, who believed the Business Advisory Council should have a more representative cross-section of industry, and that one group of business officials should not have access to government information withheld from other businessmen and the public as well. To correct this situation Hodges advocated that a public observer should attend the meetings.

For a time some effort was made to meet these objections. The Council agreed to have a government official in attendance at its closed meetings, and to permit the press to attend all sessions addressed by government representatives. Further, agendas drafted by the Secretary of Commerce would be followed by the Council. Again, future membership would include some representatives of small business.

A short time after those revisions in procedure were announced, the executive committee of the Council in a meeting with President Kennedy informed him that the BAC had severed relationship with the Department of Commerce, so that it could act in an advisory capacity to all sectors of the government.[10] This action has been interpreted to mean that the members of the BAC found the reforms suggested by Secretary Hodges not to its liking, and that even fewer restraints would hold sway in the future.

Informal pressure groups in the United States, speaking for a wide variety of economic and social interests, especially business, labor and the professions, make their influence felt on legislators and members of the executive branch of government at all levels. Informal pressure groups are also active in the European Communities.

2.

The European Social Fund

AS ARTICLE 123 OF THE TREATY OF ROME STATES, THE PURPOSE of the Social Fund is "to improve opportunities of employment of workers in the Common Market and thus contribute to raising the standard of living. . . ."[1] Toward this objective the Fund has the responsibility to encourage development of more employment facilities as well as the geographical and occupational mobility of workers. The Fund might be regarded as an attempt to set up for the European Economic Community a counterpart to the taxing power exclusively possessed by the European Coal and Steel Community. With the revenue which that Community derives from levies on coal and steel production, the High Authority has made grants to improve job opportunities for workers in addition to supporting research in social, economic and technical areas.

In effect the Fund was instituted to help overcome unemployment and underemployment within the Economic Community by financial aid to the member states in regard to projects they have fostered to retrain and resettle members of the work force victimized by plant, urban or regional reconversion. Under rules of procedure authorized for the Fund, member states will be reimbursed up to 50 per cent of costs incurred because of such projects.

RETROACTIVE GRANTS BY THE FUND

These payments by the Fund are permitted only after the workers involved have secured employment following their retraining or resettlement, or both. Moreover, they must have been fully employed on the new job for a period of six months, within a maximum period of 12 months after retraining or resettlement. In other words, reimbursement is made only if the operation is a success. Request for payments from the Social Fund become operative at least 18 months after the projects involved have been launched. Insertion of the retroactive provision for payments from the Fund was designed to persuade the member states to take the initiative on projects to overcome unemployment.[2]

It is precisely this retroactive feature of the Fund that has prompted severe criticism by trade union groups within the European Economic Community. They had insisted that an amendment be made to the Treaty of Rome permitting the Fund at the outset to finance projects by loans in member states dealing with reconversion or resettlement.[3] The percentages of financial contributions to the Fund by each member state are somewhat different from the shares in the resources of the Fund available to the same member states.[4]

The conditions required before payment is made include new jobs for the workers and a state of unemployment actually experienced by them prior to their reeducation or resettlement. Mere reinstatement or promotion following such a program of reconversion will not warrant reimbursement from the Fund. Thus under present conditions imposed by the Treaty of Rome, if the Fund finds that even some of the workers involved in the projects under which member states are requesting reimbursement had not been previously unemployed or underemployed, no payments may be made on such projects.

It is administratively difficult for the Fund to verify the observance of this Treaty regulation. In practice the Fund has used a spot check to make determinations. The percentage of violations discovered by this method is assumed to be true for the total number of requests sent to the Fund, and the amount of the demands is scaled downward in proportion to that percentage of violations.

To qualify for reimbursement, a member state must have submitted its particular plan for reconversion of a town or region in its jurisdiction in advance of implementation. There must be evidence that reemployment would be impossible for the workers involved without the program of retraining or resettlement. It is also necessary that the

Commission of the Community give prior approval to the program to be launched in a particular member state. A formal request for repayment must also be made to the Social Fund.

Besides the examination of the documents submitted to the Fund in regard to a given project, it is necessary that the national government of the particular member state verify the good faith behind the request by an "on the spot" check of the project.[5]

Though administrative problems have been considerable in authorizing disbursements for diversified projects in the several member states of the Community, notable assistance has been made available in overcoming them through the valuable counsel of the Committee of the European Social Fund.

STATUTORY BASIS FOR THE FUND

Under Regulation Nine, by which the Council of Ministers identifies the statute governing the Social Fund, this Committee is authorized to aid the Commission in its task of disbursing payments from the Fund. Membership of the Committee is made up of representatives from governments, unions and employer organizations.[6] The formation of this Committee has been termed an "opening" in the direction of a more liberal interpretation of the Treaty directives in regard to the Social Policy of the Communities. The actual terminology of the Treaty of Rome makes no provision for a special advisory committee in regard to the Social Fund, but instead includes this function in the general responsibilities of the Economic and Social Committee.

The Social Fund Committee, according to Regulation Nine, is to be consulted on all questions of general importance or of principle in regard to administration of the Fund.[7] To this end, the Committee receives all pertinent documents and information. In contrast to the Economic and Social Committee, the advisory board for the Social Fund may exercise its own initiative in regard to these issues.

To insure the effectiveness of the Committee, it is obligatory for the Commission to provide the members, in advance, with such significant documents as the annual budget of the Fund, lists of organizations eligible for grants, requests for payments pending before the Fund, projects that have received preliminary approval by the Commission and briefs on any problems facing the Fund in its efforts to encourage a common policy for vocational training.[8]

In 1962 the Committee held four meetings. In addition to advising on reimbursements to member states, it approved the draft budget for 1963, various requests for inclusion in the list of statutory organizations eligible for refunds and a proposed amendment to the statute of the Social Fund. The Committee, during those four meetings, also determined, in conjunction with the Commission staff, the standards by which the Fund would evaluate situations of underemployment when examining applications for aid. In effect these standards will enable the Fund appreciably to extend its operations, as the European Parliament has urged, in behalf of workers in areas where employment is declining, especially agriculture.[9]

Necessary financial resources to make the Fund operative actually come from the member states. France and Germany are each assessed at the rates of 32 per cent; Italy at 20 per cent; Belgium and The Netherlands at 8.8 per cent and 7 per cent respectively; and the Duchy of Luxembourg at 0.2 per cent.[10]

The unreality of the term "Fund" as a title for this organization of the Community becomes evident when it is realized that the body has no resources of its own. A more accurate designation for this institution would be that of a compensation agency. After estimating the amount of reimbursements required in a given year, the agency turns to the member states for the money. It is possible that a given member of the Community would get back almost as much as it paid. Moreover, there might be a deliberate effort to attain this objective on the part of a member state, since the payments to the Fund are obligatory in any event. Nevertheless, to get the payment returned, it was necessary for the State to have actually completed, to the satisfaction of the Social Fund, a program promoting employment.

Within a member state itself, the actual execution of a retraining or resettlement project to combat unemployment or underemployment may be the responsibility of a local or regional organization that has been given authorization by the state for this purpose.

The First Four Years

The Social Fund has been in existence for only about four years. The first payments to five of the member states were made in 1962, and by the end of that year had totaled $12,291,798. Luxembourg has made no application for reimbursement.[11]

These reimbursements related to expenses incurred in the member states during 1958–1959 for projects which enabled about 183,000 unemployed workers to find new employment. The state with the greatest number of workers to benefit in programs aided by the Fund in those years was Italy, where 69,000 workers were retrained and 79,200 were resettled in other countries, namely, 48,000 in France,

27,000 in Germany and 4,000 in the Benelux countries. By contrast only 1,400 workers in Belgium went through a retraining program related to the Fund.[12] Nevertheless, the reimbursements to France were the highest for any state, amounting to $4,624,641; Italy's were next, amounting to $3,733,198.[13] As noted earlier, by provision of the Treaty, Italy is required to pay into the Fund an amount less than is exacted of either France or Germany.

In regard to resettlement of workers in other countries, the Italian government had to pay only the travel cost incurred in Italy itself. The greater part of the expense of resettlement was paid by the receiving countries. It should be noted, therefore, that a certain part of the large reimbursement made to France and Germany was actually devoted to the cost of resettling workers from Italy. In effect, then, one may say that Italy has actually received more from the Fund than other countries of the Community. As an indication of possible future change here, the present trend in vocational retraining programs is the stress on efforts to place the unemployed in new jobs located in their home areas instead of in a foreign environment.

At the end of 1962 the total of requests for future payments amounted to $17,946,000. These requests related to projects activated in 1960 and 1961. It was estimated in 1963 that, by 1964, requests for all types of payments might reach $40,000,000.

To some degree the Social Fund is the equivalent of a social security agency in that it fosters transfers of monetary resources from the more prosperous areas of the Community to the poorer regions. In the view of M. Levi Sandri, a member of the Commission for the Economic Community, and president of the Social Affairs Division, the Fund endeavors to encourage a constant flow of financial aid from regions in the Community with high income and employment to areas where unemployment and underemployment are an obstacle to a more equitable sharing of prosperity. Sandri regards the Social Fund as tangible proof of the solidarity of purpose that animates the member states of the Community.[14]

As noted above, the poorest country of the Six, Italy, has thus far derived the greatest advantages from the Fund.[15] In a similar fashion the poorer regions within other states of the Community, because of the Fund, have gained in employment and skills. It is believed that this trend will become more pronounced, and designedly so, in the future.

FUTURE OUTLOOK

It is significant to note that of the $36,500,000 constituting the requests made to the Fund from five of the member states up to December 31, 1962, $29,000,000 had related to vocational retraining and $7,500,000 to the transfer of workers.[16] By the very nature of the activity, the expenses of retraining are much heavier than the mere transfer of workers.

The Social Fund intends to put more weight in coming years on regional development and on the concept that the local region is the normal milieu for meeting problems of unemployment and resettlement. Fortunately, regional organizations are now reviving throughout Europe and will be ready instruments of cooperation in these tasks of the Social Fund. In contrast with the situation of only 15 years ago, there is now, once more, strong regional awareness and organizational activity in such areas of France as Normandy and Brittany. As a consequence regional policy for economic and social development is becoming more important each year. It is expected, therefore, that the Social Fund will have a big impact on the regional level in the various states of the Community. Accordingly, future programs submitted to the Fund for advance approval, which take into account the regional context, will be in a favorable status.

In the European Economic Community there are two other organizations designated to give financial aid for economic and social development. The European Investment Bank grants loans and guarantees on a nonprofit basis to assist projects in less developed regions; these aids are designed to modernize or convert industrial plants. The Bank also will give financial aid to establish new activities required by the continued development of the Common Market. There is also the Association of Overseas Countries and Territories.[17]

The purpose of the Social Fund differs decidedly from the objective of the European Bank, which deals in matters of commerce and is concerned with future returns on investment. The Fund—by means of encouraging retraining, reconversion and resettlement—is designed to meet problems of social dislocation facing members of the work force.

The most important regions having received aid from the Social Fund thus far have been southern Italy, Sardinia, western France and Brittany. Certain parts of Belgium have benefited, as well as refugees from East Germany who have been helped by the Fund in West Germany, as have been refugees from Algeria who located in France.

An important question that will face administrators of the Social Fund in coming years is the matter of payment for vocational training. New regulations on this subject have been under preparation by officials of the Fund. Under present Treaty provisions the Fund only may reimburse in part the costs of retraining and resettlement, but not the costs of vocational training as such. In view of the likelihood that in the near future the Social Fund will expand its activities, thought is being given to intervention in the field of vocational training despite the silence of the Treaty on this subject. To this end a study is under way for means to allow the Fund to give financial aid to vocational training and thus contribute to the Community's policy of promoting harmonious and balanced development throughout the different regions of the Six.[18]

A factor impelling practically all six member states to seek a change in the Treaty provisions governing the Social Fund, in order to enlarge its activities, is the virtual absence of unemployment in the Community except in Italy. There is still a significant problem, however, in regard to underemployment. In Europe the transition from an agricultural society to a service and industrial economy has yet to be fully achieved. The big problem is how to find workers for the jobs already available. True, the situation in southern Italy is quite different from that of the rest of the Community.

In the accumulating demands for reimbursements by member states during the summer of 1963, amounting to $21,500,000, some projects were involved dealing with vocational training as such. Until Treaty regulations for the Fund are amended, no payments can be used to compensate for the cost of these projects. Yet, even with authorization, a difficulty that might hamper an active role for the Social Fund in vocational training is the lack of general standards or regulations throughout the member states for the formative process of this type of education for workers.

It has been urged by the European Parliament that the Fund should have competence to act promptly toward the furtherance of a common vocational training policy, especially the retraining of underemployed persons who desire to continue in self-employment. Moreover, the European Parliament desires that the Fund be allowed to encourage retraining, while employed, to prevent later unemployment among workers in declining trades.

THE COMMISSION AND THE FUND

The European Commission holds the view that the Fund, in addition to its role of compensation agency to member states for expenditures on retraining programs, should be allowed to take the initiative by actually promoting pilot retraining programs in the member countries.

For some time it has been the intention of the Commission to present to the Council practical proposals toward this objective.[19] The Social Fund itself also has been active in drafting new regulations for the consideration of the Commission that would lift the restriction which presently confines reimbursements to programs of retraining or resettlement for unemployed or underemployed workers.

In early 1965, the Commission for the Economic Community actually submitted to the Council of Ministers a series of proposals designed to improve the effectiveness of the Social Fund.[20] To show the need for these modifications the Commission stated that the experience from the first four years of operation of the Fund showed certain inadequacies in the methods and procedures governing the Fund.

As an instance, the Commission noted that despite the critical importance of promoting vocational retraining and readaptation, it is evident that the stimulating effect of the Fund has been reduced because its financial help often arrives too late in relation to the needs of a given situation. Further, it was found that the present regulations tend to prevent the Commission from adapting the application of the Fund directly toward the more immediate objectives of Community policy. In effect, the delayed response to these objectives has actually, in the last three years, caused a decline in demand for financial aid from the Social Fund even in the area of vocational retraining where the need for such programs has become even more pressing because of a lack of skilled manpower. The Commission called attention to the growing disparity between the number of workers who have received vocational retraining and the much greater number who could be potential beneficiaries of such programs that might be financed from the Fund.

In actuality, the Commission pointed out that certain functions and procedures of the Fund are no longer consonant with social and economic realities that have come about since the Treaty of Rome was signed in 1957. Here the Commission stressed that the areas of responsibility outlined for the Fund under Article 125 of the Treaty were determined in light of an economic situation characterized by serious structural unemployment and by fears that the launching of the Common Market might have a serious impact in certain areas on the level of existing employment. In contrast, the Commission noted that today structural unemployment is evident only in some restricted regions, and that the rate of general employment in the Six has actually been improved due to the influence of the Common Market.

Further, the Commission noted that to a considerable degree the progress of readaptation of workers, especially where it involves migration from one country to another, remains without lasting effect because of the difficulties facing resettled workers and their families due to lack of suitable housing and to problems of adjusting to a new social environment. Very often these factors induce an early return to the country of origin.

There was also acknowledgment that, in a general way, the less developed regions of the Community have not benefited by help from the Fund under programs originally intended to relieve congestion in overpopulated industrial areas by encouraging workers to move elsewhere. Under present regulations it has been found to be very difficult for the Fund to encourage directly the development of regional economies.

Accordingly, in the face of this situation, the Commission has proposed a revision of the regulations originally intended to meet the objectives as set by Article 123 of the Treaty of Rome. Here it was noted that those objectives are not confined to the reabsorption of unemployed workers, but are mainly concerned with the encouragement of permanent social progress as a natural accompaniment to the gradual realization of European integration. To this end, the Commission believes the Fund should help encourage more industrial facilities for employment, as well as greater geographic and vocational mobility for workers.

First of all, the proposed revisions of the Commission are designed to remove from existing procedures some residual difficulties in their applications and interpretation not evident at the time of the first revisions of Regulation Nine, which, as noted earlier, is the statute governing the Social Fund. Secondly, another group of proposed revisions aim to take into account the necessity to adapt conditions for intervention by the Fund to current developments in the labor market. Here the Commission stressed the need for skilled manpower in the Community, which could be met in part by a more careful utilization of existing potentialities on the part of present members in the work force.[21]

SUPPORT OF THE COMMISSION BY THE EUROPEAN PARLIAMENT

In June 1965 the Social Committee of the European Parliament issued its report on the proposals of the Commission to modify the regulations controlling the administration of the Social Fund. At the outset it was noted in the Committee's report that, both in 1959 and 1963, the European Parliament had urged revisions in the rules for the Fund. With directness and brevity, the report stated that the circumstances under which the rules for the Fund had been drafted are today largely irrelevant. Instead of unemployment, the predominant problem now is shortage of qualified manpower. The report stressed, however, that the Fund had not become superfluous, since divergent developments in the Community show a continued need for an instrument to promote economic and social equilibrium.

The point was made that because of the excessive prudence which had characterized the proceedings and modes of action controlling it, the Social Fund has not been able to exercise this balancing function. Accordingly, the Social Committee maintains that it is of the utmost importance that the functions and procedures for the Social Fund be brought up to date.

Referring to Article 123 of the Treaty of Rome, the Committee's report observed that the Fund has the responsibility to improve the opportunities for employment of manpower by giving support to production facilities as well as to measures encouraging geographic and vocational mobility of manpower. In large part, discharge of this responsibility should take the form of promoting vocational retraining, readaptation and encouragement of plant reconversion.

Yet, for some time it has been apparent to the Social Committee that the Fund's performance has not measured up to expectations in these areas. It was found that the procedures for the Fund do not respond to new economic conditions. In particular, the present restriction that the Fund may give financial aid only retroactively is considered a serious weakness. Though the Committee acknowledged that the measures already taken by governments of the Six have practically removed the problem of unemployment, nevertheless in some areas potential unemployment and underemployment still remain. In such instances the report notes that the Fund should be permitted to furnish funds in advance in order to encourage preventive measures. For the same reason, administrative procedures should be modified so that the Fund may provide funds in advance to promote plant reconversion.[22]

From field surveys made by the Parliament's Social Committee, there are numerous programs of readaptation in the Community destined for failure because the workers are not able to bring their families along for lack of adequate housing. The report also stresses that it is equally necessary to set up training courses for migrant workers, if it is desired over the long run to obtain from this source a type of labor supply responsive to the needs of the receiving country.

In another area, the Committee finds that the Fund is not in position to promote adequately the economic development of certain regions and thus prevent an inordinate emigration of workers from such areas. In one instance it has been discovered that as a general rule economic reconversions do not take place within existing enterprises. More often they come about through new firms with new types of production. Yet, the present regulations of the Social Fund prevent any type of contribution by it for advancing the activities of such new establishments.

The Committee has noted that the success of any program of regional development obviously depends on the existence of properly trained manpower. To meet this requirement there must be in operation an adequate number of modern retraining centers in each of these regions. It is therefore recommended that the Fund contribute financially to the construction and equipment of institutes for vocational retraining.

Regretfully, the report observes that the regulations for the Fund now in force do not permit the giving of any aid for anticipatory retraining of workers presently engaged in obsolescent trades. In general, therefore, the Committee finds that administrative rules restricting the Social Fund permit it only to give meager financial help toward improving the qualifications of workers.[23]

Over the years, from December 1960 to December 1964, the Parliament's Social Committee notes that the expenditures made by the Fund were much too small, amounting to $24,500,000. Moreover, the reimbursement by the member countries so closely matched this figure that the balance of credit outstanding at the end of 1964 was only $3,638,579. As was noted earlier, the rules now in effect require that credit not be expended by the Fund unless the member states have previously incurred the expenses of a more than corresponding amount, and over a stipulated period of time.

The European Parliament is, therefore, strongly in accord with the proposals by the Commission for the Economic Community to modify the administrative regulations of the Social Fund. In the report of the Parliament's Social Committee, it is believed that these proposals will raise the credits available from the Fund for retraining the considerable number of workers in the Economic Community needing such programs to readapt themselves to modern needs of production.

The Committee's report also indicated that acceptance of these proposals by the Council of Ministers would enable the Fund to combat situations of potential unemployment and persistent underemployment more effectively. In other words, these modifications of the rules for the Fund would make it a more useful instrument in encouraging the necessary restructuring of a large part of the labor supply in the Community.

In terms of regional development, the report observes that the European Parliament has been constantly urging a more active regional policy on the part of the Social Fund. Up to the present, the Parliament has found economic growth tending to favor more concentration in the already dense industrial centers. Accordingly, the contrast in development between different regions of the Community has been accentuated rather than diminished. By such a turn of events it has been impossible to secure an equitable sharing in regional programs among the different areas of the Community, one of the objectives in the Treaty of Rome. As a result, many workers in the retarded regions have not found new opportunities for the future. In the opinion of the Parliament's Social Committee, this circumstance makes it all the more imperative for the Social Fund, originally established to combat mass unemployment, to institute a balanced program of measures as rapidly as possible that would permit a more harmonious sharing in economic growth by the populations in all the regions of the Community.

The Committee's report notes with satisfaction that the proposals of the Commission would encourage the member states to intensify programs of retraining for the benefit of workers in obsolescent trades. In the estimation of the Committee these retraining programs are still insufficient in number and are often of only an experimental character.

As a concluding note the report observes that very likely it was intended originally to make the Social Fund an instrument for economic equilibrium. Nevertheless, such a role has been only partially fulfilled because of the restrictive procedures imposed on the Fund. In the opinion of the Social Committee, adoption of the proposed modification of regulations for the Fund would reactivate this original role by recognizing the vital needs and interests of the Community today.[24]

In all fairness, it must be pointed out that despite its financial and procedural limitations, the Social Fund in its four years of operation up to 1965 provided for half the cost of financing the vocational retraining and reemployment of 322,000 Community workers. Because of poor qualifications, these workers had been previously out of work or underemployed.

A BROADER BASE OF OPERATIONS

Assuming the Council of Ministers' approval of the first series of proposed rule modifications for the Fund, it will then be able to provide a significant portion of the work force, especially the agricultural sector, with vocational retraining for new jobs in industry and services. The key change in policy required for this new role would be authorization of the Fund to support the retraining of employed workers, not just the unemployed or underemployed.

The Council's acceptance of the second series of proposals for modifications of its rules would enable the Fund to safeguard the income level of workers in the less developed regions who, because of plant closings, have had to accept jobs at lower pay in new companies in the same area. Construction of vocational retraining centers would also be encouraged. Initiative on the part of the Fund could likewise be exercised so as to grant loans in advance relating to training programs for migrant workers, instead of merely reimbursing the member states long after they had taken such action. Financing of much needed housing programs for migrant workers would also come within the initiative of the Social Fund.[25]

3.

Vocational Training and Retraining

THE EUROPEAN ECONOMIC COMMUNITY

THERE HAS BEEN WIDE ACKNOWLEDGMENT IN THE EUROPEAN Economic Community that vocational training is one of the underlying factors to be used in the effort to achieve the main objectives of the Treaty of Rome. Such training is necessary to establish balance between expansion of population and technological change, as well as to enable the labor force to adapt itself to the varied needs of a growing economy.[1] Again vocational training is closely linked with the advancement of worker mobility, both in regard to change of occupation and to change of location.[2]

BASIC CONSIDERATIONS

The ultimate goal is to bring the levels of training among the member states to a common standard by gradually instituting comparable training programs and by fostering comparable experience. One proposal directed to this end is the use of uniform tests administered on a competitive basis in various cities of the Community.

On April 2, 1963, the Community's Council of Ministers approved a body of general principles, submitted to it by the Commission, to underlie the common European policy for vocational training of workers in the Community.[3] Prior to making this decision, the Council had given consideration to various provisions in the Treaty of Rome, especially Article 128, which states:

> The Council shall, on a proposal of the Commission and after the Economic and Social Committee has been consulted, establish general principles for the implementation of a common policy of occupational training capable of contributing to the harmonious development both of national economies and of the Common Market.[4]

In its decision of April 2, 1963, the Council of Ministers recalled that the Treaty of Rome had imposed a duty on the member states of the Community to follow an economic policy that would assure the maintenance of a high level of employment. The Council noted that the member states had also accepted the obligation to develop vocational qualifications in the work force conducive to general economic development and adaptive to changes in technologies of production. Further, there was special urgency seen by the Council in the need for consistent vocational training and retraining because of coordination of regional policies and structural changes in various economic sectors.

Again, it was acknowledged that a common policy in the Community on vocational training would lend itself to greater economic stability and to an accelerated upward trend in the standard of living for the Community. Other advantages foreseen in such a common policy among the member states included a more rapid realization of the free movement of workers within the Community, a more substantial educational base to permit advanced training at later stages and, when the need arises, readaptation to a different source of livelihood.

On the basis of these observations the Council of Ministers enunciated 10 principles to be put into effect by the Community to foster a common policy of vocational training by the member states. Some salient points in each of these principles will show their applicability to economies other than the Common Market.

1. The Council declared that, by subscribing to a common policy for vocational training, it is understood each member state will establish programs of training designed to meet the requirements set forth in the general principles approved by the Council. The result envisioned is occupational training for each worker adequate to enable him to make free choice of an occupation in the location he prefers.

2. Facilities for assuring such training are to be made available in sufficient time so that the different economic sectors will have a type of work force necessary to meet requirements. Moreover, the breadth of instruction is to include balanced development of the individual, along with courses of study leading to technical progress, familiarity

with new methods of production as well as social and economic changes. Especially concerning the young, the Council noted, there should be regard for intellectual and moral development, civic education and physical fitness.

Stress was placed on the importance of avoiding any undue delay between the completion of the period of general education and the beginning of vocational training. Even throughout the years in a given occupation, the Council stated, there should be opportunity for advanced training, duly suited to a change of occupation. Moreover, where the desire, aptitude and background are present, there should be channels available enabling workers to attain a higher level of competency in their callings to qualify themselves for promotion.

The Council emphasized that close relationships should be established between the various centers of vocational training and the economic complexes of the Community so that training programs will respond better to industrial needs and to the interests of the trainees themselves. Further, the Council foresaw that this approach would enable the training centers and the employing enterprises to share in the study and solution of each other's problems.

3. As a third principle, the Council required that an estimate be made, both on the national and the Community levels, of the future —quantitative as well as qualitative—needs for a work force in the various economic sectors. A permanent bureau of information is to be established to counsel both youngsters and adults on matters of occupational aptitudes, training and employment. The bureau is to work in close cooperation with the employing sectors, the training centers and the educational institutions.

4. The Commission for the European Economic Community has the duty to make concrete proposals to the Council and member states for the realization of the objectives set forth in the general principles. In particular the Commission is to carry on research in the area of vocational training, designed to foster a common policy for the Community on training, adequate employment centers as well as geographic and occupational mobility of the work force.

An inventory is to be taken on present facilities for occupational training as compared to present needs. The Commission is then to recommend appropriate action to the member states with due regard to priority. It is expected that joint measures by the states will be initiated through bilateral or multilateral agreements. The Commission is to follow closely the response of the states and duly inform them on the adequacy of their performance.

5. The Commission is to take the initiative in assembling, distrib-

uting and exchanging among the member states all helpful documentation and teaching materials in regard to vocational training, particularly on new methods. The member states in turn are to cooperate with the Commission by furnishing it with full information on the developments in the national systems of vocational training.

6. By means of seminars, programmed visits and even periods of residence at the different institutes for vocational training, the Commission is to encourage direct exchange of experiences among the member states, especially with respect to specialized fields and new developments.

7. The Council was particularly concerned about the adequate formation and growth in numbers of teaching personnel, inasmuch as an effective policy on vocational training is not otherwise possible. To this end the Commission is to use all suitable measures, especially to assure constant adaptation of instruction to progressive changes in the economic and technical spheres.

Emphasis was placed by the Council on the importance of training future instructors—who have the necessary qualifications—taken from the work force itself. It is expected that in the course of this training, future instructors will gain many advantages through the seminars and exchange visits authorized by the Council in the sixth principle.

It is recognized throughout the member states that new technical progress and modernization of industry particularly demand a work force qualified not only in manual skills, but in mental agility as well, to meet the changing job environments of the future.[5]

All the member states are in agreement that modern vocational training demands a better preparation for the teaching personnel involved in imparting it. Accordingly, the public authorities and organizations representing the various occupational groups are disposed to give their support to courses of instruction that are designed to raise the standards of teachers in vocational training and to establish such courses where they do not presently exist.

Significantly, the Council stipulated that teachers and instructors in vocational training, who are to be stationed in the less developed regions of the Community, should receive special attention in regard to formative preparation. Similar regard is to be shown instructors who will serve developing states and territories associated with the Community.

8. Stress was placed on the need for a common policy of occupational training to promote a close relationship and understanding among the various levels of training. Accordingly, the Commission,

in cooperation with the member states, is to establish a definite program for various occupations, consistently setting forth the basic requirements for advancement through the different levels of formation.

An agreement is to be reached on the objective conditions required for successful completion of a training program. On this basis it will be possible to recognize, throughout the Community, a certificate from any member state as proof of adequate occupational training. Further, the Council has directed the Commission to encourage the use of Community-wide examinations.

9. To assure good balance between the demand and supply of workers within the Community, after noting the forecasts required under the third principle, the member states and the Commission cooperatively are to work out adequate steps for the establishment of additional training programs where they are needed. These additional programs should also provide for accelerated training of adults, made necessary by the need for conversion and readaptation due to economic or technological changes.

10. It was recognized by the Council that in implementing general principles for a common policy on vocational training, attention must be given to special problems that will inevitably arise for certain economic sectors or categories of persons. Appropriate action should be taken to solve these problems, and the financial burden should be borne by the entire Community.

In commenting on the above 10 principles dealing with vocational training, designed to implement a common policy for the Six, Leo Crijns, director of the Division on Labor Problems for the European Economic Community, has confirmed the goal that adequate vocational training is to be available to all in addition to greater opportunity for general education.[6] Crijns said further that, with the expansion and improvement in quality for both types of education flowing from these 10 principles, he expects that the needs will be met for "full individual development" as well as for social, economic and technical progress. He stressed that intellectual and general development, including physical, is to be fostered on behalf of all those enrolled in vocational training programs.

Further, the 10 principles envision a continuing process of education throughout the worker's lifetime—even beginning, as Crijns notes, with the monition that there should be no delay between the period of general education and the start of vocational training. Moreover, throughout the worker's lifetime there is to be opportunity for retraining, specialist training, and, for those with requisite abilities and aptitudes, facilities for adaptation to higher rank in industry.

DIVISION OF VOCATIONAL TRAINING

Years before the enunciation of these principles, there was established in the European Economic Community a Division of Vocational Training. As an advisory body for this Division a tripartite committee was also formed, with representatives from the member governments, employer groups and union organizations.

The Division is still in the preparatory stages toward carrying out the mandates of the Treaty of Rome that are assigned to it. Among the big immediate tasks at present is the need to prepare ample documentation on all phases of vocational training; this function has been in progress for some time. Again, it is regarded as crucially important to discuss within the Division all phases of pending programs before they are presented to the European Parliament for discussion there. Otherwise, embarrassing delays can impede implementation of programs because of inadequate presentation before the Parliament.

With the Council's approval, April 2, 1963, of the general principle for a common policy on vocational training, a definite program was ready to be put into action. The first meetings were held in July, 1963, for the purpose of promoting the harmonization of standards of vocational training in the Community.

In the early stages of approaching this goal, a few occupations were chosen out of the 500 broad classifications in Germany, which gave indication of ready adaptation to a general program. These occupations show certain common characteristics in all the six member states and have been selected, therefore, as the pilot group for guidance in fostering harmonization in regard to other job classifications.

Another important responsibility of the Division is to develop a full knowledge of current developments in vocational training throughout the states. To this end the Division has made a close study of the existing situation in the Community.

Some of the findings brought to light are presented here. The Division has determined that the number of workers in the Community, with the exception of Italy's, who do not get some form of vocational training, is exceedingly small—4 to 5 per cent. In Germany and France the rate is even less—1.5 per cent.

In Germany, the time span for vocational training varies from one to three and one-half years. The bulk of this period of training is spent within an industrial enterprise. Exactly the contrary is true in Belgium, where most of the vocational training is obtained while the candidate is still in school. Under such an arrangement there must be allowances later for time to adapt such training to the peculiarities of a particular manufacturing company.

In France and Italy about 40 per cent of vocational training takes place within industry, and the remainder is provided in the schools. In recent years, because of the shortage of school facilities, there has been a growing tendency in France to increase the number of youngsters receiving vocational training within industry. In The Netherlands, only about 15 per cent of such training is done by industry.

Special efforts have been taken in France to recruit personnel for teaching courses in vocational training. Qualified members of the work force have been selected for this responsibility. Arrangements have been made for service credits on behalf of instructors who go on temporary leave from institutions in order to train workers. Part-time employment of married women with university degrees, as instructors, is now permitted. A special center for research on effective teaching of vocational skills has been established by the minister of national education. It has representatives from government, unions, industry and the teacher associations.[7]

THE GERMAN PROGRAM

At present in Germany there are many apprenticeships not being utilized because of the scarcity of applicants. The Division for Vocational Training in the Common Market estimates that 30 per cent of the openings for job training in Germany remain unfilled.

In German industry and commerce there are about 500 vocational patterns for training purposes authorized by the minister of economics. From these 500 basic training programs, workers are able to fit into 20,000 different types of jobs. Moreover, as new jobs are established and old ones eliminated each year, the training programs undergo corresponding revisions. This situation has been found to be similar in other member states.

In actuality vocational training programs in Germany are under the direction of a special department of the country's Chamber of Commerce, rather than under the government, even including examinations. The use of the three-year apprenticeship is widespread. However, apprentices must also attend professional schools for one or two days a week, both to accelerate the apprentice training and to provide a broader educational base.

The tradition of training along craft lines still remains strong in Germany. Notable advantages are acknowledged in this form of preparation, but its use is becoming increasingly expensive.

Of the youth in Germany between 15 and 22 years of age, 60 per cent are in apprenticeships relating to industry, commerce, agriculture, local contracting and services, railways, post office administration or medical institutes. A disadvantage for youths facing such programs in Germany is that most youngsters leave school there at the age of 14 or 15, with only about eight or nine years of formal schooling.

Nevertheless, in Germany and also in Luxembourg, all youths up to 18, whether in training or not, must have one full day a week of schooling. The requirement is similar in The Netherlands except that school attendance may take place in the evenings. The law in Germany on military service permits a deferment for young men who have not yet completed their vocational training, whether in a training school or in a recognized apprenticeship program.[8]

In each area of vocational training there is a curriculum in regard to skills and knowledge which must be completed in a determined period of time. In metal processing the same training requirements prevail for about all the semi-specialized areas. When that stage of training is finished, specialization then begins. The training time established for operatives in German filling stations is normally three to four years. However, at the completion of the apprenticeship they are fully competent in automobile maintenance and are able to give expert technical advice.

A more recent classification of job training concerns the installation of oil heating systems—of little importance in Germany until about thirty years ago. The problem here was the absence of workers who had been trained to install such equipment. To meet the situation both electricians and mechanics were put into a special job component and retrained within industry to qualify for the new job classification.

Customarily, apprentices put in 44 hours of work with their firm and 10 to 12 hours of schooling in addition. In such varied fields as commerce, industry and the professions, it is necessary at the end of the training period to obtain a certificate of competency by passing an adequate examination.

Even the first stage of the apprenticeship is characterized by a basic program that serves well in the event retraining is required in later life for some related industry. Hence, throughout Western Germany, a general pattern of training prevails for each of the authorized professions.

Though industry in Germany assumes the larger part of the responsibility for vocational training, pooled arrangements are utilized in the case of small companies in highly specialized industries. Under such circumstances not all companies may have yet installed the latest types of machinery. Therefore, to enable the apprentices in the different companies to acquire familiarity with new equipment, a system of rotating the apprentices has been put in effect.

In a plant having five to ten apprentices, the entire factory is normally adjusted to conduct their training. An older worker, perhaps a father of one of the apprentices, has the general responsibility for their training program. During the course of the apprenticeship no wage as such is paid. Instead, a supporting allowance, up to 600 marks per month, is allotted to each apprentice.

To lessen the serious lack of instructors in vocational training in Germany, the various Chambers of Commerce, both for industry and trade, have instituted three- to four-day study sessions and have established regular courses of instruction. The subject matter covered deals with pedagogical, technical and cultural themes.[9]

THE SITUATION IN OTHER MEMBER STATES

Though the regular primary schooling ends in The Netherlands at 12, a growing proportion of youths are spending two to four years more in primary technical schools before beginning formal apprenticeships. A longer period of training in the technical school serves to reduce the time required for apprenticeships in industry.

In the six member states it is expected that over the next few years a longer period of primary education will be required for all students. In France it is probable that by 1969 school attendance will be required for all until the age of 16. Germany is considering such an age limit at 15 or 16 years. In some parts of Germany the school-leaving age already is 15 years.

The age limit still remains at 14 in Holland. Nevertheless, both boys and girls in Holland are forbidden to enter the work force until 15 years of age, except for household tasks. Such a restriction in effect tends to keep Dutch youth in school for a longer period of time. For the most part the ninth and tenth grades of primary education in Holland tend to be more in the area of general education rather than technical.

Throughout the member states of the Community there is diminishing evidence of unemployed young people. The only serious exception to this observation is in Italy, and even there the situation is improving.

In southern Italy, however, little education, training or skill exists among members of the work force. The Division of Vocational Training in Brussels believes that only in Italy is it feasible to resort to short-term training programs. Though there are many Italian workers with no occupational training, they are nevertheless very adaptable to a course of training on a short-term basis, such as four to six weeks or three months.

In Italy, to encourage theoretical aspects of vocational training, often neglected in industrial training programs, the minister of labor has decided to reimburse part of the expense where industrial firms discharge this responsibility. In addition the government is endeavoring to encourage more preparatory courses for the benefit of apprentices who have had an inadequate general education.[10]

In other countries of the Community there is no evidence of such a short-term program, since the traditional system of a basic general education combined with adequate vocational training prevails. The brief course of a few weeks can only be regarded as a make-shift solution for a special situation in Italy, on the basis that it is better to give a short-term training course than not to do anything at all.

Mindful of these variations in practices and traditions in the "mixed system," there is still an effort within the Six to direct all vocational training programs along a similar course, at least to the extent of harmonization. There is no intent to have for the future a single program of education and vocational training. Instead, the member states will continue to carry on their programs in their own ways, but it is hoped that the final result in each country will show a record of accomplishment impressive in itself and also, to a degree, harmonious with the performance in other member countries.

A development in 1961, serving as a notable aid toward harmonization of vocational training in the Community, was the publication of a comparative study of terminology and definitions by the Federated Industries of the European Community. The work embraces the different levels of vocational training for the six member states.[11]

THE EUROPEAN COAL AND STEEL COMMUNITY

In the Division of Occupational Training at Luxembourg, there has been considerable concern with the need to modernize organization and methods of training. In the face of rapid technological progress in recent years, it is recognized that an urgent need exists for changing and intensifying training of the young, the older workers and even members of management.

BASIS FOR ACTION

Nevertheless, in this problem of training, the European Coal and Steel Community lacked specific authority in the Treaty of Paris—a defect avoided in the Treaty of Rome for the Common Market by the inclusion of Article 128 in that Treaty. Despite the specific omission in the Treaty of Paris, the Coal and Steel Community since 1953 has maintained that such a clause as found in Article 3 (d) of the Treaty—referring to the need to maintain conditions "which will encourage enterprises to expand and improve their ability to produce . . ."—implied the need to act in regard to vocational training programs.[12]

Accordingly, the Coal and Steel Community consulted representatives of unions, governments and industry, and told them of this conviction, also what the Community would be able to do. In effect a voluntary agreement was obtained from these representatives of management, labor and governments that the Coal and Steel Community should assume a responsibility for vocational training despite the silence of the Treaty.

For over 10 years close check has been maintained with experts in labor and employer groups to foster a consistent policy on such training and to maintain specific activities in regard to it. The European Parliament, member governments and professional organizations have all cooperated with the Community to this end.

The Community, of course, does not operate training programs, or give directives to enterprises for the exact methods of training. Even in the specialized industrial areas of coal and steel, training methods traditionally have differed among the Six, just as national systems of general education and technical training have differed.

THREEFOLD PROGRAM

Instead, the Community saw fit to devote its efforts on behalf of vocational training along three channels. First, it has initiated a systematic exchange of experience, so that the interested parties would have a better understanding of current developments within the Six, both good and bad. Meetings have therefore been held periodically in Luxembourg; seminars and study trips continue.

Research and published documentation are now provided by the Community on significant problems in the field of vocational training related to coal and steel. These publications are made available to all parties interested, including groups in the United States, South America and beyond the Iron Curtain.

Among the completed studies of the High Authority is a document treating the training of instructors, based on problems, methods and experiences within the Community industries. This particular research is the Community's first contribution to the formation of instructors for vocational training in the coal and steel industries.

The work delineates the necessary qualities which should be characteristic of the instructor. Suitable methods for selecting candidates for this profession are described as well as the type of technical and pedagogical instruction they should receive.[13]

Second, a new area of activity for the Community is the providing of investment credits for the construction of training centers. This development has considerable significance since the investment policy of the High Authority has been generally confined to technical installations as such, rather than to training centers. It is expected that this new type of investment will be enlarged over the years. There is a broad realization, shared by the Council, that a new approach to vocational training must be encouraged by such measures as modern training centers. The coal and steel industries are also aware of this need.

Third, the Community has established a technical committee to discuss reorganization of training programs. Government representatives review its findings. Further, the Division of Occupational Training in Luxembourg periodically prepares an agenda for committees of experts from industry and unions that discuss training problems and make suggestions once or twice a year; they have no power of decision.

The Coal and Steel Community is mindful of its limited role since the problems coming before it only concern directly two industries as compared to the much broader coverages entrusted to the European Economic Community. Nevertheless, there is no question that the experience and findings of the older Coal and Steel Community have put their stamp on the policies and practices of the Common Market.

Over the years the Community has submitted reports on vocational training to the member states and emphasized certain points in this field to the Council of Ministers. By these precedents and the discussion which follows, a competency has been established in the area of vocational training which the founding treaty did not specify for the Coal and Steel Community.

Three historical phases in regard to the Community's analysis of vocational training can be delineated. From 1953 to 1956 studies and publications were developed on the comparative organizations and methods of training in the Six for steelworkers and miners. From 1957 to 1960 attention was given to the problems of middle management—e.g., the problems of foremen in steel mills—and the difficulties of developing highly qualified instructors for vocational work.

For this second phase the Council requested findings in the following areas: 1) The problem of training unskilled workers who entered France, Belgium and Germany; 2) Research on cooperation between general educational systems and the coal and steel industries so as to effect a certain liaison with universities, engineering and technical schools; 3) A broad study of the structure and organization of general and technical educational systems in the Six; 4) Determination of methods to eliminate administrative and tax difficulties existing in the Community which hamper the exchange of teaching aids, such as films. Even now there are serious administrative difficulties hampering the sending of films, for instance, from Germany to France.

For the third phase, from 1960 to 1961, the Council directed the Coal and Steel Community to draft a new program on the adaptation of training methods to new technical developments in coal and steel, and promotion of more systematic measures for training of management.

Over the past several years the characteristic development in vocational training for the coal and steel industries has been toward a wider scope of activity and special efforts to adapt training programs to the new needs of industry.[14] Formerly, vocational training within industry consisted mainly of apprentice programs for the young or for the formation of instructors. Now training programs take into account the entire work force, from instructing the new employee to the advancement, specialization or readaptation of seasoned workers. Likewise there is the responsibility for the formation of instructors, technicians and managerial staff.

In the coal mining industry the increased use of mechanical and electrical equipment has intensified the need for advanced training and greater specialization. The High Authority has therefore authorized studies designed to encourage and accelerate efforts which will adapt training programs to the new trend toward mechanization and electrification.[15] Care is taken that every step toward adaptation is preceded by an evaluation of needs and the proper measures necessary to meet needs. There is a realization now of the increasing importance of adult training and of its recurring necessity throughout the work span of the employee.

As part of the third phase on training programs, the Division of Vocational Training has completed a special study on the repercussions of technical progress on methods used in training miners. There also has been published a separate study for the steel industry. The latter takes into account the impact of technical progress on the structure and quality of manpower in various sectors of the industry.

The Division, in making this study of the steel industry, has analyzed in each of the Six the impact of technology on the work force of selected companies, all of which operate modern furnaces and rolling mills. Comparable studies were made in these companies on structure and quality of manpower and especially the incidence of new jobs and modified jobs because of technological changes. The main concern of the Division was to draft the new job descriptions, determine the type of training required for them and thus establish a means of orientation for new training policies in the steel industry.

In the Division's second task for 1960–1961, concerning management, the Coal and Steel Community has made less progress than is the case in Britain and the United States. There is sharp awareness of the lag. One of the difficulties is the European tendency to look on problems of managerial training as the specific responsibility of engineering. Only the technical phases of such training gain significant attention. There is regret in the Community that in Europe, regarding management, there is not sufficient conviction that there are responsibilities relating to personnel and administrative organization along with technical phases.

As one effort to meet this problem the Division selected a representative management group from the Six to visit operations in the British steel and coal industries, with a view to observing developments in managerial training. There was a resulting acknowledgment that the British are doing more in this field than are the Six. Such an admission was considered an accomplishment.

Further, the High Authority completed a study in 1961 on the formation of managerial staff in the British steel industry, based on the 1960 visit to Britain by representatives from German, French and Italian steel industries. A parallel study was likewise published on the development of management personnel in the steel industries of the Six.[16]

Another study completed by the High Authority in 1961 deals with recent developments in vocational training among the Community's coal and steel industries and the results from changes in earlier methods.

The Division has found it difficult to get representatives from employee organizations and management around the same table in its attempts to set up a working committee on vocational training. Concerning management organizations there is the obstacle that, in some of the Six, management in coal and steel is not inclined to discuss its problems in "mixed committees," those which have union representation. Yet the official step taken by the Coal and Steel Community to establish such mixed committees is beginning to have results, seen in joint discussions by union and management representatives, despite the tradition of opposing this approach in some areas.

The Division of Vocational Training maintains that a more systematic method of training on all levels is of urgent necessity. Efforts are, accordingly, being made to persuade industrial firms to intensify their teaching programs and to adapt them to the repercussions of technological changes, such as automation and partial automation in the steel industry.

Throughout the period of its more than 10 years of activity, the Division cannot claim many direct spectacular gains, but there has been satisfactory success in indirect advances such as getting representatives of management and unions to discuss their problems on the level of the Community and to learn from the good and bad experiences of each other. Over the longer term it is hoped that this approach will result in a harmonized training system for the countries of the Coal and Steel Community.

The Community provides funds to finance training programs even though it has no direct voice in organizing them. Such programs are regarded as the main responsibility of the local authorities. Further, the Coal and Steel Community will provide funds only on the condition that the member states ask for them. Merely a request from industrial firms or unions will not suffice. There must be matched grants from the governments as well.

NEW METHODS OF TRAINING

As was the case in Brussels, in the Coal and Steel Community at Luxembourg the belief was expressed that both general education and technical training for the young should receive adequate attention in the formative period. The individual should be made aware of his responsibilities as a citizen and of his importance in the complex life of the community surrounding him.

Effort is made even in the technical area to avoid too narrow a base in order that breadth of knowledge will permit later adaptation to new technologies and techniques if the need arises. The Division is convinced that a young man will be faced in later years with changed processes; preparation for this contingency must be made even in the formative years.

The methods of training which are encouraged, therefore, endeavor to stress not so much a specific task on one machine, but a general technical development, for instance, in electronics. The broader base of technical knowledge serves then not only as preparation for specific training at the present time, but also for specialized retraining five or ten years later.

As an instance of the changed situation facing new workers in the steel industry, the contrast was drawn between old and new type steel mills. In the past steel workers were trained to qualify in the direct production of steel. Modern steel plants have greatly changed the requirements for training. Far from being directly involved today in the production and handling of steel personally, the worker in a modern plant must know how to operate machines which control the production process. The training process is vastly different now and a greater technical knowledge is required.

Similarly in the coal industry, in the old days ability to operate a compressed air hammer would have been sufficient. Today, with increasing mechanization of coal mines, it is necessary to have a much wider knowledge of mechanical operations, of general mining operations and of safety standards.

In effect there is a requirement now for workers of a higher educational standard than before. To meet this need broader education and systematic training must be the basis of future preparation for youths entering the work force. The responsibility for providing this educational background, in the view of the Community, will be first on the member governments, and then upon management in the individual firms.

In the steel industry, the Community has found that the large companies generally have had their own training centers since the 1920's. Here young men are trained over a three-year period in courses on electronics and mechanics, as well as in some 30 occupational callings.

COMMON TRAINING CENTERS

In the last 10 years the management of big steel firms has realized they must enlarge training activities to include programs so that adults become technicians, foremen, and enter types of specialized occupations for which the labor market presently has few qualified applicants. To meet these new requirements, either present training centers must be expanded or new ones constructed.

In 1963 this problem was met by joint action on the part of 10 big steel companies that set up a private association to build a new training center. A request has been made of the Coal and Steel Community for a loan to help finance the project. These 10 companies already have a training center in operation dating from 1950, but it is now inadequate.

Actually the common training center built in 1950 marked a departure from the traditional practice in Europe for each firm to have its separate training program. With the broadening of industrial markets since World War II, a trend has developed toward a new approach to training methods which did not fit in with old practices and obsolete buildings characteristic of training centers owned by individual companies.

Even new training centers that are confined to one company are vastly different from the pre-war type. In 1963 a large steel company in the Community decided to establish a modern structure housing machinery and laboratories to train varied categories of personnel, despite the rather unfavorable market for steel in 1963.

In training of foremen, the Division has found that for over 12 years the German steel industry has maintained common training centers. A common center for training foremen has existed in the French steel industry for over 14 years. A second center of the same type has recently been built to meet expanding requirements. Here modern technical training is available.

To train skilled workers in France it is still found advantageous to carry out the programs within the individual firms where apprentices are in sufficient numbers. For example, if a company has 11,000 employees it may have as many as 700 trainees, a number which justifies the maintenance of a company-owned training center.

Where the number of young men for any one firm does not warrant separate arrangements for training purposes, the Community finds that it is more feasible for several companies to pool their resources for this purpose. The obviously smaller number of candidates who would be required in a training program for foremen is indicative of why common centers have been established for this type of formation. One firm could not afford to maintain such a program for only three or four employees.

GROWTH OF RETRAINING PROGRAMS

In the original Treaty of Paris which established the Coal and Steel Community, Section 56 authorized the High Authority to finance the retraining of workers who were required to change employment because of technical changes within the general objectives specified by Community policy. However, in the Treaty amendment of 1960 this authorization was extended to retraining programs for workers obliged to change employment due to changes in marketing conditions of coal and steel not directly related to the Common Market. Hence, with the amendment of 1960, the High Authority was given a much broader scope of action for retraining than in 1951.

Some have interpreted this amendment of the 1951 Treaty as a major revision of the basic concept behind the Treaty. In other words, social adjustments financed by the Community are no longer to be limited to the transition period establishing the Common Market for coal and steel, but are to include any such future adjustments brought on by basic changes in market conditions. Instead of a shrinking role for the Division of Social Affairs, this amendment to the Treaty permits the Division to expand and adjust to new conditions.

In any event it is foreseen that hundreds of thousands of mine workers will have to turn to other types of employment because of basic changes in the coal industry. Further, structural changes in steel employment, because of automation and technological progress, will also necessitate vast retraining programs for future displaced workers. A wide transformation of skills is regarded as inevitable by the Coal and Steel Community.

As an indication of future trends, total steel production from 1955 to 1960 increased by 40 per cent. However, total employment increased by only 14 per cent. Yet of this increased total manpower of 14 per cent, the proportion in the classifications of clerical, technical and managerial had risen by 22 per cent.

Under Article 56, the High Authority has several other approaches, besides financing retraining programs, to facilitate readjustment for displaced workers. As an example, differential allowances are paid to a point where total income equals 90 per cent of the former wage to workers who obtain lower-paid employment elsewhere. If the new job means change of residence, cost of moving is borne by the Community.[17]

During 1962, the High Authority made an arrangement with West Germany to apply the measures provided in Article 56 of the Treaty to displaced iron ore miners and steel workers. In the case of France there have been increased payments made by the High Authority for unemployment compensation and for meeting lower wage differentials on new jobs in the case of displaced coal and ore miners and steel workers.[18]

During 1962, the High Authority authorized 47 applications in Germany, France and Belgium, of the broader provisions relating to readaptation of workers as in Section 2 of Article 56. The bulk of the cases related to German coal and ore miners.[19] For the Community generally, displaced coal miners remain the chief beneficiaries of readaptation programs. In France a significant program of vocational retraining has been in progress with respect to displaced coal miners preparing for reemployment in newly established industries.

VOCATIONAL TRAINING IN THE UNITED STATES

In the face of full employment in all but one of the Common Market countries and mindful of the overwhelming proportion of youth in those countries who receive vocational training adapted to modern trends in industry and trade, the economic situation confronting youth in America seems most disconcerting. In the six-month period ended March 31, 1964, over 53 per cent of 25,190 men in New York City failed to pass the preinduction Selective Service examination, a rate slightly above the average for the nation as a whole.[20] Further, about one-half of the rejections in New York City were due to educational deficiency, a rate somewhat above the national average, which is also disturbingly high.

Current unemployment data would indicate that educational deficiency is also a cause for economic rejection in the civilian work force. Despite rising productivity and rising over-all employment, persistent large scale unemployment has remained since the 1950's in many sectors of the economy. One development that has become evident during these 15 years is that in addition to willingness to work there must be capability for doing the work available. A vast number of job seekers, including millions of young people, are not thus qualified.

Today the highest unemployment rates are found among those with least education. Yet it is expected that of the some 26,000,000 young people who will enter the labor force in the 1960's, one-third will come under the designation of "dropouts."[21] One might expect that there would be hope of obtaining vocational and technical training geared to modern trends for this enormous number of youth, who will have discontinued an educational program supposedly designed as preparation for college. Unfortunately, such training programs are not readily available.

Ironically, vocational programs tied to a declining economic pattern still enjoy generous public support. It has been estimated that in the 1950's farm employment decreased by about 3,000,000 and now amounts to 7.5 per cent of the labor force. Nevertheless, in 1960 funds allocated to training in agriculture were 28 per cent of all vocational education funds.[22] It is true that there have been a series of federal vocational education acts, based on grants-in-aid to the states, since the original Morrill Act of 1862. For the most part, however, their application has been in the areas of home economics and agricultural pursuits.

The new technology, with its widespread impact on the structure of the economy, looks askance at the unskilled and the inadequately educated worker. Further, changing tastes and demands are leaving thousands of other workers with obsolete skills and no hope of reemployment. For both groups of unemployed the burgeoning fields of electronics, government work and service trades offer no encouragement, since they lack the capability to fill such jobs.

Though acknowledging that over-all expansion of production must be intensified, Gunnar Myrdal, the Swedish economist, emphasizes that to reduce the idle labor supply in America, the quality of the labor force must be improved. He finds there is a need for decided expansion of facilities for education and training. In particular, Myrdal stresses that these facilities for young people should expand at a rate greater than in proportion to the population increase because of the larger than average increase in the younger age groups.[23]

Further, Myrdal stresses that special attention in regard to education and training should be given to younger people in the chronically neglected geographical regions and social strata of America. To accomplish this objective, Myrdal, for over 20 years a close student of the American scene, deduces that no quick solution is likely since the very teachers, as well as facilities, are in short supply.

Myrdal observes that in addition to the need for greatly expanded general education, there is a particular necessity for concentration of efforts in the field of vocational training in America, but with a creative philosophy that will strive to steer young people away from blind alleys and move them to better occupations and higher responsibilities. He regrets that "training for work has in America never been made a regular part of the educational system."[24]

Myrdal acknowledges that industry in America, predominantly big industry, has extensive programs of on-the-job education and training for its employees. However, he notes that such programs are for those already employed and who initially have a high level of education and training. In effect such programs are supplemental to other education and training, dependent for their source on public institutions.

In December of 1963 Congress at long last took constructive action to modernize the Federal program regarding vocational education. Passage of the Vocational Education Act of 1963 will not only substantially increase the grants to States for vocational training, but also will bring a transition from the present emphasis on home economics and farm operations, underlining the need for training in business fields and work areas of significance for school dropouts and others still in search of their first jobs. Additional legislation in 1963 called for the construction of five residential schools to provide supervision and job training for school dropouts and other youths now handicapped by living in a demoralizing environment.[25]

4.

Conditions of Employment

FREE MOVEMENT OF WORKERS

A CENTRAL PROVISION IN THE 1957 TREATY OF ROME IS ARTIcle 48 which concerns the free movement of workers within the six member states of the Common Market. In clauses one and two of this Article it is stated that:

> The free movement of workers shall be ensured within the Community not later than at the date of the expiry of the transitional period.
> This shall involve the abolition of any discrimination based on nationality between workers of the Member States as regards employment, remuneration, and other working conditions.[1]

Additional clauses in Article 48 note, however, that qualifications can be put on this free movement of workers in the interest of public safety and health. Further, it is pointed out that within the meaning of the Treaty the phrase includes the right to accept offers of employment which actually have been made. Accordingly it is to be understood that the freedom fostered by the Treaty within the member states is for the purpose of entering into such proffered employment.

In Article 49 of the Treaty the Council of Ministers is directed to set forth necessary measures to implement the free movement of workers. Through close cooperation with national labor ministries the Council is to seek the abolition of such legal barriers as time limits, whether international or local, which restrict eligibility for employment. On the positive side, Article 49 directs the Council to set up "appropriate machinery for connecting offers of employment and requests for employment" so that a proper balance can be maintained and serious threats to the standard of living and employment in various regions may be avoided. The regulations to achieve these objectives are to follow from proposals made to the Council by the Commission of the Community and after the Economic and Social Committee has been consulted.[2]

DIRECTIVE FOR THE FIRST STAGE

Regulations for the first stage of the transition were adopted by the Council in September, 1961, and were to be in effect for two years. During this period consideration of priority in the domestic employment market was to be taken under advisement. In the following stage, however, the principle of priority would become an exception. In effect, by the end of the transitional period, that is, after 12 years, it is intended that there will be no discrimination in the clearance of employment vacancies and applications in the Community.[3]

The action of the Council in adopting this first phase of the program in 1961 was hailed as a major step in the direction of a completely free labor market. Upon the completion of two progressive stages it was expected that the traditional "national" labor markets would be eliminated by ending all restrictions in accordance with the Treaty.

Further, the new regulations embodied the principle of European Economic Community (EEC) priority in the labor markets. Thus a member country would note the availability of workers in the Six before seeking manpower from non-EEC countries. It is interesting to point out here that when this portion of the regulations was approved, a chief supplying country, Italy, interpreted the clause as an obligation under the Treaty. However, the chief employing nation, Germany, did not consider that a Treaty obligation as such was involved.

According to the regulations of 1961, it was expected that a member state with inadequate manpower would make vacancies known to other countries of the Six after openings had remained unfilled for three weeks. The countries thus notified were required to report any available labor resources within 15 days and actually to forward names of candidates within three more weeks. The regulations also provided that Common Market workers who were employed in an EEC country might take their wives and minor children and dependents with them. Further, they were entitled to join and vote in labor organizations. Work permits could be renewed in the host country for the same job after one year, and for another job in the same field after three years. After four years permits could be renewed for any job.[4]

By August of 1962, it is noteworthy to point out that a member of the EEC Commission, Levi Sandri, stated that by encouraging free movement of workers the Commission had no desire merely to promote migration or to favor density of manpower in existing industrial areas. Rather, the Commission was desirous of facilitating, when possible, the flow of capital investment to regions where unemployment was still critical. The impact of a free movement of labor was thus regarded as more likely to cause an upward leveling of wages and provide opportunity for underemployed labor to enjoy the benefits of a modern economy rather than promote mass movements of labor.[5]

In an even stronger statement during a debate in the European Parliament on the free movement of seasonal and frontier workers, Levi Sandri, referring to hopes that the Commission would foster job creation where manpower already was available, observed that the EEC had always believed free movement of labor must not be regarded as a solution to persistent unemployment problems in the Community. Instead, the achievement of this free movement was to be a first step toward recognition of a common European citizenship.[6]

By the end of 1962 Commission proposals already were before the Council in regard to rules in the second stage of the transition on free movement of labor. The new rules were to relax administrative procedure and practices among the Six in regard to manpower movements. An important feature of the proposals was the termination of priority treatment for the home labor market, apart from certain exceptions and safeguards for regions marked by unemployment. Additional steps were suggested to extend employment of migrant workers and establish their eligibility for election to representative groups within the employing firm.[7] In effect, the proposed new rules were regarded as conducive to substantial progress in the assimilation of workers into the various national work forces. Further, it was believed that these rules would prevent administrative delays concerning immigration and residence of workers.[8]

JOB DESCRIPTIONS

One of the measures the Economic Community has undertaken to encourage freer movement of workers among member states has been the compilation of job descriptions for various skilled occupations, especially in occupations where greater mobility on the part of workers is typical, as in construction and hotel work. Utilization of the same job descriptions throughout the Community is expected to assure accurate matching of requests with offers to meet them.

In the process of compiling this catalogue of job descriptions, it has been found that some occupations tend to remain stable in job content over many years while others undergo major changes. However, the total number of occupations in the first trade list was only 68, and therefore the problem of changes in job content was much less serious than in the case of the extensive glossary compiled by the International Labor Organization for a vast number of countries.

In describing the job content effort has been taken to note the individual tasks that would be required of the candidate. However, excessive detail is avoided; too comprehensive a list could require revision of the descriptions every few years. Difficulty in harmonizing job descriptions has been encountered because of different classifications in various countries. For instance, there is one trade in France for the occupation of baker. In Italy, however, six trades are involved.

THE COORDINATION OFFICE AND AUXILIARY COMMITTEE

To implement Regulation 15 of the European Community in regard to free movement of workers, the European Coordination Office has been established. In addition there are now Advisory and Technical Committees. It is the function of the Office to institute regular communications with government departments and the central employment agencies appointed by them.

Within the Office statistical data is collated which is provided quarterly by the member states in line with identical schedules drafted by the Office. At the beginning of each quarter the Office compiles and distributes a list of occupations and regions where a shortage or surplus of manpower exists.

Also on a quarterly and annual basis the Office makes reports on clearing operations and placements among the six member states. Continuing effort is being made to bring more uniformity into the methods used by Community countries to evaluate the status of the labor market. Further, the Office is studying measures by which it can give more complete information on manpower conditions in the various regions of the Community to workers, employers and labor exchanges.

The Advisory Committee has membership representing employers, workers and governments and meets two to three times a year in Brussels. In 1962 it helped prepare the Commission's drafts on regulations to advance freedom of movement by workers during the second stage of the transition. By a large majority, approval was given to the Commission's proposal to discard the priority rule for hiring in the national home labor market, as compared to migrant workers from other member states.

In 1962, the Technical Committee gave approval to the comparative glossary of trades compiled by the Community, in which is represented the greatest migration among the Six. This first volume was widely distributed, especially to national employment agencies. The experts on the Committee were unanimous in stressing the need to continue the compilation of such lists because of their high practical value in quickly determining the skills available among migrant workers. The Technical Committee has also agreed to establish a program to train staffs of specialists to operate vacancy clearing offices.

DIRECTIVE FOR THE SECOND STAGE

In October of 1962 the Commission submitted to the Council its directive for the free movement of workers in the second stage, originally intended to begin in 1963. At this point the principle of priority for Community labor had been modified to the extent that new arrangements would allow for exceptions so that there would be no upset in the balance of the labor market for a particular region or occupation. Thus hiring of labor coming from another member state might be deferred if an excess labor supply existed locally. Further, it was agreed that the principle of priority for Community labor would be applied flexibly so as not to impair the efficiency of plant operations. Nevertheless, the proposed directive was designed to make it much more likely that workers from other member states would acquire the same rights as national employees in a given state, in three significant categories.

As one instance, the Commission held that where the duration of employment for a foreign worker is extended, his full assimilation to national worker status should be accelerated. For instance, the waiting period before eligibility to vote and run for office in union and plant council elections should be reduced. Moreover, the Commission favored, with the approval of the European Parliament and the Economic and Social Committee, a reduction in the period of regular employment after which a foreign worker acquired additional rights. Accordingly, such a worker would be permitted to accept any wage-earning occupation anywhere in a member state after only two years of regular employment there.

Second, the Commission proposed that eligibility for election to factory committees in any member state should be open to workers from other states of the Community at least to the extent that such elections are governed by law and are dependent on administrative decisions. Nevertheless, the Commission stipulated that a worker would not attain such eligibility until he had been a resident for at least three years in the member state.

The third category concerned the admission of workers' families. The existing right of wives and minor children to follow the head of the family was extended in the new proposal to include all other fully dependent relatives residing in the same house with the worker. Nevertheless, the admission of a worker's family would depend on his ability to house them in a manner considered normal to workers in the area of his employment. The Commission also proposed that workers under contract for no more than three months would not have to obtain labor or resident permits.[9]

On February 7, 1964, the Council unanimously approved the draft regulation submitted in 1962 by the Commission. The new provisions were considered extensively liberalizing in regard to manpower mobility, and conducive to closer cooperation between the member states and the Commission in regard to priority consideration for Community labor. According to the new regulations, there would no longer be any discrimination against the employment of workers who are nationals of other states in the Community.

It was believed that a solution had now been established to meet the key problem of manpower within the Community. To implement the new regulation the Commission intends to prepare a report on the general situation of the labor market in the Six. In turn member states are to examine this report with the Commission so that the labor market in other member states can be noted when shaping employment policies. Thus, as far as possible, priority for Community nationals will be observed in filling job vacancies.[10]

Aware that the regulation in the second stage for the free movement of workers had been submitted to the Council in October, 1962, several speakers in the European Parliament on January 23,

1964, expressed regret at the Council's delay of more than a year in adopting the measure. Further, that same day the European Parliament discussed a report presented by M. Storch on the findings of a delegation of the Social Committee which studied problems of free movement throughout the Community. Suggestions were made on particular tasks the Community should undertake to help solve the problem of free movement. Emphasis was placed on housing needs of migrant workers, the extension of social services, vocational training and especially intensive training to fit unemployed workers in certain regions of the Community for skilled work in other areas.

Emphasis was also placed on the importance of making the free movement policy part of a general employment policy embracing regional problems. A special point was made of the need for a regional development policy which would, as much as possible, open up jobs for unemployed workers in their native areas.

The European Parliament in a subsequent resolution stated that there was a pressing need for both a European and a national effort to correct deficiencies in recruitment and placement, housing and vocational training, and sources of information. Unless shortcomings in these areas were removed, the Parliament expressed concern that long-term progress toward freedom of movement would be hampered or even undermined. True freedom of movement from depressed areas was defined as migration by choice rather than from driving necessity. As one cure for this latter cause of migration the Parliament emphasized that economic and social structures should be improved in depressed areas.[11]

A move toward more adequate information for migrant workers was taken by the Commission on February 26, 1964, when it called in worker representatives to consider the feasibility of publishing and circulating an information handbook on living and working conditions in the Six, with a digest of the basic regulations on free movement of workers. As a first step, coverage was designated only for workers in construction, metal production and processing, and agriculture. Members of the Advisory Committee agreed to provide the Commission with all pertinent information on their respective nations. For the industries initially selected, representatives agreed to establish study groups which would meet periodically.[12]

Despite Community efforts to encourage the movement of workers, Italy is still the only member of the Community that supplies a notable amount of migrant labor. However, economic growth has tended to reduce the outward movement of Italian workers in the past few years. Moreover, most Italian migrants continue to travel to Switzerland rather than to Community countries.

Each year it is estimated that a million workers migrate from southern to northern European countries. However, a considerable part of this movement is seasonal in nature. Workers who live close to international frontiers and are employed in neighboring countries are not considered migrants.

The main sources of emigrant labor in Europe are Italy, Spain, Portugal, Greece, Turkey and Yugoslavia. Community countries which look to these sources for manpower are Germany, France, Belgium and The Netherlands, in that order. The other receiving nation, besides Switzerland, is the United Kingdom.

Until 1961, Italians composed over one-half of the labor migration, but their proportion was only 42 per cent in 1963. Both France and Germany have experienced a rapid decline in Italian immigrants.[13]

For the member states of the Community itself, with the exception of the unskilled workers—particularly of southern Italy—it has been found very difficult to get workers to emigrate. The barriers to mobility, noted below, in the special study sponsored by the European Coal and Steel Community, such as language, social roots and customs, tend to anchor workers and their families in their natal regions despite declining production in obsolescent industries. As long as they have social security and hope of some kind of job in their own region, most are reluctant to relocate.

EMPLOYMENT AND THE ECONOMIC COMMUNITY

The Community has no precise mandate to affect the volume of employment within the member states. Industry and governments retain that power. For the most part the policy of the Commission is governed by Article 118 of the Treaty. This article states that it shall be the aim of the Commission to encourage close cooperation among the member states in matters of employment.[14] Only in the area of free movement of workers is there a definite policy for the Commission to follow. To this end Article 49 (d) of the Treaty indicates that by directives or regulations the Commission may encourage the free movement of workers "by setting up appropriate machinery for connecting offers of employment and requests for employment, with a view to balancing them in such a way as to avoid serious threats to the standard of living and employment in the various regions and industries."[15]

What action is taken on employment policy, in effect, depends mainly upon the enterprises within the member states. The EEC has the role of a catalytic agent. It is in a position to exercise its coordinating and promotional activities by field studies, consultation with representatives of member states, and periodic conferences sponsored by the Commission. Actually the labor ministries in the member countries have not been anxious to yield much discretion in the area of employment policy to the Brussels headquarters of EEC.

Fortunately, the issue of employment has not been a major one since the founding of the Community in 1957 because of the generally prosperous economic picture in Europe. Nevertheless, the Community has made studies of areas where pockets of unemployment persist, as well as of situations of chronic labor shortages. Attention will be given to these two problems after noting the general picture on employment in the Six.

According to Robert Marjolin, vice-president of the EEC Commission, the continued increase in the size of the Community's labor force in 1962 saw unemployment, except for certain parts of Italy, less than 1 per cent of the EEC working population.[16] For the year 1960 the number of those employed increased by 900,000 and totaled 70.7 million workers. Germany and Italy accounted for most of the increase.

For 1962 the Commission reported a total employment of 72.4 million persons which amounted to a gain of nine per cent over 1961, or 640,000 new jobs. In terms of employment in major activities, between 1958 and 1962 the percentage distribution in agriculture had fallen from 22.7 to 19.5 per cent. In services the share of Community employment increased from 35.3 to 37.4 per cent. In industry the percentage rose from 42 to 43.1 per cent.[17]

By the middle of 1962 the Community estimated that the number of unemployed was the lowest on record in almost all the six countries. The sharpest decline was in Belgium where unemployment fell 30 per cent in the first half of 1962. Though Italy had the highest rate of unemployment in the Community in 1962, in the preceding two and one-half years unemployment declined there by 29 per cent leaving 1,102,000 workers without jobs.[18]

At the end of 1963 unemployment, except for Italy, remained extremely low and even in Italy it continued to decline. Moreover, by 1963 there were quite general shortages in Italy of skilled workers, semiskilled and even unskilled workers in some regions. For 1963, the Community considered its labor market had experienced not merely a high level of employment but actually "overemployment."[19]

SCARCITY OF LABOR

Especially in the skilled trades, the scarcity of labor is regarded as one of the most significant problems confronting the Common Market. For its solution the basic proposal is to raise the quality of existing labor sources by programs in vocational training. Even as early as February, 1960, the Commission, together with the six governments, had found through a special study that a prolonged boom had practically exhausted manpower reserves in several states, such as Germany, Luxembourg and The Netherlands. Preparations were then being made for short courses in occupational training for Italian workers so as to help close the labor gaps present over wide ranges of industry.[20] Again, in 1960, the Commission drew up a program for job training in Italy for which the financial resources of the Social Fund were put into play. Under the 1960 program, 10,000 workers were involved, of which about 9,000 were destined to be employed in West Germany and 700 in The Netherlands. In the latter country they were to be allocated to trades in construction, metalworking and catering.[21]

In the fall of 1962 the Commission's third annual report on manpower trends in the EEC noted the continuing breach between supply and demand in labor, even to the extent of sometimes blocking industrial expansion. While labor reserves continued to decline, the number of unfilled jobs generally tended to increase considerably.[22]

This imbalance continued through 1962 and was augmented in regard to skilled workers. The number of vacancies for such jobs were far in excess of applications in West Germany, Holland and Luxembourg. In France, Belgium and northern Italy there were also considerable labor shortages of skilled workers.[23]

IMPROVING EMPLOYMENT CONDITIONS

Turning to the role of the Economic Community in relation to improving working conditions, the Treaty notes in Article 117 that:

> Member States hereby agree upon the necessity to promote improvement of the living and working conditions of labour so as to permit the equalisation of such conditions in an upward direction.
>
> They consider that such development will result not only from the functioning of the Common Market which will favour the harmonisation of social systems, but also from the procedures provided for under this Treaty and from the approximation of legislative and administrative provisions.[24]

The Commission declared soon after the Treaty was signed that

Article 117 did not mean an alignment of all six members along some theoretical average of harmonization which would in effect slow development in the more advanced nations until the less fortunate member states caught up. Instead, it was maintained that the Community must endeavor to persuade and help all of the Six to improve their present standards. Further, the "equalisation" sought for in Article 117 is to be achieved by more rapid improvement in areas where the need is more urgent. To this end the Commission endeavors to offer individuals, social groups, geographical and economic areas equal opportunities to participate in social advancement.

Article 117 acknowledges that though the operation of the Common Market is a necessary condition for improvement of working conditions and living standards, additional measures are required such as coordination of social policies within the member states. However, the actual work of coordination is not regarded as the responsibility of the Community, but of the social partners and governments of the member states. The Community's role is seen as one of planning studies to be carried on through other international bodies or by research institutes, and conducting consultations and conferences with government, industry and union representatives, as well as with professional experts. Thus the Community endeavors to put the problems before the parties directly concerned, and by constant effort persuade them to work out solutions compatible with the welfare of the Community.

In actuality the Treaty gives the Commission no real power over the governments or social partners to achieve this upward harmonization of working conditions. For instance, the Commission has no mandate to order the governments to coordinate their laws on weekly hours of work or paid holidays. It can only present the problems arising from lack of such coordination and recommend that remedial action be taken.

To facilitate this task the Community has launched studies covering all working conditions feasible for harmonization within the Six. A special study has been undertaken to determine the economic and social impact of new technology and of replanning of industry in order to adapt conditions of work to new requirements.[25]

By conferences and consultation, and by publishing of documentary studies, the Commission endeavors to create awareness of better working conditions present in the more advanced member states and thus stimulate the desire and effort to attain those standards in the less developed states. As one instance of the educational and per-

suasive activities of the Community, in 1962 there were 35 conferences held in Brussels under the direction of the Community for the
purpose of disseminating such knowledge to representative groups
from the member states. Before 1957 such gatherings were unknown
in the industries covered by the EEC. It is true that the International
Labor Organization has conducted tripartite conferences to study
labor conditions for many decades, but the plenary sessions occur
only every two years, and then on a global basis. Regional meetings
confined to a restricted number of countries take place in the ILO
even less frequently.

Under the auspices of the Community, industrial partners in such
countries as Germany, France, Belgium and The Netherlands are
readily accessible to each other for discussions on matters of working
conditions. It does appear therefore that the opening of the frontiers
has had a favorable impact on working conditions by tending to
harmonize them through collective bargaining based on data made
available by the Community. More than ever before negotiations now
take into account what is happening in other countries on such issues
as paid holidays, hours of work and other conditions of the job.

For the first time company and union representatives have stable
relations with their colleagues in other countries and thus are kept
informed of new developments regarding terms and conditions of
employment. Similarly the documentary studies sponsored by the
Community serve as a contribution toward harmonization.

In Belgium, for example, employers at the time of union negotiations actually consider bargaining trends in other member countries.
Belgian employers are aware that French employers have agreed to
the four-weeks vacation. While Belgian industry, because of the tight
labor market, has not felt it could make that concession, it has
weighed the alternatives used in The Netherlands, namely, payment
of extra time in lieu of additional vacation after the regular period.
This arrangement was incorporated in the 1963 Belgian inter-industry
agreement on vacations, discussed below.

EQUAL PAY FOR MEN AND WOMEN

By the end of 1961 the Commission had completed plans to assure
removal of disparities remaining between wages of men and women
in the Community. By 1960 there had taken place a gradual reduction
in this discrepancy. Equal pay for men and women is one of the
objectives of the Treaty of Rome.[26]

It is the belief of the Commission, however, that such customary

criteria as ability, age, seniority on the job and even family circumstances can be given consideration when applying the principle of
equal pay for men and women. Nevertheless the Commission holds
that job classifications should apply to both male and female workers
without distinction.[27]

For various industrial sectors in Belgium during 1960, agreements
had been reached raising wage rates for women workers to within
80 to 100 per cent of those paid to men. In Italy an agreement had
been signed in July, 1960, by representatives of employer and worker
organizations providing for sizeable increases in minimum wage rates
for women workers and the use of a single job classification for
both men and women. In January, 1961, the General Confederation
of Commerce in Italy signed an agreement with three major trade
unions, providing for the general increase of wage rates for women
workers with equal qualifications up to 95 per cent of the rates paid
to men. In The Netherlands during 1960 a number of agreements were
signed which established a notable advance toward the objective of
equal pay for women.[28]

However, by May, 1964, while considerable progress in the Community had been attained in moving toward the objective of equal pay
for women, it was already evident then that the deadline of December
31, 1964, for the removal of all pay inequalities between the sexes
would not be met unless the labor ministries in the member states
greatly intensified their efforts to effectuate Community policy.

Nevertheless, an EEC Commission report found that new Belgian
collective bargaining agreements in many industries provided for
identical pay provisions for men and women and also observed the
Community's time schedule for reaching pay equality. Yet in some
other industries wage differentials of 20 to 25 per cent remained,
despite refusal by the government to recognize agreements not
conforming to Community policy.

This Commission report also notes that in Germany wage differences between men and women on the same jobs are unlawful. Accordingly, the government and employer associations maintain there
has been no restriction on the application of wage equality in bargaining agreements. However, unions in Germany assert that certain
methods of job classification foster discrimination; for instance, where
jobs are classified by skill, women in some industries have not been
upgraded. Yet the Commission found that women's wages are actually
rising more rapidly than men's.

Rapid application of the principle of equal pay for women has taken place in France where the formal recognition of women is more extensive than in the other members of the Six. Generally, statistical findings show that in France a difference of less than 10 per cent exists between wages for men and women.

The EEC had found that, by 1964, wage rates for women in Italy had been increased by reclassification of jobs, eliminating some lower pay grades. During 1963 in certain industries collective bargaining agreements had satisfactorily met the problem of wage disparities. Although in other industries collective bargaining is still not recognized, the EEC concluded that in Italy, Community policy is being closely applied under government inspection.

It has been found that in Luxembourg, unions, employers and government are supporting collective agreements which comply with Community policy. Recent legislation there has provided for equal minimum wages for both sexes.

Because of new minimum wage laws for women in The Netherlands that incorporate rapid wage increases, wage differences between the sexes are now less than 10 per cent in many industries. Since new collective agreements without equal pay provisions are illegal, it is believed that equal wages should be quickly attained.[29]

LENGTH OF THE WORK WEEK

The average length of the work week for the Community, as late as 1960, was 45 hours. For Italy the average work week was less but most likely this was because of the greater number of public holidays. In The Netherlands the average was somewhat above 45.

In 1960 the five-day, 45-hour week was customary in Belgium. Many companies and trade unions were seeking its general adoption with overtime rates for extra hours. For West Germany most employees were on a 45-hour week or less. Though the legal limit of a 40-hour week has been in effect in France for some years, the average hours worked per week in 1960 was actually over 45.[30]

RESULTS THUS FAR

Generally speaking, progress toward the goal of harmonization of social and working conditions in the EEC has not advanced as rapidly as originally expected, especially among less economically developed regions. Greater efforts toward coordination will be necessary if the social objectives of the Treaty are to be realized.

To the criticism of union organizations that social harmonization resulting from the Treaty is not much in evidence as yet, employer associations point out that persistent differences within the member states prevent any early attainment of close harmonization in conditions for the Community as a whole.

With respect to the difficulties besetting the Communities in promoting harmonization of working conditions, mention has been made of the lack of specific language in the Treaties of Paris and Rome on this point. Yet in one instance, at least, the Treaty of Rome has been most specific. Article 119 goes into considerable detail on how equal pay for equal work without sexual discrimination is to be attained. A time table was set down in that Article to the effect that this objective should be reached by the end of the first stage in the development of the Common Market, namely January, 1962. As noted above, the objective, even when it was delayed until 1964, was not attained; considerable progress has been made nonetheless.

Moreover, Article 119 is very specific in stating that equal wages are to include a basic minimum remuneration as well as additional pay of any kind, direct or indirect. Further, the Article states that equal payment here refers to both piece rates for the same unit of measurement and time rates for the same job.

Such precise language, though quite characteristic of the Treaty in regard to commercial policy, is not generally in evidence in other sections of the Treaty's chapter dealing with social provisions. Thus Article 118, which deals with such matters as employment, labor legislation, working conditions, social security, safety and industrial health, has no timetable for its implementation. Instead, the Commission is directed to promote close collaboration among member states in the social field of areas listed in Article 118. To this end the Commission is instructed to work closely with member states "by means of studies, the issuing of opinions and the organizing of consultations. . . ."[31]

There is the possibility that opening of borders to greater competition between member states caused certain governments to demand that social provisions in the Treaty which bore directly on costs of production, such as equal pay for men and women and length of paid vacations, be harmonized at an early stage, and on a rather definite basis.

Thus it would seem that provisions put in the Treaty for social policy alone, tend to be general in language. However, matters of social policy which are inserted primarily for competitive reasons, tend to be rather specific. Generally social legislation is an area of jealous concern to the national governments. To surrender final determination of policies on employment, working conditions and similar matters to the Commission would have been regarded as giving up sovereignty over a much larger area than member governments were willing to do when the Treaty was signed in 1957.

Nevertheless, the European Parliament, in a resolution on social harmonization, has urged the Commission as well as employer and worker organizations to foster, in accordance with Article 118, the establishment of more mixed committees and greater activity by existent committees to promote harmonization in living and working conditions; they are requested to make use of the studies made by the Commission. The same resolution also urged European governments to take more energetic measures toward social harmonization as provided under the Treaties.[32]

In 1962 M. Levi Sandri, a Commission member, stated that the executive body of the Community fully supported the views of the European Parliament and that no restrictive interpretations should be put on Article 119 which deals with equal pay for men and women. Further, he stressed that it was an unacceptable position to hold that a member state was only obliged to meet its commitments under Article 119 to the degree that other States did likewise.[33] It is apparent that the national governments, especially their legislatures, are basically responsible for the rather slow advance toward harmonization of social legislation in the Six, and not the executive bodies of the Communities.

THE EUROPEAN COAL AND STEEL COMMUNITY

LABOR MOBILITY

While the EEC was established to break down barriers hampering the movement of men and materials in almost the entire economy of the six member states, by the Treaty of Rome it still has to depend on inter-governmental cooperation to achieve these ends. Likewise, in the case of the European Coal and Steel Community there was full awareness that Article 69 had reserved no power of decision to the High Authority on labor mobility. It was up to the sovereign states to take the necessary measures toward implementing this Article of the Treaty of Paris. The High Authority saw its role here as one of orientating and facilitating action by the member states, and then only for the industries of steel, coal and iron ore.

Free movement of labor therefore, within the European Coal and Steel Community, envisioned a more restricted area than was planned for the Common Market. Further qualifications were also added in

Article 69 of the Treaty of Paris, which deals with labor mobility. It reads thus:

1. The Member States bind themselves to renounce any restriction, based on nationality, on the employment in the coal and steel industries of workers of recognized qualifications for positions in such industries possessing the nationality of one of the Member States; this commitment shall be subject to the limitations imposed by the fundamental needs of health and public order.

What is implied in Section 1 of this Article is made plain in Section 2 since there the member states are directed to draft a common definition of "skilled jobs and conditions of qualification. . . ." Only when expansion of production in the coal and steel industries might be impeded by a shortage of unskilled labor will immigration restrictions on such workers be modified so as to ease the labor situation. In that contingency special effort is to be directed toward obtaining coal and steel labor from other member states. With these qualifications established, Section 4 of the Article then directs the states to ban any discrimination in wages and working conditions between foreign and national workers.[34]

In accordance with the directive of Article 69, the governments adopted an agreement in August, 1957, which went into effect the following month. Because of the application only to skilled workers, it was estimated the coverage would apply to not more than one-sixth of 1.6 million workers employed in the coal and steel industries in 1956.[35]

At least this group of select workers were supposedly free to take jobs in other countries of the Six and the governments had the duty to avoid regulations which would hamper their movement. In actuality, the workers eligible to exercise this freedom were those most in demand in their home countries and were the highest paid because of their skills. In consequence there has been very little inclination to emigrate to another state, even though the same type of employment at good wages would be offered to them.

Nevertheless, to meet the requirements of Article 69 a special Council of Ministers adopted in 1954 a list of 56 trades in which workers could exercise free movement in the European Coal and Steel Community. A worker practicing one of these trades henceforth had the right to demand a labor card which would permit him to choose employment anywhere in the Community. This trade list represented the first stage in attaining free employment of manpower in the coal and steel industries.

As a further step in this direction an intergovernmental commission was appointed which met from November 7 to 9, 1960. At that time a decision was made to seek approval from the Six of a second list of 116 trades. The list divided into 87 trades for the steel industry and 29 for the coal industry.[36] A modified version of this list was approved by the member governments in 1963.

In actuality even these skilled workers could not go to another member state and simply ask for a job. However, if a company in France wanted a skilled worker living in Belgium, the Belgian government would not be free to oppose his moving to France.

The results from the institution of the work card have been decidedly unimpressive. Of a possible 160,000 workers in the coal and steel industries who would be eligible for these cards, the vast majority have never even requested them. According to the data supplied to the High Authority by the employment services in the Six, the number of labor cards distributed was 18 for the period September 1 to December 1, 1957, 406 in 1958, 728 in 1959, and only 190 for the first nine months in 1960. Further, the actual number of these skilled workers carrying such a card who obtained employment in another country of the Community either directly or through an employment office was only 285 by September 30, 1960. As one might surmise, the labor card was requested especially by a skilled worker who already had located employment in the Community outside his native country. By September, 1960, the greater part of the cards issued had been in Belgium and Holland, 509 and 471 respectively. For Germany, France and Italy the order was 112, 7 and 243. No card had been issued in Luxembourg.[37] Of 1,767 labor cards issued up to September 30, 1963, only 119 were in the iron and steel industries; the remainder were held by mine workers.[38]

Actually, a considerable number of workers, with the "recognized qualifications" the Treaty of Paris requires, who are employed in a community outside their native country have obtained their jobs by bilateral agreements and thus have not bothered to apply for a labor card. Further, many kinds of existing arrangements accommodate regular crossings of borders by frontier workers and thus they consider the Community labor card unnecessary. Again, for natives of a Benelux nation, working within the Benelux area, the labor card is also unnecessary.

By 1963 the only workers in the Community not entitled to the benefit of freedom of movement were those in jobs not specifically in mining or iron and steel production, or not requiring any particular training. Since July 5, 1963, this Treaty provision has covered 174 occupations.[39]

True, there are provisions for benefits to meet moving costs and other expenses when workers laid off in one country emigrate to another member state for employment. Moreover, these benefits are also available to laid-off workers in coal and steel who must move to another part of the same country to obtain employment. In such circumstances the High Authority has defrayed half the expense of moving and extra expenses involved in maintaining the family at the first domicile until suitable housing has been secured in the new city. To be certain of the sincerity in the choice of the new job location the High Authority has paid only one-half of its commitment at the time of moving and the other half six months later.

In any event, the initiative must be taken by the government concerned by informing the Coal and Steel Community that it will pay the other 50 per cent of the expenses involved in moving a worker and his family to another job. Until such action is taken the Community can do nothing. For workers who, of their own choice, accept work in another country without first having been laid off in their own nation, these benefits are not available. Thus most migrants do not qualify for "free movement" benefits under the Treaty.

The High Authority has long held that two factors have tended to limit its effectiveness in stimulating greater mobility of labor. First, the terms of the Treaty are considered to be much weaker in regard to social objectives than on the economic aspects of the coal and steel industries. Second, it has been pointed out that an attempt to establish a common labor market for workers in the Coal and Steel Community could not be adequately realized until an integrated program for all industries had been established by the EEC.[40]

It also is acknowledged that the founders of the European Coal and Steel Community hesitated, in 1951, to give over collective bargaining powers in industrial relations to an agency with no previous experience in such matters. Accordingly the final decisions on social policy remain with employers, union organizations and governments.

RESEARCH ON LABOR MOBILITY

As a means to offset its lack of specific powers in the Treaty to formulate and implement a fully rounded social policy, the High Authority has intensified its support of research projects in this field carried on by universities and other scientific institutes in the member states. A significant study relating to the free movement of labor under sponsorship by the High Authority was published in 1956, based on separate studies made on labor mobility by universities and research institutes in Germany, France, Italy, Belgium and Holland, under the direction of the UNESCO Institute of Social Sciences at Cologne.[41] Of special relevance here is the section dealing with skilled workers, since they are the particular concern of Article 69.

The study notes that skilled workers are best qualified and most in demand for employment in other countries and regions. Nevertheless, these workers have the lowest rate of mobility in practice. Even in Italy where emigration is the highest in the European Coal and Steel Community, skilled workers have shown a turnover of only 6.9 per cent a year. It has been found generally that the highly qualified worker has an unusually stable way of life and therefore shuns the thought of pulling up roots and moving to another country despite the possibility of promotion.[42]

The joint study notes other obstacles to labor mobility, some of them inherent in the nature of things and others which are subject to remedial action. Measures which the Community has taken in the latter direction will be discussed later.

In regard to personal factors it was found that aptitude for mobility was chiefly a characteristic of the young, whether the transfer related to region, employer or type of work. Moreover, heads of families with children of pre-school age were more inclined to move than where difficulties might be encountered when the worker's children would have to change schools.[43]

The degree of attachment to a given locality was found to be a big influence in deciding whether or not to move elsewhere. Certain workers are strongly rooted to their native village, their friends at the corner café, their music societies and the personal influence of their social group on them. Those less sensible to such attachments or in a spirit of revolt against the demands of their social group are more likely to emigrate.

All the scholars engaged in this study on mobility were in agreement that workers are deeply concerned about the ability to spend free time in the new region on the same basis as in the present locality. Leisure was found often to be the occasion on which the individual expressed his creative personality, by caring for his garden, his pigeons, or his livestock. Similar expansion of personality has been exercised in trade union activities, religious or political associations. A study made in the chief coal regions of Western Germany vividly projected this demand for self-expression where 73 per cent of the miners were facing loss of their private gardens, and 82 per cent the loss of stock-raising as a hobby.

The French report emphasized that the most serious material

obstacle to labor mobility was a concern that adequate housing facilities would be unavailable. The Belgian report also noted the necessity to change dwellings has been the most frequent reason for reluctance to move to a new location. Home ownership in Western Europe is considered a strong inducement to immobility. On the other hand, assurance that a new home would be waiting for the worker's family often is the determining factor.[44]

On a par with the importance of suitable housing is the problem of what has been called social infrastructure: in other words, workers are often unwilling to move unless they are confident of finding adequate shopping centers, schools, hospitals and clinics awaiting them. Mediocre facilities of this type in new regions have often discouraged workers from leaving older industrial areas or cities, especially when there was a question about education for the children.[45]

Among collective factors shaping the individual's attitude toward mobility, the study put stress on the amalgam of common traits of a population, the attitude and behavior in a given milieu, or what might be called socio-cultural traits. Inevitably ethnic, linguistic, geographic and climatic factors have a part to play, as well as family and religious influences.

The German report pointed out that the language barrier was a serious handicap for many immigrants. While they might take hold at once in the duties of their new job, socially they remained outsiders and were even subjected to raillery by their fellow workers.

Even in the small country of The Netherlands there is a sharp cultural and religious distinction between the northern Dutch and the Brabantines at Eindhoven. So marked is this contrast that workers from the north are not inclined to move into the Eindhoven region. Further, the Brabantines have little enthusiasm for industrial development in their territory and show their resentment in the attitude taken toward outsiders who obtain work as a result of it.[46]

Socio-cultural distance between native groups and migrants in the same region of a country actually can be as retarding for internal migrations as they are for international migration. Besides the situation in Holland, the Community's study on mobility also cited the people in southern France as contrasted with those in eastern France. Attention was also given to the classic example of the lack of desire on the part of the Flemish and Walloons in Belgium to live in the same neighborhood.[47]

The study did not overlook the pressures, through placards and vocal protests, from shopkeepers fearful of losing their patrons, which have been put on workers in older regions not to move to new locations. Arguments have been presented pointing out the threat to local well being from such an exodus. Political, labor and religious leaders have also emphasized the advantages of local attachments and the hazards involved in going to a strange country.[48]

These findings do not deny the fact that despite such grave obstacles some companies have succeeded in persuading highly trained personnel from other countries to fill the void in areas where skilled native workers were lacking. For instance, in the Philips plant at Eindhoven, Holland, over half the skilled workers came from outside the country.

Actually, movement of labor does occur on a large scale among nations of the Community, but for the most part among less skilled groups because of environmental factors. For instance, demographic pressure was cited in the Community study as cause for the high rate of emigration characteristic of two member states, Holland and Italy. Added to the excessive population in Italy, especially in the south, is a scarcity of raw materials. As a consequence, in recent years there has been a huge migration from rural southern Italy to the industrial north and to other countries of Europe. Note was taken in this study that Holland's rate of population growth from 1900 to 1950 was 100 per cent while for the rest of Europe it had been only 27 per cent.

For receiving countries of the Community, however, instead of population pressure there is a serious lack of native manpower for the heavy industries, particularly in West Germany and Belgium. In these countries an improved standard of living and full employment have caused workers in the old industrial regions to spurn the drudgery and danger of coal mines and the more difficult jobs in the steel industry. Inevitably, foreign workers were given the jobs no longer desired by the nationals of these countries.[49] Even at the present time in Germany, while there are about 800,000 foreign workers employed, most of them have menial jobs.

A factor which causes reverse mobility, or return to place of origin, is the regulation in many European countries that as soon as the labor contract expires under which a foreign worker was employed, he is obliged to return to his home country. Moreover, in recent years with the industrial upsurge in Italy, skilled Italian workers have been returning home on a permanent basis because of attractive offers.

Turning to recent data on the disbursement of nonnationals in the coal and steel industries of the Community, it becomes apparent that these industries do not generally have a heavy percentage of immigrants. Of the 1,321,000 workers in these industries on June 30, 1962, only 12 per cent of them were nonnationals. In Belgium and France, however, they constituted 33 per cent and 23 per cent of the coal and steel work force. At the other extreme the percentages were 16.6 and 3.5 for Luxembourg, Holland and West Germany.[50] Though West Germany has the largest number of foreign workers and the largest coal and steel work force in the Community—671,300 in 1962—only 22,500 foreign workers were employed in coal and steel. France, with a coal and steel work force about one-half that of Germany had 81,800 foreign workers in those industries in 1962.[51]

Regarding the countries of origin for these workers, Italy still predominates, but with a decrease from 43.1 per cent in 1957 to 41.1 per cent in 1962. For all other member states there has been a slight decrease in the same years from 13.4 per cent to 12.6 per cent. Other nationalities, such as from North Africa, Poland, Spain and Greece accounted for 46.3 per cent of the foreign workers in coal and steel.[52]

GROWTH OF THE WORK FORCE

In terms of overall employment in the European Coal and Steel Community, there has been a continued increase in recent years in the work force but technical progress has so increased the rate of productivity that work force growth is no longer comparable with mounting production volume. True, from December, 1959, to September, 1960, the work force increased from 550,100 to 571,600, or a growth of 3.9 per cent in nine months. In the three countries of the Benelux region, however, employment in steel had become somewhat stabilized by 1960 although for West Germany, France and Italy the steel industry showed a rate of increase in employment above that of 1959.[53]

While steel production in the Community in 1960 was 20 per cent above that of 1959, the increase in the steel work force was only 4.5 per cent. Moreover, the program of modernization in the ore mines over the past few years has continued to lessen the need for iron ore miners. Another factor accounting for reduced employment in the ore mines is the better and cheaper iron ore now available in South America and Africa; French mines in northeast France are selling less ore to the Belgian steel companies. Germany has reduced its iron ore production even more than France. In terms of transportation costs, the German ore mines are more at a disadvantage than similar mines in France.

It is significant to note here that the strong pressure put on the

French government, which owns the ore mines, not to close the pits does not generally stem from fear that employment in some other industry will not be available. Rather, the protests against the closings are traced to the fact that wages of ore miners are higher than for workers in other industries.

Despite efforts by the High Authority and various governments to improve the situation, the total work force in the coal mines continues to decrease. However, in Belgium in 1963 attempts were made to call back to the mines some of the 35,000 workers who had lost their jobs since 1958 due to the closing of obsolete coal pits. The recall met with little success because the laid-off miners had readily found employment either in other mines or in different industries in their localities.

It is likely that the continued decline of employment in the coal industry of the Community is due not so much to mechanization as to the changing sources of energy for Europe. Strong competition from fuel oil producers has put a considerable part of the coal mines in a weak competitive position.

Actually, for the industries of the European Coal and Steel Community the employment figure of 1,372,000 for September 1963 was notably less than the figure of 1,415,600 of a year earlier. Though on a much lower rate proportionally than for coal and iron ore mining, there was even a decrease in employment of 5,100 in the steel industry from September, 1962, to September, 1963. The countries sustaining most of these declines were Belgium and Germany. In contrast, employment in steel and coal increased in Italy, Holland and France.[54]

POLICY OF HARMONIZATION

Regarding harmonization of working conditions for the industries of the European Coal and Steel Community, the Treaty of Paris, like the Treaty of Rome is not very specific in giving directives to the High Authority for attaining this objective. The term harmonization has been put to use here in recognition that while equalization of working conditions is still a remote goal for all the member states, effort must be made to lessen extreme imbalances. Advocates of the term emphasize that without slowing progress in the more advanced areas, the tempo of social improvement should be increased in the less progressive areas. Stress, however, is placed in the Treaty on one point, harmonization of wages under certain conditions. Thus Article 68 states:

2. If the High Authority finds that abnormally low prices practised by one or several enterprises, are the result of wages fixed by these enterprises at an abnormally low level as compared with the actual wage level in the same region, it shall address the necessary recommendations to the interested enterprises after consulting the Consultative Committee. . . .

3. If the High Authority finds that a lowering of wages entails a drop in the standard of living of the labour force and at the same time is being used as a means of permanent economic adjustment by enterprises or as a means of competition among enterprises, it shall address to the enterprise or government concerned, after consulting the Consultative Committee, a recommendation intended to assure the payment to the workers of compensation by the enterprise in question.

Again in Article 3 of the Treaty, the High Authority is directed to:

(e) promote the improvement of the living and working conditions of the labour force in each of the industries under its jurisdiction so as to harmonize those conditions in an upward direction. . . .

Nevertheless, definitive steps to achieve these objectives are left to the respective governments and the industrial partners. Article 5 merely directs the Community to "assist the interested parties to take action by collecting information, organizing consultations and defining general objectives; . . ." The data which has been gathered by the High Authority has been made available both to management and worker groups in these industries. The social partners are now familiar with the working conditions in the various member states, a necessary step to the promotion of harmonization. Moreover, before these studies were undertaken by the High Authority, such knowledge of conditions in other countries was not available. Nevertheless, except for the competitive situation in regard to wages, as noted in Article 68, the High Authority has no mandate to improve working conditions directly.

As one instance of the contribution made here by the High Authority, a study has been sponsored to determine the factors relating to turnover of coal miners.[55] Apart from the obvious factor of the hard work required of miners, the High Authority has endeavored to analyze turnover in terms of distribution according to age, amount of training, length of service and mine location. The high cost of training coal miners makes the problem of turnover a serious one in the mining industry.

As another example of its indirect influence in improving conditions of work, the Community has learned that Italian trade unions made use of data on hours of work, furnished them by the High

Authority, when they negotiated a reduction in hours of work in Italy.

In terms of arranging joint meetings sponsored by the High Authority for discussion of working conditions by the interested parties, it is necessary to find out subjects in advance which will be acceptable to both management and unions. With respect to conditions of work in the coal and steel industries, it has been said that German trade unions take less interest in comparative data of the Six than do unions in Italy. For a country like Germany, which believes its work standards are the best in the Community, there is little curiosity about conditions in a less advanced member state. Contrariwise, Italian trade unions note the data on working conditions in Germany and France carefully since this information is useful in collective bargaining as a lever to obtain more favorable working conditions.

THE PROPOSED STATUTE FOR MINERS

There is strong interest and support by the trade unions generally for adoption of the proposed European Statute for Miners which would accelerate the harmonization of working conditions and compensation in coal mines in the Community. One of the results hoped for by the advocates of this proposal would be a reduction in the turnover of miners which is a serious, industrywide burden at present.[56]

The proposed statute has been under consideration in the European Coal and Steel Community since 1956. Conferences to discuss such a code for European miners have been encouraged by the High Authority. At a rally of 20,000 miners in Dortmund, Germany, July 4, 1964, the president of the High Authority, Dino Del Bo, urged that there be a renewal of talks on a European miners' code.

At the Dortmund rally resolutions were passed advocating a Community energy policy, a "social Europe" and a miners' charter. On the first, concern was expressed over the little progress since discussions began in October, 1957, toward a policy on Community energy. Particular stress was placed on the miners' desire for an assured recognition of the coal industry in any policy on energy adopted by the Community. It was assumed that such recognition would involve subsidies for the coal industry from each of the member states as a means to improve living and working standards for miners.

The second resolution urged the High Authority to intensify its efforts in social matters and to continue its favorable interpretation of the Treaty in this direction. The same resolution, however, expressed dissatisfaction over the progress made in applying the social principles of the Treaty.

With reference to the resolution on the miners' code, strong disapproval was shown to what was termed the negative attitude and lack of foresight by coal mining companies and certain member governments. The view was expressed that the miners' code would effectively remove the uncertainty over workers' future security as miners and would also improve their working conditions.[57]

Difficulty has long been encountered by the High Authority in its efforts to get company representatives to discuss the proposed European Statute with the worker representatives. As one objection, the companies state that by such a code the unions would endeavor to obtain a number of demands which they thus far have not been able to get on the national level. Further, the companies maintain that by this proposed statute the miners are endeavoring to set the standards for working conditions at the level of the most advanced member country in the Six though at present there is a marked variation from country to country. At present it appears that Germany has the highest benefits for pensions and illness. For old age insurance France has the highest benefits.

Another argument used by the coal companies is that before there can be any meaningful discussion on a European miners' statute, there must first be a policy of coordination for European energy. The producers maintain that only by such a policy will there be any assurance of the volume of coal to be produced in the future and the income to expect. Until these matters are settled, more social benefits cannot be considered.

A similar attitude of disinterest toward the proposal for a European miners' code has been characteristic of governments in the Community. In France the mines are under government ownership and operation. It is maintained that any increase in benefits granted to government employees in the coal industry would also be demanded by government employees in other nationalized industries and services.

LENGTH OF THE WORK WEEK AND WORK DAY

In the mining industry, for the workers underground, the length of the work week in 1953 was 48 hours in Belgium and Italy. For West Germany and The Netherlands, the work week was 45 hours and 46 hours respectively. The legal limit in France was 38 hours, 40 minutes. By 1962 Germany and The Netherlands had adopted the 5-day, 40-hour week and Belgium was very close to this standard. The reduction in the work week for miners is regarded as a significant improvement in their working conditions.[58]

In 1961, notable progress was made toward the observance of the 40-hour week in two countries in the steel industry. The German metal industry negotiated an agreement providing for its introduction by stages. A similar arrangement was concluded in The Netherlands.[59]

For the steel industry as a whole, the progress toward a shorter work week from 1953 to 1962 has been much less apparent than in the coal industry. In 1953 the length of the work week was about the same in all member states, averaging 48 hours, including France, despite the legal maximum of 40 hours.

Collective bargaining agreements negotiated earlier, provided that the 40-hour week would be introduced in Germany in 1965. In 1962 the German steel industry was on a 42-hour week. Belgium and Italy had work weeks of 45 and 46.5 hours respectively. Luxembourg was on a 43-hour week and in Holland the hours ranged from 48 to 45.[60]

By 1964 the work day at the surface in the German coal fields, other than the Saar, had been reduced from 8½ hours to 8 hours, amounting to a reduction of 64 hours in the year and a 40-hour week. Also in 1964 the 40-hour, 5-day week was put in effect for underground mine workers in Italy. Surface personnel in Italian coal mines in 1964 had their work week reduced from 45.5 hours to 44 hours.

As a result of a decision by a mines board in Holland, surface personnel after January 1, 1964, were no longer required to work eight Saturdays in the year.

Collective bargaining agreements for the iron and steel industry now provide for a work week of 44 hours in state-owned and partially state-owned plants, and 45 hours in privately owned plants. For both categories, the work week was reduced to 43 hours after July 1, 1965.

All workers in West Germany are entitled to a minimum of 15 days paid vacation per year as of 1963 by virtue of a Federal act. For both surface and underground mine workers in the Saar a 1963 agreement raised the annual minimum vacation from 12 to 18 working days. Workers with 10 years of service at a mine had their vacations extended from 24 to 26 working days in 1965 and to 28 days in 1966.

In Belgium, through a national inter-industry agreement, a three-weeks vacation each year was negotiated on December 12, 1963, which went into effect in 1965, with five weeks of pay during the three weeks of vacation. Nevertheless, France continues to lead the other members of the Community on annual vacations. In France, for all workers in coal mining, iron-ore and the iron and steel industries, the vacation period has been extended from 18 to 24 days, with extra days of leave on a graduated basis for workers with 10 to 30 years of service.

OVERTIME WORKED

Little overtime is worked below ground through most of the coal mining industry in the Community—no more than 1 to 2 per cent of a normal work day—but the proportion was as high as 6 per cent in Germany in 1962. For surface workers in coal mining the proportion of overtime is frequently as high as 5 per cent.

For the iron and steel industry the percentage of overtime worked of normal hours has tended to decline between 1954 and 1962, with the exception of France. However, the very high overtime worked in France is largely explained by the statutory 40-hour work week in effect since 1936. For the French iron and steel industries, overtime worked in 1954 and 1962 amounted to 22.9 and 28.1 per cent of normal working time. For the other members of the Community, iron and steel workers in 1962 ranged between 1.5 and 5 per cent in overtime, with the exception of Luxembourg where the rate was 8 per cent.

For Germany, Belgium and Holland time and one-quarter is paid for the first two hours of overtime in both coal mining and the steel industry. For France and Italy the lower rate prevails for a longer period than the first two hours.[61]

An issue which overshadows much of the discussion on working conditions is the likelihood that thousands of coal miners will face loss of occupation and will need to find other employment. Even in the steel industry it appears that workers must rapidly adjust to transformation of skills because of mounting production by new methods with a disproportionately small increase in demand for steel labor. But present indications point to a remarkable ability on the part of the economy of the communities to adjust to these transformations in the work force by continued full employment and highly developed programs for readaptation of workers. By September, 1964, the Coal and Steel Community had given aid for retraining 150,000 workers facing unemployment because of the closing of coal and iron mines and obsolete steel plants.[62]

COMPARISON WITH THE UNITED STATES

The central point of contrast between the United States and the European Communities in regard to conditions of employment is the impressively small rate of unemployment in the Six, less than 1 per cent apart from Italy, and the high rate of unemployment in the United States, 4 per cent in March, 1966. Various efforts have been made to explain away this embarrassing difference but they are not adequate.

Such factors in this country as greater efficiency, automation, differences from Europe in types of employment, greater productivity per worker, have been considered as possible bases for discounting the much higher employment ratio in Europe. Some of these factors may serve to qualify somewhat the greater proportionate volume of European employment, but they do not alter the conclusion that the unemployment level in the Six is basically low while ours is basically high.

Further, while there may be some difference in methods of computation, there is little warrant for holding that European statistical offices actually undercount the number of unemployed; this point was acknowledged in 1962 by the President's Committee to Appraise Employment and Unemployment Statistics.

In actuality there seem to be significant differences regarding employment policy between the United States and the countries of Western Europe. On the basis of his findings, R. A. Gordon of the University of California has concluded that there is no advanced economy in Western Europe which puts such a low priority on the goal of full employment, or interprets it so loosely as does the United States.

Generally in Europe there is agreement that unemployment should not be more than 2 per cent. Yet in the United States, Gordon finds there is the common assumption that we would attain full employment and meet the requirement of the Employment Act of 1946 if the unemployment rate could be held to very near 4 per cent. Moreover, since in the seven years prior to 1966 the rate remained over 5 per cent, some in America have regarded even that percentage as equivalent to full employment, on the assumption that 5 per cent was an irreducible minimum.[63] While the overall unemployment figure in the United States dropped to 4 per cent in January, 1966, high unemployment remained within particular groups of the work force.[64] As instances for that month and year, the unemployment rate for teenagers stood at 13 per cent and for nonwhites at 7.3 per cent.[65]

There has been some criticism leveled at the European Communities by observers in this country because of the rather slow progress toward harmonization of working conditions and social legislation among the member states. A more tolerant attitude might well be shown here when one recalls the disturbing variations in these same sectors, and within our state jurisdictions, that have persisted for a longer period than the few years of the Common Market's existence. Even in the domain of our national government, where Constitutional authority has been available to increase the coverage of workers under federal standards for working conditions, millions of workers still remain outside the jurisdiction of the Fair Labor Standards Act.

As noted earlier, the Treaties of Paris and Rome have given the executive authorities of the Communities very little mandatory power in the social field. Instead, for the advances already achieved, recourse had to be made to persuasion and education. It may well be possible that from greater knowledge and communication, made possible by the facilities of the Communities, the parties at the bargaining table will contribute more to the ultimate achievement of social harmonization in the Six than the slower and more cumbersome deliberations of the various legislatures of the member states.

5.

Industrial Health and Safety

THE EUROPEAN ECONOMIC COMMUNITY

IN COMPARISON WITH THE COAL AND STEEL COMMUNITY AND Atomic Energy Community, the Economic Community ranks third in terms of achievement in the area of industrial health and safety. Various factors account for this situation, but most significant are the less specific provisions on this subject in the Treaty of Rome. Article 118 does state, however, that it shall be the aim of the Commission to promote close collaboration between member states in the social field, particularly in matters relating to:

—protection against occupational accidents and diseases,
—industrial hygiene, ...
   For this purpose, the Commission shall act in close contact with Member States by means of studies, the issuing of opinions, and the organising of consultations both on problems arising at the national level and on those of concern to international organizations.[1]

Moreover the Commission, by virtue of Article 155, is empowered in the field of industrial health and safety to "formulate recommendations or opinions which are the subject of this Treaty, where the latter expressly so provides or where the Commission considers it necessary. . . ."[2]

Another provision of the Treaty of Rome invoked to advance

activity in the field of industrial health and safety is Article 235 which states:

> If any action by the Community appears necessary to achieve, in the functioning of the Common Market, one of the aims of the Community in cases where this Treaty has not provided for the requisite powers of action, the Council, acting by means of a unanimous vote on a proposal of the Commission and after the Assembly has been consulted, shall enact the appropriate provisions.[3]

Though the Treaty of Rome was signed in 1957, it was not until 1962 that the Health and Safety Division was established at Brussels for the Economic Community, "with a view to strengthening and expediting current measures to harmonize industrial safety arrangements. . . ."[4] Up to that time there was a less formal approach to the problems in this field.

Unlike the Coal and Steel Community, no funds could be made available in the area of industrial health and safety unless appropriated by the Council. The Council has been more inclined to authorize funds for the protection of health and safety in behalf of the Atomic Energy Community (Euratom) than for the use of the Economic Community.

Nevertheless with the creation of the Division in 1962, a significant advance was made in the responsibility to be assumed by the EEC in this area. In preparation for a larger role, the Division has established close contacts with the International Labor Organization and the World Health Organization, both located in Geneva.

Over the years the EEC has followed closely the work of the Coal and Steel Community and Euratom in the field of industrial health and safety. Obviously, research on problems of health and safety, directly relating to the industries embraced by these latter two Communities, has not been duplicated by the Economic Community.

THE GROWING PROBLEM OF HEALTH AND SAFETY

The Commission is mindful of its increasing responsibility in the field of health and safety.This general problem was highlighted May 11, 1962, at a session of the European Parliament, when M. Friedensburg and M. Storch of Germany "urged that all steps should be taken to reduce the growing incidence of industrial diseases and accidents; . . ."[5]

One of the first tasks undertaken by the new Division was to make an inventory, on the basis of information supplied by governments and industrial groups, of dangerous environments relating to the operation of "machinery, appliances, installations and products of every description."[6] The European Parliament has urged that problems of industrial safety be settled by the Economic Community through appropriate measures enacted in virtue of Article 235, which permits action on critical situations where specific Treaty language is lacking, if the Council should unanimously approve a proposal by the Commission. The European Parliament has suggested that an alternative toward standardizing safety provisions might be adoption of a convention by the Six.

In accordance with the Economic Community's responsibility under the Treaty, to advance the social situation of the member states, the European Parliament in 1961 acknowledged the impressive results achieved by the Commission in "compiling comprehensive documentation on the present situation as regards industrial health and safety in the Community; . . ."[7]

At present the central effort of EEC on industrial health and safety is to secure the adoption of permanent regulations consonant with scientific and technical progress in this field. In the view of the EEC, a basic problem of special urgency is to coordinate effectively the many efforts of the governments and national technical commissions. Moreover, the goal of a European code on industrial health and safety will become of increasing urgency as greater freedom in the circulation of workers, goods and services develops.[8]

An example of cooperation toward a Community standard has been cited by the EEC in the efforts of the Benelux nations to coordinate their own regulations. Special study groups with representatives of these three countries meet each month for the purpose of drafting uniform regulations for the Benelux nations. Already discussions have covered safety regulations for elevators (passenger and freight) and acetylene generators. Other subjects on the agenda relate to the handling of compressed and liquified gas, building construction, metal scaffolding and various types of machinery. In the judgment of the EEC these preparatory sessions have had their influence in recent legislation passed in Belgium and The Netherlands.[9]

Closer cooperation among all of the Community members will be necessary not only to remove existing diversities among them, but to prevent inconsistencies in future legislation, thus preventing additional complex problems. The Economic Community emphasizes that it takes much less time and effort to agree on standard provisions for such legislation in advance than it does to revise, in accordance with a common standard, legislation which has already become law.

Opportunity for fruitful collaboration between Belgium and Germany was pointed out by the EEC, referring to 1962 plans by both nations to revise safety laws on elevators and steam engines. It was the belief of the EEC that almost no area covered by the voluminous legislation on health and safety in the six member states had failed to undergo some modification during 1962.[10]

RECOMMENDATIONS TO MEMBER GOVERNMENTS

In August, 1962, after favorable opinions from the European Parliament and the Economic and Social Committee, the Commission made two recommendations to the governments on industrial health.[11] The first applied to medicine and urged the provision of compulsory industrial medical service in member states—in all branches of industry—with immediate application to sectors where the labor force is considerable and the frequency of risk is highest. This recommendation also proposed regular inspection of plants for hygiene, and institution of medical units in the factories, with provision for adequate first aid and periodic physical examination of employees.

Nevertheless, M. Levi Sandri, a member of the Commission, cautioned the European Parliament on May 11, 1962, that while he agreed with the need for greater medical services, he feared that a shortage of qualified physicians might seriously hamper the introduction of plant medical services. Accordingly, he considered it necessary to allow for a phasing pattern to effect such services.[12]

Present regulations concerning industrial medicine in the Six vary in terminology and conditions of application. The Commission of the EEC has urged that steps be taken to standardize national legislation in the field of industrial medicine.[13] In particular the European Parliament has recommended to the EEC that every organization of plant medical services should have the equipment, auxiliary staff and facilities deemed essential in recommendation 112 of the International Labor Organization in Geneva.[14]

In teaching industrial medicine, the European Parliament has suggested to the EEC that university chairs of industrial medicine should be founded in all medical faculties, and that regional institutes of industrial medicine should be established in all Community countries. These latter would be at the direct disposal of local industry, to maintain channels between academic and applied industrial medicine.[15]

The second recommendation made by the EEC Commission to member states in August, 1962, urged adoption of a European list of occupational diseases, not only with the view to compensation but to institute compulsory preventive measures, encourage more strict supervision and thus eliminate dangerous working conditions.[16] It is the opinion of Levi Sandri, member of the EEC Commission for Social Affairs, that the adoption of a European list will contribute greatly toward unifying the social systems of the member governments. Another desirable result would be the strengthening of the Community's program for free movement of workers.[17]

As part of this second recommendation a request was made that the EEC be informed of what action the governments decided to take on the proposed list. The West German government replied in 1963 that it had adopted the list of occupational diseases sent out by the EEC. In the case of Belgium, the Division was told the Government had decided to recognize silicosis legally as an occupational disease.

Under this same recommendation, each nation is requested to inform the Division of any new additions to the official list of occupational diseases and of any new types of illness that may be related to an industrial environment.

Studies have been promoted by the EEC concerning causes of such occupational diseases as certain types of cancer, skin infection, rheumatism, and illnesses peculiar to those who work with compressed air. Studies are being sponsored to determine causes of industrial accidents, with a view to reducing the rate of accidents involving electrical machinery, scaffolding, and construction workers. Particular emphasis has been placed on devising an international code of signals so migrants would be subjected to fewer hazards in crane and elevator operations.

The factor of safety, in the view of the Division, concerns not only the working conditions of a manufacturing plant, but also the control of hazards involved in the product itself, wherever it may be used. Accordingly, the EEC urges that manufacturers of machinery equip their products with adequate safety devices for workers who will use them later. Here it might be noted that certain machine tools produced in Italy, with three speeds of operation, are not legally saleable in Germany because German law requires four shifts of speed as added safety protection.

THE EUROPEAN COAL AND STEEL COMMUNITY

Since the Coal and Steel Community was established in 1951, seven years before the foundation of the EEC, and at a time in political history when the nations of Europe were inclined to yield sovereignty to a regional industrial community, it is not surprising that the Coal and Steel Community today finds itself in a better position to cope with industrial health and safety problems than the EEC.

TREATY PROVISIONS

A specific provision contained in the Treaty of Paris amply affirms the autonomy of the Community in the field of health and safety. A key provision, not contained in the treaty for the Economic Community, is the power to tax and spend, as set forth in Article 49, which states:

> The High Authority is empowered to procure the funds necessary to the accomplishment of its mission:
> —by imposing levies on the production of coal and steel;
> —by borrowing.
> It may also receive grants.[18]

Because of this financial provision, the Community has been able to be significantly thorough in the application of other articles of the Treaty which are relevant to industrial health and safety. Article 3 (e) directs the Community to: "promote the improvement of the living and working conditions of the labour force in each of the industries under its jurisdiction so as to harmonize those conditions in an upward direction; . . ."[19]

Authorization to obtain relevant data in these areas and publish the findings is contained in Article 46 (5), which permits the High Authority to "gather any information required to assess the possibilities of improving the living and working conditions of the labour force in the industries under its jurisdiction, and the risks menacing their living conditions. . . ." Further, the Community may publish the reports based on these investigations.[20]

Specifically covering industrial safety, the Treaty states (Article 55) that:

> 1. The High Authority must encourage technical and economic research concerning . . . workers' safety in these industries. To this end, it shall organize all appropriate contacts among existing research organizations.
> 2. After consultation with the Consultative Committee, the High Authority may initiate and facilitate the development of such research work:
> (a) by encouraging joint financing by the enterprise concerned or;
> (b) by earmarking for that purpose any grants it may receive; or
> (c) (with the agreement of the Council) by earmarking for that purpose funds derived from the levies provided for in Article 50, without, however, going beyond the limit defined in section 2 of that Article.[21]

The funds available for promotion of industrial health and safety programs are largely channeled through the division of industrial medicine and hygiene and the division of industrial safety.

GRANTS FOR RESEARCH ON HEALTH AND SAFETY

From the establishment of the Community, it has been the opinion of the High Authority that the members should endeavor to coordinate efforts to advance industrial health and safety. A policy has thus been adopted of persuading industry, unions and governments that they stand to benefit mutually from the experience of each government, industry and health organization. The 1955 decision of the High Authority to grant financial aid for scientific research on industrial health and safety has proved to be an extremely effective measure.

The Community does not carry on this research but makes grants to research institutes if the projects they are pursuing fit into a clearly defined framework laid down by the Community. For example, if an institute informs the Community that it is conducting a study on skin diseases, the High Authority would have a committee of experts determine if the particular project was relevant to the Community's existing framework program. If an affirmative decision resulted, the institute would be considered for financial aid.

Such a procedure keeps a specific program designed to advance industrial health and safety in focus. The Community has found that in order to finance specific objectives and avoid dispersion it is necessary to have all research concentrated on clearly defined fields within the framework program. However, the framework program only sets down the objectives sought, not the means by which they are to be obtained; there is no attempt by the Community to direct the research as such.

The first framework program on health and safety was launched in 1954–1955 after consultation with about 200 European experts during 20 to 30 meetings. Once the program was adopted by the High Authority, it was published in various scientific journals. In this fashion European research institutes became fully briefed on the problems in which the High Authority was particularly interested.

In the 1954–1955 framework program stress was placed on two occupational diseases, namely, silicosis and carbon-monoxide poisoning. Need for research on physiological hazards from noise and high-temperature conditions was also emphasized.

Institutes which subsequently informed the High Authority of their intention to pursue the objectives laid down became eligible for financial aid. Such institutes were enabled to hire recent university graduates and acquire new equipment which, under ordinary conditions, might have been considered too costly.

Also from publication of the 1954–1955 framework program, many institutes, impressed by the objectives of the program, began scientific research in these areas on their own. This factor has helped explain why in the Six there is now such a marked reduction in mortality from silicosis. Ten or more years ago workers often died within one year after contracting this disease. At present the lives of such workers have been extended 10 to 15 years because of advances in prognosis and therapy. In effect Europe has now become one of the major research centers for silicosis as contrasted to decades before when most research was done in the United States.

Research for the first framework program extended from 1955 to 1959. Seventy-two institutes took part and carried on 164 research projects. Publications available from these scientific inquiries include 250 booklets, 164 reports, and 1500 other pooled documents.

A second research framework was approved for the years 1960–1964; it placed stress on dust prevention, human factors involving job accidents and rehabilitation of the physically handicapped. Because of the need for pioneering work in these fields, even greater preparation was given the framework program than in the initial program. Moreover, the Community provided funds to enable teams of young scientists to make study trips to the highly industrialized countries of the United States and Great Britain to obtain data on accident prevention, thus accelerating developments among the member states.

Early in 1960, five of the approved projects studied individual worker safeguards such as protective shoes for miners. Three other projects concerned the attitude of workers toward the safety devices at their disposal.[22] In 1961 the High Authority approved six additional research projects relating to the "human factor and safety."[23] Nine other projects were devoted to safety problems arising in the selection and training of workers in the coal and steel industries.[24] By 1960 eleven institutes had received financial aid from the High Authority to study the effects of such diseases as emphysema and bronchitis among coal and steel workers.[25]

In 1963, for the second framework program, with 65 institutes and 220 research scientists taking part in 114 research projects, 177 reports had already been made available to interested groups throughout the world.

On June 13, 1962, the High Authority approved a document with the title *Promotion of Studies and Research Concerning Safety and Industrial Medicine*. This document summarizes the activities in this field sponsored by the High Authority, and also indicates future research to be encouraged. Deservedly, much stress is given to the complex systems of consultation used by the High Authority for the large number of participants.

The motivation behind this cautious approach to devising research programs is a desire to avoid compromising scientific or social value in any sponsored research. Accordingly, in the detailed preparation of its programs, consultation is held with representatives of professional organizations, governments and special experts. In this way judicious use of finances in effective research is assured. Another advantage of consultation with numerous groups has been a noticeable improvement in the cooperation and coordination of scientific research conducted in the countries of the Community.

Though the basic principles of administration and objectives in research policy have remained intact since 1955, the High Authority has modified procedure in launching the programs. Instead of making all phases of the framework program available to applicants on an equal basis, the High Authority has decided that cases of complex research demand highly specialized resources. Thus, certain institutes known to be especially qualified to undertake such projects will directly be invited to participate. For other types of research, the High Authority will continue to publish the framework programs for the consideration of all organizations interested in undertaking such projects.

After almost a decade of association with research institutes in the study of industrial health and safety, the Community considers it has detailed knowledge of their resources and capabilities. It therefore appears most logical to approach directly the institutes most qualified rather than resort to a long and complicated procedure of selection through public competition.[26]

Turning to objectives and accomplishments of research on health and safety, in 1955 the Research Committee on Industrial Health and Medicine, composed of representatives from producers and workers, unanimously held that efforts to overcome silicosis should be the main objective of the Community because of the technical, human and economic factors at stake.[27]

. In 1963 the High Authority reported that specialists' opinions in the treatment of silicosis are now generally in agreement. In a quite complex area of medicine, this development is considered indicative of considerable advancement in understanding the disease. Further, at a Munster congress, April, 1962, it was reported that a reduction in new cases of silicosis had taken place in several coal regions of the Community. Reports and discussion at the Munster conference also indicated that research on silicosis has been developing favorably and that prophylactic and therapeutic measures against this disease are much more effective today than formerly. Moreover, preventive measures today are so effective that the virulence of the disease has radically lessened.[28]

The second most serious occupational disease in the coal and steel industries is pneumoconiosis; a study group reported that progress in radiological technology now permits the early detection of microscopic nodules in the lungs. This advance has been of great significance in the prompt diagnosis and prevention of pneumoconiosis.[29]

If the X-ray examination discloses these microscopic shadows in the lungs of a miner, he is immediately transferred from his job at the coal pit and the progress of the disease is thus arrested. Since employment elsewhere is assured to such workers they do not object to the system of early diagnosis through X-ray examination. This attitude toward physical examinations is in marked contrast with the suspicion held by workers ten or more years ago of such examination. New cases of pneumoconiosis annually have declined from about 7,000 in 1957 to 2,000 in 1963. Efforts are still being expended to reduce the incidence to the vanishing point.

In November, 1961, the High Authority conducted a two-day session in Brussels on pneumoconiosis where discussion was devoted to the many respiratory ailments which can affect organs of workers from inhalation of dust. Some 700 delegates and experts were in attendance representing European institutions, the International Labor Organization, the Council of Europe, and governmental, professional and medical personnel from the member states. Representatives of Britain, Austria and the United States were also present. At this two-day meeting views were exchanged on the research work of the previous five years that had been sponsored by the Community in an attempt to make results known to participants and organizations dedicated to reducing occupational diseases.[30]

A growing hazard responsible for many cases of respiratory disease among steel workers is the accumulation of red dust in modern steel plants. The great quantities of oxygen used under a new process of steel production, at temperatures twice that previously required, leaves large amounts of this red dust in the air. The Community, June 20,

1962, set aside a fund to support five research projects on the Community's program to combat this hazard in the steel industry.[31] These projects were undertaken by specially qualified institutes in four of the member countries.[32]

Behind these research efforts is a two-fold aim: first, to abolish the red dust as a hazard for the workers, and second, to remove the hazard from the neighborhood of the steel plant. The Community has been sponsoring research in Germany and France, utilizing different processes and equipment, to study ways of controlling this hazard.[33] It is believed that a change in the mixture of oxygen and air will serve to avoid the precipitation of red dust. In one French plant progress has advanced so far that used air is now purer than when it entered the plant.

With the growing trend to locate steel plants on the coast line, to be more accessible to American coal, civil authorities have demanded that the dust hazard be reduced. Often, as a condition for approving a plant site, there is an understanding that the steel company will take measures to control red dust.

Dust in coal mines causes pneumoconiosis among mine workers, and the High Authority is aware that current research must place great emphasis on the analysis of the mineral contents of coal dust.[34] To this end, four study groups have periodically taken account of research progress and have endeavored to coordinate efforts to achieve dust prevention in coal mines of the Community.

One study group has been concerned with the different instruments and methods used to measure and analyze mine dust. Two groups have looked to the means used to control the causes of such dust in the mines, and later in the piling and crushing of the coal. Another study group, in personnel protection, seeks to compare the nature and density of the dust which miners have been exposed to from the physical examination data of such miners. Through comparison of the data it is hoped that the danger level of dust accumulation for silicosis can be determined.[35]

One of the difficulties is that present instruments used to measure mine dust vary in their findings, mainly because they were designed to measure something other than coal dust. While the Community now knows which types of dust are dangerous and which are not, it is still necessary to measure exactly the amount of dangerous mine dust. Better instruments and better ways of using them remain a necessary objective. To this end the High Authority has sponsored research to perfect more accurate instruments to measure coal dust in order to make more meaningful a Community standard of tolerance.

Perfection of other types of instruments, which the High Authority is encouraging by financial aid, relate to the measurement of coal gas and oxygen in the air. Efforts are also being supported by the Community to devise a mechanism to provide fresh air every hour even in a contaminated atmosphere. As the result of international efforts over two years time, the Community has had very good results in obtaining model instruments, except for measuring oxygen in the air.

The Community has sponsored international competition for an instrument to measure oxygen, involving scientists, inventors and manufacturing firms in the member states, Britain and the United States. This approach has helped to advance understanding both by academicians and technicians concerning the instruments needed in the coal and steel industries to assure health and safety.

At present, one of the most effective ways to prevent dust at the coal face is to water the coal, but this method is not equally adaptable under all conditions. Complications and dangers result from differences in the depths of mines and the type of earth and stone nearby. Thus, the Community has provided funds to explore the possibilities of applying water to coal faces without causing stone falls. Another difficulty in the use of water here is the need to be certain that no mine gas is present since an explosion might result.

The Community has found that mechanisms and methods used to inject water into coal veins for dust control vary in the degree of performance in loose, irregular or mixed veins of coal. Moreover, the growing mechanization of coal mine operations has necessitated frequent revisions in methods of dust control, especially for massive injections of water.[36]

A hazard to health and safety stemming from increased mechanization of European mines has been the difficulty of providing adequate air holes in deep shafts where mining machinery now operates 24 hours a day. The Community has sponsored a costly program to demonstrate new methods of ventilation for new types of production.

An even more serious problem is that designers of mining machinery have given little attention to the creation of dust in the process of getting out coal more easily and rapidly. The Community has therefore financed experiments so that the knives of the new machines are adjusted in various ways, according to size and position, to permit water to flow at or near the knife edge. These adjustments require much time and must be done at the coal face.

Another hazard concerns noise and vibrations. In 1962 a research team examining these factors concluded that recent investigations confirm the impact of resonant vibrations of sound not only on the ear, but on the entire human organism.[37] The Electro Technical Institute at Turin, Italy, has now in operation a portable instrument which can determine the impact of noise at the work site on the basis of three gradations: hazardous, disturbing and tolerable.

Physiopathological research on animals has helped to determine the effect of noise on emotional balance. It has been learned that noise can cause disturbance of the endocrine glands. At the University of Milan research has discovered the impact of noise on steel workers in rolling mills and foundries. Some loss of hearing among workers has been noted.

From the psychological point of view an analysis by the Institute of Physiology at Dortmund, Germany, has disclosed that among 1,000 workers, of those exposed to considerable noise, 12 per cent had grievances about disturbances in human relations. Of those working under less noisy conditions such grievances amounted to only 6 per cent.

Since many occupations in the coal and steel industries involve working in high temperatures, the Community has financed research at various institutes to determine the physical effects of such conditions on the workers involved. By 1959 many findings had been obtained through the use of new types of instruments to measure caloric radiations and the movement of air. It has been learned that work at high temperatures tends to affect the renal secretion in the kidneys. The Institute of the Physiology of Labor at Dortmund attributes this phenomenon to a loss of renal blood flow, because of blood movement toward the skin and muscles of the worker. The Institute of the Physiopathology of Labor at Strasbourg has been able to determine that effects under high temperatures can be traced to accompanying thermic restriction and loss of sleep. It is now believed that workers so affected are exposed to abnormal risks.[38]

The Community has financed research to establish criteria for determining the tolerance to heat for rescue workers in coal mines. It has been found that individual resistance to high temperatures varies considerably. This finding has also been borne out among survivors of accidents involving intense heat.[39]

Several factors seem to account for the growing number of certain types of accidents. While in the coal mines, the total incidence of accidents has not changed appreciably, there has been an increase in the number of accidents involving the use of machinery and electricity. New methods of production have brought with them new types of accidents. In the past 20 years job duties have altered greatly in the European coal mines because of the necessity to approximate a competitive basis with other fuels such as oil and natural gas. As a consequence there has been a great need for new types of safety recommendations to be circulated throughout the mining areas.

For some years the High Authority has been making such safety recommendations to the member states. The governments are free to accept or reject them. However, they are required annually to inform the Community of what is being done on such proposals. Thus the recommendations must be given formal consideration by the member states.

By 1962 the High Authority had sponsored an extensive program of research to develop a fuller understanding of the factors and circumstances at the origin of industrial accidents in the Community. Among the salient points of investigation was the analysis of job duties and their possible safety hazards, and systematic examination of the thesis that accidents can result from the combined effects of multiple factors, some of which are traceable directly to the worker himself. Other areas of this research program included analysis of the factors which influence the hazards, namely the interrelation of medical, psycho-sociological and technical considerations.

Study was given to the material and psychological conditions of the job and the attitudes of personnel concerned, which covered a wider range than just the workers who had been involved in accidents. Particular attention was placed on securing the understanding, approval and active cooperation of management in the execution of this research program.

The administration of the program was developed on two levels. Nationally, the director of each research team conducted investigations according to the definite operation under his responsibility. The areas of investigation assigned to particular research teams included such sectors as haulage, transport, work under high temperatures, and employment in rolling mills. On the Community level, research activities were evaluated in accordance with the jurisdiction of the Committee of Directors of Community Research. Here the main thrust of endeavor was to develop comparable methods and norms of observation and assure the application of results and their synthesis by reports specialized according to industry.[40] The directors of research teams were in agreement on the establishment of two specialized committees, for the mining and steel industries; for each industry these committees would centralize organization and establish a secretariat.[41]

Two disasters in 1962, one at the Luisenthal mine in the Saar on February 7, with 299 victims, and another at the Sachsen mine in Westphalia on March 9, with 31 fatalities, stirred up demands in the Community that the Permanent Commission for Safety in the Mines be given more adequate means of action to fulfill its duties. Since then the European Parliament, the miners' unions and the High Authority have increased their efforts to improve standards of safety in the coal mines.[42]

The Permanent Commission is composed of 24 members. For each of the six member states there are two designated government representatives, an employer representative and a union representative. Delegates on a consultative basis are also invited from the International Labor Organization in Geneva.[43]

In February, 1962, the European Parliament congratulated the West German government for inviting the High Authority and the Permanent Commission to participate in the probe to determine the causes of the Volklingen disaster. It also suggested that in the case of similar catastrophes the other member governments should follow this precedent. The action by the European Parliament sought to enable the Permanent Commission to judge the security measures in force in the mines and participate in future investigations on the causes and circumstances of serious accidents.

The Union representatives on the Permanent Commission insist that it should be given wider jurisdiction in the area of safety. Accordingly, they have held that miners should be safeguarded not only against risk of accidents, but also against the danger of sickness since they are victims in one case as much as in the other.

The High Authority has also urged that the Permanent Commission should have the right to inform itself at the work site and that it should participate in probes conducted by national governments. In this fashion it is believed better results will be obtained for providing means to avoid repetition of disasters. As at present the member governments would still retain full responsibility for the application of safety regulations.[44]

Periodically the Permanent Commission brings to light what action, if any, has been taken by the governments on its recommendations. From evaluation of reports on recent accidents, it directed one of its study groups to examine the technical problems involved.

On May 15, 1962, the Mineworkers' Union in West Germany

wrote a letter to the High Authority urging that the Permanent Commission be given a wider field of responsibility, with stronger means to discharge its duties. Thus four specific areas were recommended for action on the part of the Permanent Commission: injuries from firedamp and dust; problems of health and health protection; necessary power for the control and gathering of information; and publication of results from the Commission's studies for the benefit of interested parties.[45]

For several years the Permanent Commission of the Community has given consideration to comparative studies of technical problems related to accidents. On accidents involving electricity, electrical engineers have been consulted to find a more satisfactory way to protect coal miners from such hazards. The Permanent Commission is aware that different methods prevail in France, Germany and the United Kingdom. It is the desire of this agency to choose the best of such methods as a basis for recommendations to member governments.

As the result of competition for prizes from 1957 to 1962, sponsored by the High Authority, a jury had selected eight safety devices of which two were portable meters to detect firedamp, and one was an alarm to make the critical percentage of permissible firedamp known. Three of the instruments registered amounts of oxidized carbon and two represented a notable advance in efforts to achieve full protection against all toxic gases and against the lack of oxygen. However, there is not yet an entirely satisfactory device to reveal lack of oxygen; for perfection of such a device the High Authority extended the competition for prizes.[46]

In its efforts to prevent fires in deep coal pits, in 1962 the High Authority endorsed, by financial aid, a program of practice tests for fire control in deep mines through sprinkling mechanisms. The tests also concerned the disruption of ventilation which such fires or sprinklings could provoke. In the view of the High Authority these problems are still poorly understood, but are of capital importance to safety in coal mines.[47]

As another means to prevent fires in coal mines, the High Authority has supported efforts to establish criteria for oil which could be used in coal mines but would not be readily inflammable. A full reexamination has been undertaken with the cooperation of representatives from coal producers, the chemical industry, and manufacturers of mining equipment.[48] The parties were aware that the type of oil desired would not only have to be relatively noninflammable but would have to satisfy technical requirements for use in coal mining machinery.

On the basis of suggestions from the research committee and from committees representing government experts, producers and workers, the High Authority on January 28, 1959, adopted a study program concerning research of human factors and industrial safety. From subsequent consultation five distinct subjects of research have been listed in this field. They concern the accident-prone individual, the psychological and sociological conditions of the work environment, the adaptation of the work to the man, the selection and promotion of personnel, and the methods of over-all protection.

The High Authority has given encouragement to research on the selection and formation of personnel and on the methods for individual protection against accidents. As noted earlier, there has also been substantial help given to basic research on the nature, causes and circumstances of accidents. The High Authority has found other subjects suggested for research more difficult to subsidize directly because the problems involved are more complex and depend on a great number of factors.

Among the research projects sponsored by the High Authority at the beginning of 1960, five related to methods for individual protection against accidents. Three other projects dealt with the attitude of workers toward the use of safety devices and factors which will induce workers to utilize them. Effort was made to learn whether reasons for not using safety devices were based on psychological influences or physiological intolerances. Nine other projects were devoted to the problems of selecting and training personnel with a view to advancing safety standards in the coal and steel industries.

For these research projects, the High Authority has sought to encourage cooperation among the research groups and the scientific and professional centers to define problems of methodology as closely as possible.[49]

In 1959, the Permanent Commission had set up four study groups in which representatives of workers, employers and governments took part in analysis of several problems bearing on human factors and safety.

One area of study concerned the relation between methods of payment and safety. It has been found that some methods tend to encourage imprudence in work performance. Another study concerned the length of the work day under laborious or unhealthful conditions such as excessive heat or humidity or restricted space. Measures have been taken to have the workers themselves recognize dangers in psychological and sociological factors and take steps to avoid them. The advancement of safety in medical service at the mines has also been examined.[50]

For the programs formulated in 1963, researchers were asked to study the selection and training of workers in regard to safety, with particular stress on cooperation concerning safety between those responsible for training and those charged with directing operations. It was found highly desirable that the lessons on safety obtained in training courses be adapted to the actual conditions of work and not be regarded as merely theoretical. It is acknowledged that methods of individual protection are effective but have been little used generally in industry, even when they are of obligation.

Two causes have been found at the base of this situation. First, all the problems stemming from putting the safety devices into use have not been resolved beforehand. Second, the methods of protection are not adapted to the many diverse tasks which confront a worker.

Another 1963 research program of the Community put stress on collective aspects of safety such as allowance for rest periods and psychological factors which can aid in preventing accidents. Under collective aspects attention was also given to the structure and dependability of equipment and its adaptability to workers of different training and language. Rest periods were studied from the point of view not only of within the day, but also in terms of the continuous work cycle. By psychological studies note was taken of the worker's attitude toward his work environment and the work process confronting him.[51]

Today, there is a far greater tendency for management to take human factors into consideration, especially on matters of health and safety. The cultural level of many groups, including workers, has been notably improved in recent years and it is one of the changes which has given them a higher status in the industrial community. Accordingly, the past callous attitude of some foremen toward the safety of their employees now would appear glaringly out of harmony due to this narrowing cultural gap.

For many years the Division on Industrial Medicine and Hygiene has been following the progress made in the United States in rehabilitation. Particular attention has been given to the pioneering work of Dr. Howard A. Rusk of New York.

While not strictly at the stage of rehabilitation, the Community has been impressed with the prompt aid given the injured American worker to reduce loss of time from the job. Account has been taken of the efficiency of emergency transportation to avoid neglect of the patient during the critical moments immediately after an accident so that the interval before surgery will be as brief as possible. Such measures are recognized as an invaluable aid to rehabilitation later.

The Community also looks with favor upon the American practice of an active convalescence period to enable the injured worker to achieve complete physical and psychological recovery.

Numerous study trips have been made to the United States by teams of doctors from the Community to learn current practices in rehabilitation. Research specialists in the treatment of burns have made repeated visits to America and American specialists have visited research centers of the Community. Such exchanges have considerably advanced progress in rehabilitation.

Among research grants authorized by the Community in 1960 were 53 projects devoted to the rehabilitation of victims of industrial accidents and occupational diseases.[52] Of research projects completed in 1960, there were several which had been conducted at the Bergmannsheil Hospital at Bochum, Germany, relating to traumatisms of the vertebral column and serious cases showing symptoms of loss of will power, along with victims of minor accidents who evinced no desire to return to work.

Of the vertebral cases at Bochum only 3 per cent resumed regular work. Others within this category did not resume work because of their physical handicap. But a second group did not return to regular work from fear of loss of benefits. In this latter group it was believed that neurosis and lack of will among such patients ought to be reexamined in the light of personal motives which can condition the attitude toward affliction.

The Center for Traumatology at the Faculty at Lille, France, has researched early rehabilitation of paraplegics and has verified benefits obtained by prompt surgical treatment each time there is indication of suppression of the marrow. It has been found that surgical techniques have so improved that risk of serious complication has become very slight.

Among other research projects completed, the Clinic of the Surgical University of Amsterdam has ended its clinical-histological and experimental studies on deep hand burns. The findings have important relevance to rehabilitation.

For deep burns generally, a special commission has been appointed for basic research to coordinate and stimulate European studies in physiology and therapeutics. A group of directors of industrial medicine from corporations have studied the subject of burns to coordinate emergency transportation and establish a European organization for mutual aid in major disasters.

Organized relations have been established among specialists in rehabilitation for study of fractures of the vertebral column and maladies relating to the muscular function in the case of traumatists.[53]

On January 4, 1961, the High Authority authorized grants to finance nine additional research projects for the rehabilitation of victims of industrial accidents and of occupational diseases.[54]

In the Community's *General Report* for 1962 it is noted that several researchers have found that definite improvement can be obtained for workers with respiratory handicaps through the lessening of infections and circulatory complications. In addition, by techniques of reeducation the physical capacity of victims of emphysema and pneumoconiosis has been improved.[55]

It is essential, according to the High Authority, to assure a solid scientific base for rehabilitation and therefore research must be advanced in regard to traumatology. Special stress has been placed on studies relating to diagnosis and treatment of injuries. In regard to recovery from injuries the Community, as noted earlier, has given particular attention to physiological and psychological factors. Great importance is also attached to improving the various techniques which enable workers themselves to facilitate efforts at recovery.[56]

It has been the constant objective of the High Authority to keep the groups adequately informed which are directly concerned with results obtained. The High Authority has also organized periodic exchanges of information and experience for the benefit of the industrial partners.

For several years a bibliographic service and an analysis of medical documents has been in operation. As of 1960, over 1500 file cards had been reprinted and distributed in regard to articles from world literature on the subject of pneumoconiosis. Reprints of publications sponsored by the High Authority have been sent to universities, to ministries of labor and to industry for the purpose of informing the specialists concerned. The program of industrial medicine has made the distribution of over 250 publications possible. In December, 1961, a synthesis in the form of a monograph was published which contained the findings of health and safety research sponsored by the High Authority from 1956 to 1960. The monograph was distributed to practitioners and clinicians.[57]

Findings from scientific studies have been the subject of discussions organized under the title, "Inquiry on Industrial Medicine in the Coal and Steel Industries," and have been confined to a restricted number of experts. In October, 1959, three days of study were given over to informing more than 100 doctors in industrial medicine, as well as safety engineers, of research findings on high temperatures and noise.[58]

From colloquia and symposia held at Luxembourg under the sponsorship of the High Authority research specialists have been encouraged to exchange views frankly on their investigations. It was noted at the outset of these conferences that research workers were quite suspicious of each other and feared that by speaking of their work they might be copied and the originality of their research lost. Over the years these suspicions have tended to disappear and researchers in different countries, even former enemy countries, have become friends.

Another advantage from the conferences is the realization that less progressive industries in certain countries have learned by systematic exchange of views among the Six that there is much to learn from the experience of others. The understanding has come that no one country is superior in all areas and that varied achievements of several nations offer fruitful avenues of knowledge to the inquirer.

Numerous research study groups which the High Authority regularly has called together, have continued to develop scientific cooperation. A considerable part of the preliminary results from the investigations of these groups was published in September, 1962, under the title, "State of Research Work Relating to Safety, Hygiene and Industrial Medicine, in the Community, Sponsored by Grants from the High Authority."[59]

THE EUROPEAN ATOMIC ENERGY COMMUNITY

From the establishment of Euratom in 1957, there has been a constant effort to achieve satisfactory standards of protection against radiation both for workers in the nuclear plants and for citizens in general. The Rome Treaty which founded Euratom has numerous provisions looking to this objective.

In Chapter III, "Health Protection," Article 30 states:

Basic standards for the protection of the health of workers and of the general public from the dangers arising from ionising radiation shall be established within the Community.

The term "basic standards" shall mean:

(a) the maximum doses compatible with adequate safety;

(b) the maximum permissible degree of exposure and contamination; and

(c) the fundamental principles governing the medical supervision of workers.[60]

In Article 31 the Commission for Euratom was instructed to work out these basic standards after it had secured the opinion of competent authorities appointed by Euratom's Scientific and Technical Committee from among scientific personnel, especially public health experts of the member states. Further, the Commission was directed to request an opinion on the proposed standards from the Economic and Social Committee.[61]

Once the basic standards had been approved, Articles 33 and 219 required that each member state enact "the legislative and administrative provisions" necessary to assure conformance with them. The standards were to be fixed by April 17, 1958.[62] Further, each member was directed to take the necessary steps concerning instruction, education and vocational training for this same purpose.[63]

In terms of enforcement the Commission is empowered by Article 81 to "send inspectors into the territories of Member States," who at any time shall have "access to all places and data and to any person who by reason of his occupation deals with materials, equipment or facilities" related to nuclear fission.[64]

In its first *General Report,* September 12, 1958, the Commission outlined what it considered the main requirements of a policy for health protection. Attention was first given to the permissible increase in radioactivity compatible with the health of workers and the public at large. Second, the need was recognized to design and apply a method of protection and control to safeguard the health of workers exposed to ionizing radiation. Third, the Commission acknowledged the necessity of preventing as far as possible the risks which might arise from "contamination of the atmosphere, water or soil."[65]

In the second *General Report* of Euratom, March 14, 1959, it was announced that in accordance with the time limit set by the Treaty, the Council of Ministers had established basic standards for health protection during the last quarter of 1958. In the process, an opinion had been obtained from the Economic and Social Committee and there had been consultation with the European Parliament. These standards had thus become a "compulsory basis for national legislation" by the member states.[66]

The Commission emphasized in the second *General Report* that, because of the clear wording of the Treaty, for the first time it had been possible to devise a set of standards for the protection of the health of workers and public which had the force of law. Euratom has thus become a "pilot organization" for directives bearing on health protection against the hazards of radiation. A wider international agreement based on Euratom's standards may develop in the future through cooperation of the International Agency on Atomic Energy in Vienna and the International Labor Organization at Geneva.[67]

The Euratom Commission in 1959 immediately took up the work of harmonizing pertinent legislative provisions of member states with the official basic standards. Under Article 33 Euratom has the right to make recommendations for that purpose.[68]

The system of health protection desired by Euratom—besides setting down permissible maximum doses—also includes maximum permissible exposure and maximum contamination. Principles controlling medical supervision and permanent control of the level of radioactivity in the air, water and earth are also defined.

On December 1, 1960, the German Federal Republic became the first member state to incorporate a specific set of regulations in harmony with the basic standards.[69] During 1963, the Commission noted that an important advance had been made in legislation adopted by the member states in accordance with the basic standards; in May, 1963, the Belgian Government promulgated two decrees looking to the protection of workers and the public; in March, 1963, The Netherlands also enacted a law for protection against ionizing radiation. France responded in December, 1963. At the beginning of 1964 approval was given by the Italian government to a measure for the safety of nuclear installations and the protection of workers and public. It was expected that Luxembourg's draft legislation would also be promulgated in 1964. With action taken by that member state the Commission believed that all six members would then have on their law books one or more statutes putting the basic standards in effect.[70]

In its own functions, the Commission has acknowledged its special responsibility in the fields of nuclear medicine and radiation hygiene. Accordingly Articles 23 to 27 of the basic standards set forth criteria for national governments by which they could organize medical supervision for nuclear workers along consistent principles.

In the course of the consultation with the European Parliament in November, 1958, the Commission was requested to state more precisely the problems related to safety controls, principles of hygiene and regulations for nuclear workers and their medical inspection. These various problems have since been given study, including a consultation with twelve experts. An irradiation card for nuclear workers has been approved and accepted by the control services in the member states. A notebook on irradiation, to benefit nuclear workers and facilitate application of certain basic standards nationally was under study in 1960. Publication was also started then of a small volume giving comments on the basic standards and discussing problems of radiological protection. It has been written for the medical fraternity and health officials responsible for the control and inspection of nuclear installations.

In response to another request of the European Parliament, the Commission convoked a scientific colloquium in 1960 which discussed the type of regulations best suited for medical supervision of nuclear workers and for physical control over radiation.[71]

In accordance with the Commission's right to issue opinions on health and safety of workers, in 1962 the Commission rendered opinions concerning workers and the public from studies of the SENN reactor at Chooz (France and Belgium) and of the KRB reactor at Gundremmingen, Germany. A second study of the SENN project was underway in 1963, along with evaluation of the EUROCHEMIC installation in Belgium.

In the Munich symposium, sponsored by the Commission in October, 1962, four specific problems were discussed relating to safeguarding workers from radioactive contamination. They dealt with accident control, prevention, protection and organization. About 300 delegates from member states and other nations, as well as representatives from international organizations were in attendance.[72]

Of special concern to the Commission is provision for the safety of workers exposed to ionizing radiations, the chief anxiety of workers in nuclear plants. The Commission is constantly preoccupied with measures to advance the system in force for the medical supervision of nuclear workers to the highest possible standards. Valuable suggestions made at the Stresa Conference, and also at the Munich Conference, for improving these standards were scheduled for application in 1963.[73] The trend is to drop the level of permissible radiation even below what is allowed by treaty in the interest of stronger safety measures and because the genetic effects of radiation are not well known.

6.

Trends in Wage Standards

WHILE THE TREATY OF ROME IS NOT AS SPECIFIC IN SETTING forth the responsibilities of the European Community in regard to wages as is the treaty establishing the European Coal and Steel Community, nevertheless there are provisions which authorize the EEC to make periodic analyses of wage trends in the member countries. In Article 118 of the Treaty of Rome it is stated that the Commission shall aim "to promote close collaboration between Member States," on matters relating to "employment" and "working conditions." Thus, the Commission was empowered to institute "studies" and organize "consultations."[1] Another provision which has justified extensive research by the European Community in regard to wages is Article 213 which states:

> For the performance of the tasks entrusted to it, the Commission may collect any information and verify any matters within the limit and under the conditions laid down by the Council in accordance with the provisions of this Treaty.[2]

BASIC WAGE RATES

Evaluating wage trends for industries in the member countries— apart from those related to the European Coal and Steel Community

111

—the Commission reported in 1961 that basic wage rates in 1960 had increased to a greater extent than in 1959. The largest gains occurred in West Germany and The Netherlands and were prompted by a shortage of manpower. Another factor was the growing use of shorter work weeks in some of the member states. For West Germany the gross hourly wage in 1960 was 9 per cent above that of 1959. In The Netherlands the increase was 8 per cent.

In the harmonization of working conditions in the member countries the wage gains in 1960 tended to narrow the dispersion among the Six. Thus German wages tended to rise to a level approaching that in Belgium; in some industries they were even somewhat higher. Again, wage levels in France and The Netherlands moved nearer those in Belgium. For industrialized areas of northern Italy wage levels actually met those in France and The Netherlands. On the basis of these findings, the Commission concluded that labor expenditures in several countries had become close to similar outlays in Britain and Switzerland, but still were below wage levels in Sweden.

Putting wages in terms of purchasing power, in all the member countries, and especially in West Germany and The Netherlands, there had been a considerable advance in real wages from 1959 to 1960. The cost of living had advanced 2 to 3 per cent in four of the member countries—(France, West Germany, The Netherlands and Italy)—but larger wage payments kept well in advance of the rise in living costs. However, in Belgium and Luxembourg, where increases in the cost of living were most evident there was no significant wage rise. As a result wage levels tended to come closer together.

The Commission held that throughout the member countries higher wages had raised purchasing power by 2 to 6 per cent in 1960. Nevertheless, it was believed that the greatest benefits had been enjoyed by the most economically advanced and heavily industrialized regions. Thus, there was an admission that a more coordinated policy would be necessary to obtain the greater harmonization required by the social aims of the Treaty of Rome.[3]

HOURLY LABOR COSTS

On total hourly costs, a survey by the Statistical Office of the European Communities disclosed that the average hourly wages—including employer contributions for fringe benefits—for 14 industries in West Germany, France and Belgium during 1959 approximated 80 cents an hour. For The Netherlands and Italy the rates were 15 to 25 per cent lower.

The survey of the 14 industries covered all establishments having 50 or more employees in all the member countries except Luxembourg. The particular industries were:

Chemicals	Automobiles
Synthetic fiber	Cement
Paper pulp, paper and	Rubber
paperboard	Pottery, porcelain and
Cotton spinning	earthenware
Wool spinning	Machine tools
Sugar	Electrical engineering
Brewing and malting	Ship building and ship repair

The selection of industries for the survey was made through the cooperation of government experts and representatives of management and labor. As basis for the use of this list of industries it was estimated that, except for Luxembourg, they included at least 30 per cent of the wage earners in manufacturing industries. To facilitate international comparison the data was expressed in Belgian francs. As mentioned earlier, for the purpose of the study both direct and indirect labor charges against the employer were included. Accordingly, all such charges, whether by law, by collective bargaining contract, or by unilateral decision were in the computation. Note was taken of such items as bonuses, paid holidays, social security payments, cost of labor recruitment and training, and even benefits in kind.

In terms of American currency (which expresses the Belgian franc as 2¢) the average hourly wages for 1959 plus employer contributions for fringe benefits would be as follows:

West Germany	$.8084
France	.7988
Belgium	.7918
Netherlands	.6902
Italy	.6482

Nevertheless, it was the conclusion of the Commission, from this study, that the geographical factor is of less significance than the structural factor. In other words the data showed that wages in the same industry for the various member countries tend to be more homogeneous than wage costs in different industries even in the same country. Of the 14 industries surveyed, the highest wage costs were most commonly in the automobile industry and shipbuilding. The lowest wage costs were in industries producing pottery, cotton goods, woolens, porcelain and earthenware.[4]

Concerning the direct costs or wage outlays for labor expenditures, the countries of West Germany, Belgium and The Netherlands spent around 80 per cent of total labor cost for wages; the remaining 20 per cent went for indirect charges or fringe benefits. In France and Italy direct labor costs or wages came to 70 per cent and indirect costs were 30 per cent.

Nevertheless, the Commission found that the relative proportion of direct and indirect labor cost had no appreciable bearing on the total wage levels in the member countries. Thus in The Netherlands, where total labor costs are comparable with those in Italy, the breakdown between direct and indirect labor costs is actually similar to West Germany and Belgium where total labor costs are much higher. Again, France has a structural division between direct and indirect labor costs very similar to that in Italy. Yet, unlike Italy, France is in the group of member countries with high total labor expenditures.[5]

INITIAL REAL INCOME STUDY

As contrasted to total hourly labor costs to the employer, noted above, the Economic Community published in 1962 the findings on the first large scale comparative study of the real incomes of European workers by country and industry. For 13 industries surveyed in the six member countries, the French and Belgian workers had greater purchasing power than those in other member countries. The incomes of Dutch workers occupied a middle position, with the Germans in the next place. Italian workers, with the exception of those in the high wage rubber industry, were most often at or near the bottom position. Luxembourg workers in breweries and in the steel and iron mining industries were the highest paid of all Community workers.

The survey dealt with a comparison of male workers' incomes, with separate data for workers having families of one to five children. To determine workers' final net income the study took note not only of gross cash income, but also of such benefits as family allowances, social security payments, and income tax deductions. For the entire Community, workers with two children were generally best off in France, where average net incomes in 10 of the 13 industries were highest. Belgium had first place in two of the three remaining industries and second place in six industries.

Both in terms of gross and net income the lowest real income levels were found most often in Italy. Nevertheless, total Italian net incomes were higher in the rubber industry than in any other member country for bachelors and married workers with one child or none. However, in the case of larger families the greater family allowance payments in France and Belgium overcame the Italian's advantage of higher net wages in the Italian rubber industry.

For the 13 industries the net incomes of Dutch workers were usually close to the Community average. But workers in the Dutch rubber industry were among the lowest paid group. Dutch wool and cotton spinners, with no families or one child, tended to be a little better off in purchasing power than in other member countries.

German workers, for five of the 13 industries in the survey who were married men with two children, generally had the lowest income in the Community. Moreover, in seven other industries married men with two children had the second lowest income.[6]

Labor Costs and Worker Income

By 1964 the first surveys on the level and structure of labor costs and workers' incomes had been completed by the Statistical Office. These surveys, which had begun in 1959, have now covered 35 industries. In effect they have included almost the entire industrial sector. Uniform principles and definitions were applied throughout the surveys and for the first time it is possible to make an international comparison both of labor costs and workers' real income. Such data is of utmost importance for a meaningful study of the economic and social situation in the Community.

Through meetings with workers and employer representatives, the Commission has examined and discussed the findings of the initial 1959 wage survey. In addition to other phases of the work relationship, the Commission is preparing monographs on the wage structure in three industries: cotton spinning, rubber, and shipbuilding and repairs. In these current studies efforts will be made to determine the reasons for the sometimes unusual divergencies in the structure and level of labor costs.[7]

For 1963 the increase in wage levels in most of the member countries was higher than in 1962. However, in West Germany the notable wage increases of 1962 were followed by mild increases in 1963. The Netherlands' wage increases of 1963 were not exceptional, but wage agreements made at the end of 1963 meant sizeable increases for the year 1964. These increases took place despite new reductions in the work week and extensions of the annual vacation.

It appears that all the member countries have experienced notable gains in the share of income going to wage earners for the three years preceding July, 1964. For a considerable time the number of active wage earners in all the member countries has been increasing at a high rate because of constant immigration and also because of the transition from agriculture to other forms of employment. Thus the unemployed segment of the population has declined both in percentage and in absolute numbers due to this structural change in the work force.

In regard to factors behind the actual increases in wage rates, the Commission has found that new wage agreements in all the member countries are of considerable significance. For 1963 the agreed minimum wage in Germany, Belgium and The Netherlands had increased on an average of more than 7 per cent. Moreover, agricultural and female workers generally received even higher increases. In Italy negotiated wages had advanced 15 per cent on the average from the end of 1962 to the end of 1963.

Actually, the negotiated wage increases have been surpassed by additional wage gains resulting from the pressures of the labor market. Only referring to manufacturing, the greatest 1962–1963 wage increase—18 per cent—took place in Italy. The most moderate increase was in West Germany: 7.2 per cent. However in Germany from 1959 to 1963 the increase in gross hourly earnings in manufacturing was 44 per cent. During this same period, though, from a lower base, manufacturing wage gains in Italy had been 56 per cent.

Since in most of the member countries the rising wage rates have been accompanied by substantial improvement in fringe benefits, the total costs of manpower have thus increased in a higher proportion than the hourly wage rates. Thus by 1963 a guaranteed weekly wage was required by Belgian law. France instituted the fourth week of paid vacation. Further, higher charges on the employers for social security are in effect in Belgium and Italy. In total hourly costs of manpower in manufacturing, Italy had advanced most sharply from 1962 to 1963: 19.5 per cent.

Bearing on real income, the gains in hourly wages have been accompanied by increases in the cost of living, at a higher rate for 1963 than for 1962. The smallest increase of 2.1 per cent was in Belgium and the highest increase was for Italy: 7.5 per cent. But the gains in real income for industrial wage earners continued to take place in all the member countries from 1962 to 1963. Italy and Belgium were at the top with Italy ranging from 5 to 10 per cent and Belgium 6 to 8 per cent. In other member countries the increase in real income ranged from 2 to 4.5 per cent. From 1959 to 1963 the gains in real income have been high in all the member countries as indicated by the table below:

Increase of Annual Average Real Income (including Family Allowances) for Industrial Workers (In per cent).[8]

Country	From 1962 to 1963	From 1961 to 1962	From 1959 to 1963
Belgium	6–8	3½–4½	16–22
West Germany	2–3	6–7	24–30
France	3½–4½	3½–4	15–18
Italy	5–10	2–4	12–22
Luxembourg	3½–4½	3½–5	18–21
The Netherlands	2–3	4–6	14–18

THE EUROPEAN COAL AND STEEL COMMUNITY

Since the founding of this Community in 1951, the High Authority has been aware of its duty to gather and publish data on the wages of workers in the coal, steel and iron ore industries. A specific provision in the Treaty of Paris setting forth this responsibility is Article 46 (5) which directs the High Authority to:

> gather any information required to assess the possibilities of improving the living and working conditions of the labour force in the industries under its jurisdiction. . . .

Nevertheless, Article 68 clearly states that the application of the Treaty gives no mandate to the High Authority permitting it to affect the methods of fixing wages already in force within the member states. However, under one condition the Community may recommend to certain enterprises that wages be increased. This situation refers to cases where the High Authority "finds that abnormally low prices practised by one or several enterprises are the result of wages fixed by these enterprises at an abnormally low level as compared with the actual wage level in the same region. . . ."[9]

REAL INCOMES

In 1955 the High Authority published the findings obtained from a preliminary study regarding the real income of miners and steelworkers in 1954. Based on this initial survey, it was concluded that divergencies in real incomes between one member country and another in the Community were not so great as had been assumed previously. In actuality, it was found that they do not exceed the variations at times existing within a particular country between different types of industry or different industrial areas. At all events it appeared from the data then available that divergencies in the real income of miners and steelworkers had declined between the years 1953 and 1955.[10]

From comparison of data available in 1956, the High Authority maintained that the levels of living in Luxembourg, Belgium, The Netherlands, France and Germany were very close to one another. It was acknowledged, however, that by contrast the data from Italy showed that conditions there were somewhat less favorable.[11]

Particular indicators which are considered as significant in determining levels of living are life expectancy, rate of infant mortality, calories available per day per person and consumption of steel per capita. In the case of females, The Netherlands had the highest life expectancy at birth, 72.9 years, as against Italy with the lowest, 57.5 years. For the other member states, they ranked respectively: France, Germany, Belgium and Luxembourg. The range was considerably higher than the average life expectancy for women in the less favorable parts of Europe, which was 46.8 years. Complete data was not available in this study for the life expectancy of males.

With respect to infant mortality, per thousand, The Netherlands had the low figure of 21.1 compared to the high rate of 52.8 for Italy. The other member countries were all close to the figure of 42 per thousand.

Available calories per day per capita showed Italy with the low figure of 2595 and all the other countries close to 2900, except for France which was at 2795. In terms of steel consumption per capita, an index of industrial development, in the year 1954 Germany ranked highest with 319 kilograms, and Italy lowest, with 101 kilograms. For the other countries the order of rank was Belgium, Luxembourg, France and The Netherlands.[12]

In general this study on the comparison of real income among workers showed that, as contrasted with variations among countries, even more significant differences existed between industries and between families with two as against several children.

For coal miners, the three top countries in terms of high income were the German Saar, Belgium and The Netherlands. These three countries were within a range of 90 to 100 per cent of each other. France was in an intermediate position. For a French married couple without children, the income was 80 to 90 per cent of what miners received in the top three countries. For a French miner's family with two children, the real income was close to the top level in the Community. In Germany the coal miners were generally within 70 to 80 per cent of the top level. Italian coal miners had real incomes ranging between 60 and 70 per cent of the top level.[13]

The findings on comparative real incomes for steelworkers in 1954 showed a much closer relationship than for coal miners. Luxembourg was in top position, with Belgium about 10 per cent lower. However, all the other member countries were within 70 per cent of Luxembourg.[14]

But for iron ore miners, while Luxembourg was on the highest level of real income for all categories of such families, there was considerable divergence in the other member countries. French iron ore miners were in second place with about 10 per cent less income than miners in Luxembourg. Italy and Germany were in last place with about one-half the income of iron ore miners in Luxembourg.

The results on real income in this study were obtained by comparing purchasing power in the member countries through pricing the contents of representative national "market baskets."[15]

By 1960 the average net real income in each country for a married man with two children showed that Luxembourg had the highest income in the steel and iron ore industries. Belgium had the highest real income for coal miners and second place for steel workers. French steelworkers and coal miners were close to Belgian levels. Iron ore miners in France were in second place to the top position held by Luxembourg.

Since this study was completed, Community experts have estimated that real wages from 1958 to the first half of 1961 have advanced at the rate of 33 per cent for Germany, 27 per cent for France, 20 per cent for The Netherlands and 17 per cent for Italy. Also on the basis of these estimates it was concluded in 1963 that real per capita income in the United States was likely about twice as high as the average for Western Europe.[16]

TOTAL LABOR COST

Since 1952, in cooperation with the industries of the Community, the High Authority has made an annual survey of hourly wage cost to the employer. Note has been taken also of all other expenses properly related to workers. In 1960 the Office of Statistics for the European Communities re-examined this data for the seven years from 1952 to 1958, and observed some significant trends in wage developments.

To make the comparison of wage trends more meaningful from

country to country the data was expressed not in the national currencies of the different countries, but in relation to Belgian francs. The total expenses in wages and charges on employers relating to workers were considered. For the latter category payments by the employer for social security, family allowances, costs for recruitment and training of workers, medical and social services were included.

LABOR COSTS FOR COAL MINING

For coal miners, from 1952 through 1958, variations in labor costs were somewhat irregular, and labor payments in the Italian coal mines were the lowest. In six of the seven years the Saar Basin mines had the highest wage costs. Some notable variations took place in other countries during this period. France occupied second place for six of the seven years. Belgium for five years was in third place. West Germany, in four of the seven years, occupied the fourth position. The Netherlands during four of the seven years was in fifth place. The High Authority concluded from these findings that the policies of the different member countries on the matter of wage costs for miners are not yet coordinated. Sooner or later, however, wage changes in one country provoke similar changes in the other countries.[17]

Between 1952 and 1958 hourly wages have advanced the least in countries where, in 1952, their level was relatively high. On the other hand, wages for miners have advanced most notably from the 1952 level in countries where the level in that year was relatively low.[18]

Another equalizing tendency is shown by the dispersion in total coal mining labor costs which has been diminishing from country to country. The coefficient of variation among the Six for such costs in 1952 was 22 per cent. By 1958 it had been reduced to 15.4 per cent. The High Authority regarded this reduction of about 30 per cent dispersion as a significant index of a closer agreement among the member countries on outlays for labor costs in the coal mines.[19]

Additional data considered important by the High Authority in indicating wage trends compare total hours worked and average wages per hour. In 1952, 1.9 billion hours were worked at an average hourly expense of 41.38 Belgian francs, or about 82 cents.[20] Payment for this work, including wages and social charges, amounted to 80 billion Belgian francs or 1.6 billion dollars. By 1958 the hours worked in the coal mines (in round figures) amounted to 1.66 billion hours, with an average hourly wage of 60.86 Belgian francs or about $1.32. The total outlay of labor cost in 1958 was about 101 billion Belgian francs, or well over 2 billion dollars.[21]

TRENDS IN STEEL LABOR PAYMENTS

Between 1952 and 1958 steel industry labor payments were highest in Luxembourg. Counting the Saar Basin as added to the six countries, Italy, after the first three years, exchanged its sixth lowest place with Holland's seventh lowest place for the remaining four years. Belgium held the second position in steel labor payments for all years except 1956 and 1958 when it was in third place. France was in fourth place for most of the period, except for 1957 and 1958 when it was in fifth place. While Germany was in fifth place for the steel industry in 1952 and two additional years, it was in the fourth position in the last two years, 1957 and 1958.[22]

The Netherlands, sharing with Italy the lowest ranking for labor payments, had the highest percentage increase in payments, 79 per cent. However, Italy experienced an increase of only 34 per cent. Germany, in fifth position in more than four of the seven years, had a percentage increase of 52 per cent. As with the coal industry, the countries with the highest labor payments in steel had the lowest percentage increase in labor payments—Luxembourg and Belgium with increases of 35 and 33 per cent.[23]

And again the variations between member countries for total labor payments tended to modify between 1952 and 1958. The coefficient of variation was 17.8 in 1952 and was 12.7 in 1958. Even in 1952 this dispersion in the steel industry was much less than was the case with the coal industry.[24]

Interestingly enough, the total number of hours worked in the steel industry in 1952—around 0.9 billion—had not increased appreciably in 1958. Nevertheless the average labor payment per hour, including fringe benefits, had advanced from 35.90 Belgian francs in 1952 to 51.49 Belgian francs in 1958, or from 72 cents to $1.02. Total labor payments had thus increased from 32 billion Belgian francs in 1952 ($640,000,000) to 47 billion Belgian francs in 1958 ($940,000,000).

It is the belief of the High Authority that indirect labor charges— except for Italy where they are unusually high—tended to somewhat equalize between 1952 and 1958.[25]

LABOR COSTS IN ORE MINING

The data on labor payments gathered by the Statistical Office showed wide variations among the four member countries involved in iron ore mining. Even in the final year of the period under study, 1958, hourly rates of about 85 Belgian francs for France and Luxembourg were far removed from the rates of 44.74 and 33.91 paid in West Germany and Italy. It was the view of the Statistical Office that this great disparity really reflected the difference in the ore mining conditions of France and Luxembourg as against those of Italy and Germany. They are comparable neither from method of operation, size of the enterprise, nor from position and size of ore strata. Moreover, from 1952 to 1958, despite some increase in the level of labor payments, the disparity existing in 1952 was practically the same in 1958.[26]

CONTRASTS WITHIN THREE INDUSTRIES

For these three industries—coal mining, steel and iron ore mining —total hours worked in 1952 were about 2.9 billion, as compared to 2.7 billion in 1958. This reduction in hours worked possibly reflects the past efforts of trade unions to reduce the duration of the work week. Nevertheless, while total 1952 labor payments were 116 billion Belgian francs ($2,320,000,000), they had increased to 154 billion Belgian francs ($3,080,000,000) in 1958. The average hourly labor payments (direct and indirect) were highest in iron ore mines, with the coal mines and the steel industry following.[27]

From 1953 to 1961 the changes have been notably different in hourly wages and total labor payments for the coal and steel industries. The increases in wages and total labor payments in West Germany, France and The Netherlands have tended to be more pronounced than in Belgium, Italy and Luxembourg, especially for coal mining and iron ore mining.

Among the three industries the changes in hourly wages and total labor payments appear to have been least rapid for coal mining. In The Netherlands, however, the difference between the steel industry and the coal mines has been less noticeable in the area of direct wage payments. In Italy, wage costs have changed more sharply for coal miners than for steel workers or iron ore miners.

HOURLY WAGE COSTS IN BELGIAN FRANCS

Utilizing the more meaningful index for comparison—i.e., Belgian francs—the High Authority found the hourly wage costs increased strongly for all the member countries between 1953 and 1960. By 1960 only Italy showed a wage cost significantly lower than the other member countries.

Comparing coal industry data for the first nine months of 1961 with the figures for 1960, it was evident that direct wage outlays for miners had increased sharply in Germany and The Netherlands at 13 and 12 per cent respectively. During the same period the increase for direct wage expenditures in France was 4 per cent, in Italy 5 per cent and in Belgium 2 per cent. Actually, these greater wage increases in Germany and The Netherlands were due in part to currency re-evaluation in those two countries in 1961. The effect of these changes was to cause wage increases for coal miners (expressed in Belgian francs), in Germany and Holland to appear greater than if they had been expressed in marks or florins.

On the basis of direct wage increases it was apparent in 1961 that hourly wage costs for German coal miners surpassed costs in France where, until that time, such costs had been higher. The relative positions of France and Italy on direct wage outlays remained about the same, though there was some widening between France and Belgium.

In the steel industry the variance in total hourly wage expenditures for the member countries narrowed somewhat between 1953 and 1955 and then tended to stabilize. Luxembourg continued to be the extreme point with total labor outlays 15 to 20 per cent higher than second place Belgium.

From 1960 through the first nine months of 1961, direct steel wages (in Belgian francs) increased 10 per cent in West Germany and 13 per cent in The Netherlands. These changes contrasted with the more moderate increases of 8 per cent in France, 6 per cent in Italy, 3 per cent in Luxembourg and 2 per cent in Belgium. On the basis of this data, it can be said that all member countries except Belgium, have moved some degree closer to the top rate of Luxembourg. To this extent the dispersion in steel wages has been mildly decreased.

There has also been a moderate narrowing of the dispersion for labor expenditures in the iron ore industry, but the variance still remains sizable, showing relatively high costs in Luxembourg and France, contrasted to relatively low outlays in Germany and Italy.

Data obtained by the High Authority indicates that the trend of real income for wage earners in the three industries of the Community, was upward from 1954 to 1957. A period of stability ensued between 1957 and 1959, but the upward trend resumed in 1960. Nevertheless, for the coal miners of Germany, Belgium and Italy, income diminished notably in 1958 and 1959 because of partial unemployment from declining markets. However, wage income reduction was compensated by benefits from unemployment insurance and, particularly in Belgium, by special allocation of funds by the Community.[28]

WAGE STANDARDS IN THE UNITED STATES

At first appraisal, there appears to be a vast chasm between the modest average hourly wage of 1959 in West Germany, France and Belgium—about 80 cents an hour, including employer contributions to benefits—and the gross average hourly earnings for manufacturing in the United States of $2.19 for the same year, which does not include employer contribution to benefits.[29] Nevertheless, in terms of real wages, as was noted above, the EEC has estimated that, due to advances in wages, by 1963 real per capita income in Western Europe had increased to about one-half that for the United States.

Moreover, it would be quite inaccurate to assume that the average wage for manufacturing in the United States is typical for occupations in other forms of employment. Thus, in 1959 average gross hourly earnings for retail trade was found to be only $1.57.[30] Again, the much higher rate of unemployment in the United States, as compared to most of the Common Market countries, inevitably reduces annual wage income here. In other words, it would not be justified to assume that annual income in the United States is the average hourly wage multiplied by 2,000 hours.

Moreover, even in manufacturing, a comparatively high wage paying sector, considerable variations in wage rates exist for different sections of the country, such as the southeast compared to the north central area.

Comparing family needs with family income in the United States, there are some rather disconcerting findings. In 1962 the Social Security Administration estimated that to meet the requirements for a "low-cost" budget for a non-farm family of four, an income of $3,955 was necessary.[31] Yet in 1962 the Department of Commerce reported that 20 per cent of the families in the United States had incomes of less than $3,000.

On the basis of these figures the President's Council of Economic Advisors, when discussing the problem of poverty in America in its 1964 annual report, concluded that "one-fifth of our families and nearly one-fifth of our total population are poor." Moreover, poverty on the farm, severe enough in itself, accounted for only 16 per cent of the poor sector of the total population, estimated at 38,000,000 people.[32]

Conscious of such barriers as inadequate education, poor health and demoralizing environment, which tend to "trap" so many people in the poverty classification, Gunnar Myrdal refers to this segment of

American citizens as the "under-class" in our society.[33]

Despite a rather impressively high hourly wage for manufacturing in America, levels of living for large portions of our population leave much to be desired; one might note that the 1960 census reported 27 per cent of the total housing supply in the United States was substandard.[34] In New York City alone the mentally ill, the aged, the sick and their children subsisting on public aid number 300,000.[35] Though spending their lives in a country known for its high average hourly wages, one-half of the aged in America do not have the means to obtain decent shelter, adequate nutrition, proper medical care, or minimum recreation.[36]

While operating o a higher wage level and actually in a much less restricted environment than the Common Market countries, the American economy faces a serious problem of inadequate income for a large sector of its population. There is no reason to look upon policies pursued by the European Communities to correct imbalances and foster upward harmonization of income distribution with patronizing complacency.

7.

Improving Patterns
for Social Security

THE GENERAL LANGUAGE OF ARTICLES 117 AND 118 OF THE Treaty of Rome applies to social security for most of those who remain employed within their native countries.[1] In this connection the Community is to encourage harmonization of social security systems in an upward direction by promoting close cooperation among the member states through research, consultative meetings and recommendations to member governments.

MIGRANT WORKERS

However, for the migrant from another member country, the Treaty is quite specific on the role of the Commission in regard to Social Security. Thus Article 51 reads:

> The Council, acting by means of a unanimous vote on a proposal of the Commission, shall, in the field of social security, adopt the measures necessary to effect the free movement of workers, in particular, by introducing a system which permits an assurance to be given to migrant workers and their beneficiaries:
>
> (a) that, for the purpose of qualifying for and retaining the right to benefits and of the calculation of these benefits, all periods taken into consideration by the respective municipal law of the countries concerned shall be added together; and

(b) that these benefits will be paid to persons resident in the territories of the Member States.[2]

In effect, the Commission of the Economic Community must wait
upon the member governments to take action to harmonize social
security programs covering citizens. Yet where two or more member
countries are involved in problems of social security regarding the
same migrant workers because of employment in more than one
country, the Commission has actual power to determine solutions by
means of supra-national regulations. Once a draft regulation of the
Commission concerning social security benefits for migrant workers
has been adopted by the Council of Ministers it has the binding force
of law upon the member states without the intervention of their
respective parliaments. The number of migrant workers, including
their families, concerned with such social security payments is over
1,700,000.

In 1958 two regulations on social security for migrant workers,
numbers three and four, were submitted by the Commission for the
Community and were adopted by the Council. Basically Regulation
Three lays down principles on social security for migrant workers,[3]
and Regulation Four makes the applications by which benefits are to
be paid to migrants and their families.[4] These regulations also determine the proportionate obligation for the member states involved.

In this fashion, as an example, claims are settled for natives of
Italy who have worked for some period of time in France, Germany
and also in Italy. The benefits involved might concern health insurance, invalidity allowances, pensions, industrial accidents, occupational
disease, family allowances, unemployment or death claims. It is possible that a worker's family might have remained in Italy while the
father was employed in Germany. Regulations Three and Four are
designed to establish the amount of payments the German and Italian
social security systems would be obliged to pay the worker and his
dependents for one or several types of coverage under social security.

THE ADMINISTRATIVE COMMITTEE

Because of the many complexities in determining social security
benefits for migrant workers in the Six, Regulation Three provides
for the establishment of an Administrative Committee. Among its
duties, the Committee has the responsibility to settle all administrative
questions and issues of interpretation arising out of Regulation Three
and Four and all later regulations or agreements. Further, the Committee actually makes the transfers of benefit payments at the request

of the appropriate authorities of a member state by means of a central clearing system, unless the countries involved in a given case wish to make direct settlements.

On a broader level the Committee is directed to advance and strengthen cooperation in social security, especially on matters of health and hazards of common concern. To this end the Committee has been instructed to submit proposals to the Commission for revision of Regulations Three and Four and later regulations as well.

Membership on the Committee is made up of one representative, assisted by a technical advisor, for each of the member states. The same type of representation is accorded the Commission of the Economic Community, and the High Authority of the Coal and Steel Community. On the basis of a special agreement, two technical advisors have also been assigned to the Committee from the International Labor Organization in Geneva.[5]

For the purpose of the Committee, the term "frontier" worker is used to indicate a wage earner who maintains his permanent residence in one member state, and normally returns there daily or at least weekly, but is employed in another state of the Community.[6] The term "seasonal worker" indicates one who has employment in a member state other than his own for a period of less than 12 months without changing residence to the second state.[7]

For both types of workers, present or past coverage under social security legislation of one or more member states is required, and, normally, citizenship in a member state. However, eligibility has been broadened under Regulations Three and Four and is thus extended to stateless persons and refugees.

By 1961 the Committee had held 25 meetings and was in the process of examining preliminary drafts of additional regulations on social security for frontier and seasonal workers to correct instances of incomplete protection.[8] By December, 1961, the draft regulations had been approved by the Commission and adopted by the Council. They had thus become supplementary law for the member states in regard to frontier and seasonal workers.[9]

During the Committee's meeting in Luxembourg in 1961 it initiated enquiries on the results thus far from using the Regulations for both long term benefits (survivors, old age, invalidity) and short term benefits (industrial accidents and diseases, sickness, maternity, family allowances and unemployment).[10]

At sessions 45 and 46 of the Committee, held in Brussels and The Hague during June and July, 1963, government representatives reached agreement on what bilateral agreements covering frontier workers between member states would remain in effect, despite the promulgation of Regulations Three and Four. This accord by the government representatives was in recognition of the stipulation made by the Council, that Council regulations will replace those made through bilateral conventions of states, except where the latter are generally conceded to be more favorable. Thus certain bilateral agreements might be mentioned in regard to health insurance benefits for international transport workers.[11]

In 1959 the Committee, at Brussels, worked out several problems on the application of existing regulations for payment of family allowances for dependents of migrant workers.[12] Upon first consideration by the Committee, the Council, in 1961, determined the method of calculating family allowances for a frontier worker who had been employed during the same calendar month in two member states. Provision for adjustment was also made for a member state which may have paid the family allowance in advance.[13] In May, 1962, the Committee adopted the draft of a supplementary regulation to assure that family allowances would be paid the children of workers employed on a temporary basis outside the country of their normal employment.[14]

At Brussels in January, 1962, the Committee, during session 30, gave approval to the texts for a second series of guides for family allowance systems in the member countries. These booklets were designed to inform migrant workers of the allowances to which they are entitled and the procedure they must use to obtain them.[15] In line with its objective of improving and simplifying Regulations Three and Four the Commission in July, 1963, proposed a new regulation to the Council for granting family allowances for children in order to simplify the existing complex procedures. Favorable action was taken on this proposal by the Council on December 18, 1963.[16]

INDUSTRIAL DISEASES AND ACCIDENTS

The European Community has long been concerned with the risk which a migrant worker may face by loss of coverage on an occupational disease in a given industry as he moves to another country and obtains work in the same industry. While the worker might have been entitled to benefits if he contracted the disease on the job in his own country, the same malady might not be recognized as an industrial disease in the country to which he migrated. To remove this hazard, Regulation Three allows the worker benefits despite the fact that the second country does not recognize the illness as an industrial disease.[17]

In line with this regulation the Economic Community has prepared a very complete European list of industrial diseases. Surprisingly, while there are at least 45 diseases on the European list, until recently not more than about 10 of them were to be found on all the national lists of the six member states.

In November, 1960, the director general of Social Affairs convoked a meeting of medical experts and technicians from the Six. Also in attendance were representatives from the European Coal and Steel Community and the International Social Security Association. The meeting was to consider a uniform list of occupational diseases drafted by Professor Vigliani of the Occupational Disease Clinic at the University of Milan. The Vigliani list was adopted by the experts after thorough study. A supplementary list was also approved as desirable to incorporate in future legislation.[18]

In March, 1961 the uniform list of industrial diseases and a list of the noxious agents likely to cause them were presented at a meeting composed of government experts and representatives of both sides of industry. General agreement in favor of the Commission's list was expressed at this time.[19]

By July, 1961, a meeting of government experts had approved the motion to prepare a Commission draft recommendation for the institution of a uniform list of occupational diseases.[20] On July 23, 1962, after consulting the Economic and Social Committee and the European Parliament, the Commission adopted a recommendation for the establishment of an official European list of occupational diseases. This recommendation was then sent to the member states, requesting them to adopt a uniform European list of occupational diseases. The action was regarded as a first measure in harmonizing present statutory and administrative provisions for protection against industrial diseases and for possible compensation. The Commission was concerned that, because of existing discrepancies among the lists of diseases recognized in the laws of the Six, unwarranted divergencies might result both in safeguards available to workers and in compensation for industrial diseases.[21]

Three main points were included in the recommendation: 1) National lists of occupational diseases were to be extended for closer accord with the European list suggested by the Commission. 2) Member countries should accept the "combined" system, by which workers would be compensated when they contracted diseases on the national list of their own country, though not on the national list of the country where they were currently employed. 3) They should encourage recognition of new occupational diseases and promote measures to prevent them; appropriate information on hazards and remedies should be exchanged among the member states.

During 1963 a meeting of government representatives took place in Luxembourg to appraise the action taken in the member countries on the Commission's recommendation of July, 1962. It was found that in Germany the law of May 5, 1963, had introduced the use of the "combined" system for industrial diseases. Germany's own national list, which was revised in 1962, is now considered one of the most comprehensive in the Community. Since July, 1962, Belgium had introduced a bill to include silicosis as an occupational disease for miners. France had added two more diseases to her national list and improved the description of four others, so that the scope of compensation would be broadened. In addition, France, in 1963, was preparing a list of diseases considered as occupational in origin and which, by doctor's decision, could become legally compensable. This new list was based on the Commission's. Italy had instituted studies aiming to recognize certain diseases as occupational. A special committee was set up in Luxembourg to study the entire European list of occupational diseases and determine if there should be legislation establishing the "combined" system in Luxembourg. In The Netherlands it was decided to use the European list of occupational diseases as the basis for instituting preventive measures.

With respect to the exchange of information, Germany, France, and Italy had already submitted specific questions on the occupational incidence of certain diseases which were forwarded to the other member countries of the Six.

The "European list" of industrial diseases was the first recommendation made by the Commission in the field of social security. Judging from the response made by the member governments and the efforts put forth in the following year to enact new legislation in accord with this recommendation, it was believed that the outlook for continued cooperation was most satisfactory.[22]

In 1961 a study group was appointed by the Administrative Committee to find a solution to difficulties in compensation for occupational diseases where the worker was exposed to risks in two or more member states.[23]

A second meeting of this study group was held in June, 1961. At that time consideration was given to the financial obligations of the member states involved. Procedures were worked out under which claims for benefits, to be paid by more than one member country, could be filed under these circumstances.[24] Drafts of these procedures were approved by the Administrative Committee during its May meeting in Paris, 1962.[25]

Among the provisions on social security for "frontier workers" adopted by the Council in 1961 was Article 16; it states that an injury incurred by a frontier worker between his regular home and the frontier in the course of the normal trip to his place of work, or on return, shall, under the law of the appropriate country where he is employed, be regarded as an industrial injury taking place in the territory of that country. For the purpose of compensation, adequate enquiry is to be made to ascertain that the conditions set forth in Article 16, concerning the place and time of the injury, were actually present.

COMPLEMENTARY SOCIAL SECURITY PROGRAMS

To encourage general improvements in the administration of social security, representatives of both sides of industry, at a meeting called by the Commission in Brussels on February 7, 1961, expressed approval and support of the proposed study on complementary social security systems for all types of industrial risks involving migrant or frontier workers employed outside their native member country. The outline of the study had been submitted to this group for examination at an earlier meeting. The initial phase of the study was to be confined to such industries as construction and public works, chemicals, printing, paper pulp and automobiles.[26] Officials from unions and management in a number of these industries later met to determine methods for drafting joint reports for each country and industry. Another meeting of representatives from labor and management during May, 1961, showed wide agreement on the proposal to draft a program of studies on social security,[27] in accordance with Articles 117 and 118, which urge improvement of working standards by closer collaboration among member states in social security.[28]

IMPROVED COVERAGE AND BENEFITS

During 1961 the Community found that substantial progress had been made toward the improvement of social security programs. Coverage had been extended to new groups of citizens and benefits had been improved for those already possessing social security. A notable extension of coverage had been made for self-employed workers, especially health insurance for small shopkeepers in Italy. Better standards for this same group were applied in Belgium in regard to

pension programs. In West Germany the pension program for crafts-
men was revised. The French government extended health and disability insurance to farm workers. In The Netherlands a measure was
introduced to extend family allowances to the entire population.

Likewise during 1961 pension benefits were increased in West
Germany, France and The Netherlands. The system of old age pensions was expanded in Luxembourg. In France and The Netherlands,
additions were made to family allowances. With regard to unemployment benefits, increases were made by France, Belgium and Italy.
France also broadened its health insurance coverage and Germany
improved its insurance program for industrial accidents.[29]

RAISING ADMINISTRATIVE STANDARDS

To facilitate procedures for migrant workers in social security programs, the Administrative Committee in 1962 published an initial
series of handbooks on health insurance in each of the six member
states, in an attempt to enable these workers to understand the rights
accorded to them.[30] The handbooks give workers all the necessary
information on their rights to health insurance and the procedures by
which they may claim benefits. For the same purpose the Committee
in October, 1962, gave its approval to informational texts (one for
each member country) outlining unemployment benefits in each of
the Six.[31] During 1964 a series of meetings were held for independent experts of the member countries who were preparing the definitive edition of the glossary of terms used in social security programs
of the member states.[32]

Another approach to better administration, sponsored jointly by
the Economic Community and the European Coal and Steel Community, was the meeting (November, 1960) in Florence of directors of
social security institutions from the Six. Also present were representatives of European trade unions and employer organizations. An
objective of this conference was to plan training sessions for 1961
(under the organization of the Commission) for staff members of
social security institutions. The conference also discussed the Commission proposal for exchange of trainees among various social security institutions and ministries in the Six. This proposal will be discussed
more extensively when treating of the European Coal and Steel
Community.

DOCUMENTARY STUDIES ON SOCIAL SECURITY

Even before the European Conference on Social Security, sponsored by the Communities in 1962, the Commission, acting in cooperation with the High Authority, had entrusted independent experts with the task of rounding out a series of monographs on social security; these monographs had been confined initially to the coal and steel industries. Comparative tables on laws dealing with occupational diseases were compiled. In cooperation with the High Authority, other comparative tables were prepared relating to the hazards of old age and disability, family allowances, industrial accidents and unemployment insurance.

A study of the general character of social security at the beginning of the Common Market was under way by 1960. The initial version in four languages of a lexicon of technical terms used in social security was also being compiled at that time. A number of research projects were also in progress by 1960, dealing with the economic aspect of coordinating social security programs and comparing sources for financing social security. Another study underway then dealt with the problem of harmonizing social security programs according to industries, especially in regard to occupational diseases.[33]

THE EUROPEAN COAL AND STEEL COMMUNITY

The Treaty of Paris has a number of definite procedures for the High Authority to follow in regard to standards for social security programs. Article 69 (4) of the Treaty places a particular obligation on the member states; surveillance over its observation is entrusted to the High Authority. As Article 69 says, the member states:

> will prohibit any discrimination in payment and working conditions as between national and foreign workers, without prejudice to special measures concerning frontier workers; in particular, they will work out among themselves any arrangements so that social security measures do not stand in the way of the movement of labour.[34]

In this connection Articles 68 (5) and 67 (2) direct that if in a member state's provisions for the financing of social security or for dealing with unemployment are so modified that they would likely "provoke a serious disequilibrium by substantially increasing differences in cost of production otherwise than through variations in productivity," the High Authority may put other provisions in Article 67 (2) in effect. In other words, if it is found that modifications in social security are causing such harmful effects to coal and steel enterprises in a given member state, the High Authority "may authorize that State to grant subsidies to such enterprises. . . ." This authorization is necessary, since under the Treaty, the European Coal and Steel Community endeavors to prevent unfair competitive advantage by one country over another within the Common Market. If the harmful effects are incurred by coal or steel enterprises in other member states, the High Authority may recommend that the state responsible for the situation apply an appropriate remedy.[35]

Obviously the Community also is aware that encouragement of better standards in social security for coal and steel workers is part of its general responsibility under Article 3(e) of the Treaty which directs the High Authority to:

> promote the improvement of the living and working conditions of the labour force in each of the industries under its jurisdiction so as to harmonize those conditions in an upward direction.[36]

In 1962 the High Authority felt it was difficult to determine if more or less harmonization in social security standards had resulted since the signing of the Treaty in 1951. It was noted that if one should assume some harmonization was attained in each of the several facets of conditions of living and employment, it would still be very difficult from these partial harmonizations to assess the total. Here the weight which each country places on this or that aspect of social security legislation was regarded as too divergent for general assessment.

Difficulties in comparison of standards in regard to social security were found to have several causes. As one instance, in each member country social security does not constitute a uniform system under one organization. Instead a certain number of institutions coexist, partly independent, in order to meet the various risks and payments entrusted to them. The High Authority has learned that it cannot proceed from one country to another and just compare different types of social security, such as health insurance or old age insurance. The comparisons inevitably remain fragmentary.

Moreover, social security is governed almost exclusively by the adequacy of legislative determination, which depends in large part on the proficiency of the governments. It may be that in order to improve the national law on social security, a government should be guided by the experiences of other countries. However, the measures it puts in effect may be based on obsolete economic and political data. The High Authority acknowledged, therefore, that the direct impact of economic integration in the Six on the development of social security is much less than on prices, wages and working conditions.[37]

MIGRANT WORKERS

In June 1960, a meeting of the Administrative Committee on Social Security for Migrant Workers was held in Luxembourg at the invitation of the High Authority. On that occasion Paul Finet, then president of the High Authority, recalled that the convention on social security for migrant workers, instituted by the ministers of labor of the member states, provided the forerunner of the regulations of the Council. Finet stressed the importance of the task entrusted to the Administrative Committee, which is to transform into concrete measures the principles contained in the regulations. He pointed out that because of such practical measures, workers recognize that notable progress has been realized and the result redounds to an improvement in living standards.[38]

In cooperation with the Administrative Committee on Social Security of the European Community, the High Authority has made a special study of Regulations Numbers Three and Four in regard to "frontier workers." A motivation for this study was the fact that national frontiers cut directly across regions important in the production of both coal and steel. As a consequence "frontier workers" form a significant part of the labor force in the industries of the Community.

For a better understanding among miners of their rights to benefits, the Community has distributed comparative tables on social security for miners in the member states. The essential points in the different laws are emphasized as well as the method by which they are financed. Annual evaluation is made by the High Authority of the protection available to miners and their families under social security in the member countries. A similar study is also made of complementary benefit systems for miners who have social security credits in more than one country.[39]

ILLNESS AND ACCIDENTS

The Community has maintained a close interest in a special problem here which has yet to be adequately solved by present regulations, namely, health benefits for migrant workers (especially miners) who have contracted an occupational disease. It is the desire of the High Authority to work for a solution to this problem based on the advancement of a common European social policy.[40]

In regard to health insurance the Community has found that the basic types of benefits in the Six are quite similar. Thus, for steelworkers, three countries—Belgium, France and Luxembourg—use the principle of reimbursement within limits, for costs of illness. Two countries, Germany and The Netherlands, make gratuitous allowances for this expense. In Italy there is a combination of these methods.

In all the member countries, it has been found that the problems posed by the need to improve benefits and coverage for medical costs has given rise to prolonged, and at times lively, political controversy. In Italy the so-called "minor reform" of 1959, secured by the National Institute of Health Insurance, amounted to an improvement and standardization of insurance benefits for different categories of beneficiaries. A closer approach to the regulations in other countries was the result.

In France the "Act" of May 12, 1960, put in effect several measures which promise to assure a given level of reimbursement for medical fees and provide much greater financial responsibility for the individual case. As of 1962 extensive reforms in health insurance projected for West Germany and Belgium had not yet been fully realized.

For mine workers, there are numerous common characteristics in the health insurance programs of the member countries. As one example, miners afflicted with illness are generally treated without charge.

Except for Belgium, where disability insurance is handled administratively along with health insurance, this type of social security is associated in all the other member countries with old age insurance.[41]

In Belgium there is no compulsory compensation for industrial accidents, but in all the other member countries the employer is obliged to take out private insurance on a cooperative basis differentiated according to industries. However, in France insurance covering industrial accidents has been made part of the centralized administration of social security. Nevertheless, the payments are scaled according to various criteria, such as the type of risk involved. Throughout the member countries there is considerable difference in the assessment of the degree of invalidity and the conditions required for eligibility to benefits.[42]

PENSIONS AND FAMILY ALLOWANCES

A measure which has attained a certain degree of harmonization in the different social security systems of the Community is West Germany's "dynamic pension" of 1957. It corresponds to the French formula of regular increases in the level of pension benefits. Germany gears increases to the increases taking place in France. In 1957 West Germany and France also instituted a system of complementary retirement based on a collective agreement for a given industry. Thus the years of service by a worker in the same industry, but with the time divided between two countries, would now coalesce for the purpose of determining pension rights. Generally, the High Authority has found that pension formulas in the Six tend to show very close similarities.[43]

The High Authority believes that the institution of family allowance benefits in West Germany in 1954 tended to make the policy on these payments somewhat more uniform throughout the Six. Though considerable differences still remain in regard to increased allowances, eligibility and demographic policy, there is a general tendency toward improving the social and material well being of the family, extending the right to coverage and adjusting payments to increases in the cost of living and to higher volume of revenue.

Another type of social security which has marked similarity among at least four member countries is compulsory unemployment insurance. However, in France and Luxembourg there has been merely a public policy of assistance in time of unemployment. Nevertheless, in France a regulation on unemployment benefits incorporated in collective bargaining contracts has been officially declared generally applicable. Since 1958 these agreements have been systematized into a contributory program for both industry and business. Though this regulation is not applicable in the mining industry, a different system for unemployment payments is in force in that industry.[44]

MEASURES TO IMPROVE SOCIAL SECURITY

Mindful that the Treaty imposes the duty on the High Authority to promote social progress, particular attention has been given to social security since it has been more and more important in the standard of living of man in the midst of modern industrial society. Desirous that its actions should achieve practical results, the High Authority sees the great advantage in working closely with the Commission of the Economic Community and the Administrative Committee for Social Security of Migrant Workers.

In accordance with Article 3, in 1961 the High Authority prepared a new edition of its monograph, first published in 1957, concerning social security programs for workers in coal and steel in the member states of the Community and in Great Britain.[45] So that the practices in the member states might be balanced and harmonized in every possible way, the services of the High Authority and the Commission have been devoted to revising the texts dealing with regulations for social security to increase their practical usefulness.[46] The staff of the European Community revised the explanatory texts in areas other than in the coal and steel industries.

Jointly with the Commission, the High Authority has helped establish training courses for staff members in social security administrations throughout the Six. The courses are intended to help these government workers apply more accurately the regulations on migrant workers and promote a better comprehension of harmonization for the various social security systems.

The training courses seek to form specialists for three types of institutions: the regular social security administration; the liaison groups concerned with the application of social security rules to migrant workers; and the ministries of the member countries. The trainees specialize not only on the general rules on social security for migrant workers, but also on their application in a given member nation so that the administration in that country will have experts capable of meeting situations concerning each country from which migrant workers come.

The initial training sessions are conducted in the offices of the High Authority in Luxembourg and in the offices of the Commission in Brussels. Later training is carried on in one or more of the administrations for social security in a member country of the Community. The period of training may be either six weeks, spending one week with the High Authority or the European Community and the balance in a social security administration; or three months, spending one month with the High Authority or the Commission and two months in a social security administration.

While at the High Authority (actually in the general directorate for "Labor Problems and Reconversion"), or at the Commission, (actually in the general directorate for "Social Affairs") the trainees study the organization and objectives of the Communities, Regulations Three and Four for migrant workers, and the laws on social security of the particular member countries where the second phase of the training period will take place. This second phase permits the candidates to work in the principal bureaus of the service which receives them, and especially in the offices particularly concerned with migrant workers.

The High Authority has noted that in May, 1961, the Administrative Committee for migrant workers had completed its study of the tentative drafts of two complementary regulations on social security, one for "seasonal workers" and the other for "frontier workers."

Upon consulting the European Coal and Steel Community as well as experts from governments, management and unions, the Commission submitted the drafts to the Council. In due course the new regulations were put in force after they were unanimously adopted by the Council. By the end of 1961 it was already obvious that "frontier workers" in both Communities had obtained advantages in regard to employer responsibility under social security which were analogous to those assured migrant workers. Thus for long term benefits, such as old age insurance, the rules revert simply to Regulations Three and Four, discussed above. However, particular cases taking into account the specific situation of "frontier workers" are viewed on the basis of short term payments, also covered under Regulations Three and Four, such as sickness, disability, industrial diseases and accidents, unemployment and family allowances.[47] For short term benefits the area of liability may be narrower for countries and employers than for a long term benefit such as old age insurance.

In the estimation of the High Authority, these 1961 regulations aid in meeting the directive of Article 69. Thus they tend to harmonize social security measures for "frontier workers" so that the movement of labor will not be impeded.[48]

The High Authority, in 1962, noted that several governments and coal producers of the Community had thought that action should be taken in social security analogous to measures toward modernization and integration in the coal industry. It has been acknowledged that, with no overall distribution of costs for the entire field of social security, when the coal industry of the four great producing countries in the Community reduces its aging work force, it actually assumes heavier burdens. In other words, pension benefits and other forms of payments must then be paid by this industry to retirees, who ultimately, may become more numerous than the number of active employees because of increasing mechanization.

The High Authority maintains, therefore, that social security programs impose higher charges on coal mining enterprises than on general industry. Such disparity handicaps the coal industry in competition with other sources of energy. Accordingly, since 1960 the High Authority has undertaken, in cooperation with government agencies, a comparative study of social security taxes for the coal industry as contrasted with other industries. In 1961 the governments concerned made available the pertinent statistical data for making an objective comparison. By February 27, 1962, government experts had undertaken a preliminary examination of the data which had previously been abstracted by the staff of the High Authority and depicted in the form of 30 statistical tables.

As another step toward improving Community standards in regard to social security programs, in 1962 the Commissions of both the Economic Community and Euratom, as well as the High Authority, sponsored the first European Conference on Social Security, which convened in Brussels from December 10 to 15, 1962. Attending the sessions were representatives of management, unions and social security administrations of governments. Other officials taking part represented family associations, medical societies, international institutions such as the International Labor Organization and observers from non-member nations including Great Britain, Ireland, Denmark, Greece and Sweden.

The conference was of a consultative nature and sought to obtain proposals on aims and methods for harmonizing social security. The findings of the conference are being utilized by the Communities to extend their activities dealing with social security and orientate them for the future.

After consultation with representatives from governments, management and unions, the following agenda was determined for the conference:

1. Extension of the Area of Application for Social Security
2. Financing of Social Security
3. Aims and Methods to Harmonize Benefits

A general report was made on each of these points, supplemented by special reports on particular problems in the different branches of social security. In addition to these specific areas of discussion, a study was presented on the scientific character of population changes and their effect on social security.[49]

During the conference, special study groups examined problems on social security unique in transport, agriculture and mining. For the High Authority the mining study was of prime consideration because of the difficulties both in retaining employees and attracting new workers to this industry. Moreover, the competitive situation now facing the coal industry is greatly reducing the feasibility of charging the financing of increasing social security benefits to net cost of coal. Further, labor cost as such in the coal industry amounts to a much larger part of the total cost than in other types of industry. Nevertheless, the High Authority is aware that special labor charges are warranted in the coal industry because accidents and disease have more serious consequences for miners than for other types of workers.[50]

At the start of the conference differences between employer and union representatives were rather extensive. Union officials placed emphasis on the need to level social security benefits upwards, though it was acknowledged that "harmonization" did not connote actual uniformity of social security systems. Nevertheless, the term was taken to mean more than just coordination. Employer representatives held to the view that each country's social security system must be assessed in the light of the national environment, with due attention to wage levels, taxation and other factors determining the workers' social situation.

As the conference proceeded diverging positions were narrowed by looking at harmonization more in the nature of equivalence in measures to meet contingencies. Opportunity was acknowledged for harmonizing short term benefits for migrant workers on such risks as sickness, accidents, and unemployment, which had been stressed earlier in Regulations Three and Four, concerning social security for migrant workers. Because of ample documentary material, compiled by the Economic Community and the High Authority, experts from the participating countries became more familiar with the operation of social security systems in other member states of the Six.

The value of this conference, sponsored by the Communities rather than management and labor directly, was acknowledged in the joint declaration by delegates from management and unions. They noted that such opportunities for discussion and joint study should again be provided by the Commission and the High Authority. Though the government representatives were present only as observers, they were mindful of the dynamic nature of the problems relating to social security and of the realistic approach to them desired by union and management representatives.[51]

One of the most significant contributions of the conference was the extensive documentation on important aspects of social security relating to each of the member countries. No individual country would have had the resources or budget to carry through such a project. For one who now wishes to make a profound study of social security in the member states, the necessary documents are available in the four languages of the Communities. Moreover, the data will be revised periodically. For briefer analysis condensed tabulation of the principal aspects have been compiled in every branch of social security. Thus through the help of experts from each of the member countries, syntheses have been made available giving comparative schedules of benefits. Preparation of the comparative studies of existing social security systems was an essential first step to advance toward harmonization. To achieve that objective it is not enough for one government to know its own system. Member countries must also have a close familiarity with neighboring systems.

The general report on the extension of the field of social security was considered a basis for a fruitful exchange of ideas on social security during the time of the conference.[52] In terms of specific areas relating to social security numerous suggestions were proposed for improving health benefits and maternity benefits where harmonization of benefits was considered possible.[53] Another special report dealt with common problems concerning benefits for disability, old age and survivors and how harmonization could be achieved.[54]

With respect to industrial accidents and diseases, note was taken of the need for employees to be given coverage in Italy. Improvement throughout the Community, in regard to payments to both victims and survivors, was also proposed for this type of industrial risk.[55] For family allowances stress was placed on the imbalance between the industrial and agricultural sectors of the member countries.[56]

Considerably less favorable standards for unemployment protection were found in two member countries, Belgium and Italy. In terms of a basic solution, the study on this form of industrial risk urged that the Communities encourage a policy of industrial investment in less developed regions of the member states and that they promote more programs of training and retraining.[57]

One of the most significant studies on social security was published in 1962 by the Economic Community. It was based on national reports by impartial experts in each of the Six.[58] In its concluding remarks the study emphasized that for every country the system of social security is closely aligned with the sociological context, which differs notably from nation to nation. Moreover, each country's system of social security tends to develop on a largely empirical basis in the face of very complex historical, political, economic and demographic factors. Again, far from being fixed in their characteristics over a long period of time, programs of social security tend to undergo frequent revision to cope with new conditions.

In the last few years legislative changes have been unusually frequent. For instance in West Germany recently there has been a very sizable increase in old age benefits. Here planned measures include pre-retirement programs and extensive reforms in health insurance; stress is placed on prevention and early treatment of illness.

Belgium may soon put a uniform old age pension program for the entire population in effect. In Belgium, the branch of social security responsible for unemployment insurance is now in charge of programs on job retraining and for the encouragement of new enterprises.

The French government is preparing to reform its system of family allowances and is making a study of all the problems relating to the aged. Italy is seeking to bring under a single administration all its varied social security programs. Besides improving benefits an effort is being made to reduce impersonalization in Italy's social services by democratizing the administration of social security. In The Netherlands proposed changes in benefits will take into account not only salary loss but also the degree of disability. The Dutch legislature has considered applying family allowances to the entire population.

These current changes in social security were cited in the general report as an indication of the permanent transition which is characteristic of social security—and the consequent difficulty in making a comparative study of this institution.

Another handicap in making a comparative study of social security was the distinct laws for different categories of social security in each country. Common terms of reference have been difficult to formulate.

Even with these obstacles, a certain number of conclusions of at least indicative value have been set down by the study group appointed by the Community. For instance, there is a far greater similarity in methods for according protection of social security to workers employed by others than to the self-employed. In the first category there has been an historical development of protection against industrial accidents, occupational diseases, and other types of risk, with stress on employer responsibility. Moreover, for this type of worker, in all the member countries, the common goal has been to assure income to replace loss of wages due to any of the industrial risks covered by social security.

A far different picture in the member countries relates to self-employed workers, who generally are not protected in any legal fashion against the typical hazards of the industrial age. Historically it has been found that these workers have been more difficult to fit into a social security plan. Again, for self-employed workers, there has been more development of voluntary protective measures, making state intervention less urgent. Nevertheless, in certain member countries efforts are being made to establish some balance between the lesser degree of protection now available to self-employed workers and the much broader protection available to the employees.

The study found there was a common tendency in industrial risks for the member countries to stress compulsory measures where voluntary programs have not proved sufficiently effective, notably concerning income for the aged and family allowances. Lumped together, the entire outlay for social security was estimated to cause a redistribution of national incomes varying from 13 to 18 per cent.

Nevertheless, for any particular risk, one country may provide a larger degree of protection than another. Thus family allowances in France amount to larger outlays than in other countries. West Germany and Luxembourg place somewhat more emphasis on security for the aged. Belgium has made considerable advances in adopting important measures for the unemployed.

A smaller proportion of the burden of governmental financing of social security costs is borne by the government in The Netherlands, as compared with the much larger share sustained by the government in Belgium. Public participation in meeting the cost of illness is very slight in Italy and Germany, but decidedly pronounced in the case of Belgium.

Besides these general variations, more specialized differentiations can be discerned in the categories of persons given protection. Here the irregular status of self-employed workers is in point. They are not always protected against the same risks in every member country. Again, methods differ in calculating payments for employees in covered employment.

Nevertheless, the preoccupation of administrators concerns the same general problems: the ever-increasing cost of medical care; the economic status of the aged; and the protection of various segments of the population, such as agricultural workers who are most disadvantaged by new economic developments.

The study on social security, supported by the Economic Community, noted that laws, administration and resources were not always adaptable to the needs of the hour. Moreover, the most urgent and pressing question remaining after a problem has been identified and analyzed is that of financing. Decisions must be made on just what proportion of national revenue should be devoted to social security payments and on the amount of direct contribution by the State and the assessment from taxation.

To attain the goal of harmonization of social security legislation as required by Article 117 the study endorsed the practice of exchanging publications on social security between the member countries. Approval was given to the training courses relating to Regulations Three and Four on social security for migrant workers as an excellent method to develop understanding of administrative practice in other countries. Mutual consultation among the States at the different periods of development for social security services was thought to be a constructive influence on administrative policy.[59]

SOCIAL SECURITY IN THE UNITED STATES

An immediate point of difference which comes to mind in relation to social security programs is that in several categories we have 50 varying types of legislation; there are only six variations in the Common Market countries. Though we rarely use the phrase "harmonization in an upward direction," the need for such application is plainly evident in regard to state and federal-state types of social security.

One of our earliest efforts toward some form of social security, workmen's compensation for industrial accidents, is especially in need of upward harmonization. These laws, which first began to appear on the statute books over 50 years ago, aimed to provide weekly benefits of from one-half to two-thirds of the worker's wage at the time of his injury. Though weekly benefits today for industrial injuries are much greater than decades ago they have not kept pace with the higher cost of living and the greater amount of weekly wages lost because of injury. It has been estimated that of fifty workmen's compensation laws in the United States, only six restore 60 per cent of the average weekly wage.[60] In effect the burden of risk for industrial accidents bears more heavily on the victim today than originally intended when this type of insurance was first enacted in the United States.

Moreover, there are great disparities in standards among the 50 state jurisdictions both in amount and duration of benefits and in the extent of coverage. Standards among the states also vary widely in the time interval before benefits are forthcoming.

In contrast to the Common Market countries we have few social insurance programs to meet the hazards of illness. It is true that the outlook in the United States now appears promising for a limited program to meet health costs for the aged because of the passage of the Medicare Bill, but there is little contemplated in terms of social health insurance for the working population as a whole.

Another area where extreme disparity of benefits exists among the 50 state jurisdictions is in old-age allowances and aid to dependent children who are not covered by federal social insurance. Though the federal government also contributes substantially to these programs, the absolute amount of the federal payment is limited by the economic status and the willingness of the particular state to use its own funds for this purpose. Resulting inadequacies of allowances because of these circumstances are especially evident in the South. The north central region of the country also faces some unmet needs but to a lesser extent than in the South.[61]

"Harmonization in an upward direction" might well be adopted as a goal for the 50 federal-state programs of unemployment insurance which are part of the Social Security coverage in this country. Originally intended to replace 50 per cent of the wage loss each week due to unemployment, the benefits paid in most states now range between 33 and 35 per cent, with a higher standard in some of the northern states.[62] Nevertheless, a somewhat compensating factor here has been the extension of duration of benefits. By 1960 it had been lengthened to a median figure of 26 weeks.

Of the various types of Social Security programs in the United States, the one adjudged to have most nearly attained its original objective is the Old Age and Survivors Insurance program under the Social Security Act of 1935, based on joint contributions of employers and employees. Since 1956, because of an additional feature, it has been given the title, Old Age, Survivors and Disability Insurance. Unlike Old Age Assistance and Unemployment Insurance, the administration of this form of Social Security is not shared with the 50 states. An exclusively federal statute and agency directs its operation. Free of the conflicting pressures among the states which have sometimes held back improvement of standards, Congress on occasion has raised benefits and coverage and added new features to meet the realistic needs of citizens who enjoy coverage under this provision of the Social Security Act.

Though the Common Market countries are beset with difficulties in their efforts to develop more harmonization among the social security programs of the six member states, there is little room for complaisance in the United States where, besides the federal government, 50 state jurisdictions share in the administration of many areas of Social Security. Some have termed the Social Security Act relating to unemployment, old age insurance and old age assistance the most cumbersome legislation of its kind in any industrial nation of the world. Accordingly, there is ample basis for concluding that we can take advantage from the efforts of the Common Market countries to achieve "harmonization in an upward direction" in our own Social Security programs.

8.

Worker Housing Developments
in the Communities

IN ARTICLE 117 OF THE TREATY OF ROME IT IS NOTED THAT the "Member States hereby agree upon the necessity to promote improvement of the living and working conditions of labour so as to permit the equalisation of such conditions in an upward direction."[1] In line with this provision housing conditions for workers have long been a matter of serious concern for the Economic Community. Moreover, the EEC is mindful that the presence or absence of adequate housing facilities is a predominant factor in influencing the willingness of workers to move to new locations where there is a need of additional labor supply.

THE 1961 STUDY SESSIONS ON HOUSING

One of the earliest measures taken by the Economic Community to implement its Treaty obligations in regard to housing was the sponsorship of a meeting of experts on family affairs. This conference held on March 13 and 14, 1961, was attended by officials from government ministries of the Six dealing with family questions, representatives of national family movements, as well as delegates from the European secretariats of international employers' and workers' organizations. Among the problems under study at this 1961 meeting

151

were family aspects of housing and especially the provision of social facilities for extensive housing units.

During March 23 and 24 of the same year the Commission sponsored a meeting of government experts on housing policy in Brussels. Representatives were again present from the European secretariats of employers' and workers' organizations.

On the agenda at the March meeting of government experts was a review of 1960 data relating to the number of dwellings completed, credits utilized and the significant legislation on housing enacted in the member states. Attention was also given to difficulties arising from land policy, and especially trends in the cost of building sites. Discussion then turned to programs and activities relating to housing which the Economic Community had either launched or had in the planning stage.[2]

On October 9, 1961, the Commission organized another meeting on housing in Brussels; experts from the research institutes which had conducted a survey on housing conditions of migrant workers in the countries of Belgium, the German Federal Republic and France met at this time. The main purpose of the meeting was to evaluate the synthesis of the three national reports, made by the Commission's staff. At the conclusion of the session the research experts expressed approval of the summary report.[3]

FINDINGS IN THE HOUSING RESEARCH REPORTS

In the synthesis of the reports from three countries of the Six, it was acknowledged that the housing factor was an important determinant affecting the movements of workers from one country to another. Accordingly, it was seen as quite proper that the Economic Community, committed to the goal of promoting free movement of persons, should have sponsored a research study on the problem of housing as an obstacle to migration of workers within the Community. For this purpose three institutes of sociology in the principal countries of immigration, Belgium, Germany and France, had been commissioned to conduct a housing investigation along very specific lines.

Among the objectives of the study was a determination of the disposition of laws and rules on housing, the extent of possible discrimination both towards nationals and foreigners in the three countries. For this purpose the researchers sought the views of government officials, consultants and representatives of unions and social service organizations on both housing problems and their possible solutions. As a possible control measure, a direct pilot study of housing conditions on a small scale was set up to verify, in a measure, the data gathered by the larger study based on interviews with housing officials.[4]

From the findings of the research study it was concluded that in the legal sphere discrimination on principle is exceptional. Nevertheless, numerous instances were apparent of discrimination in practice. It was found, as well, that the problem of housing workers is conditioned, in a given instance, by the characteristics of the immigrants, the differences in their mode of living and the general status of housing in the receiving country.

For Belgium the general condition of lodging was considered rather favorable and foreign workers in the building industry appeared to be occupying relatively satisfactory housing accommodations which met their basic needs. In effect foreign workers were lodged about as well as Belgian workers who worked at the less sought after jobs.

In West Germany, housing conditions were obviously found to be worse for the large influx of immigrants in recent years, induced as the result of the scarcity of German manpower in various occupations and regions. Special problems had arisen in Germany concerning Italian immigrants because their customs differed so markedly from those of the Germans and even other immigrants, such as the Dutch who integrated more readily with the Germans. The study found that the German housing conditions for Italians in the group settlements was of a variable standard and in certain cases was decidedly unfavorable.

With respect to France, the research study showed that since 1959 the annual flow of immigrants had been between 50,000 and 70,000, primarily Italian and secondarily Spanish. These immigrants tended to concentrate in the more industrialized areas, especially in the region of Paris where 30 per cent of the nonagricultural immigrants settled. Grave inadequacies were discovered in the housing accommodations for these workers. Save for some localized exceptions, the problem of family housing for these immigrants was regarded as still unsolved. It was acknowledged that improvement of housing conditions for migrant workers in France was ultimately dependent on improvement of the general housing situation there.

The Belgian report acknowledged that despite absence of any legal discrimination in principle, existing laws and rules did not always enable certain foreigners to escape discrimination. More effort was recommended to extend the benefits of public housing to foreign workers who are resident in Belgium, if not permanently, at least over a period of several years. A similar point was contained in the French report to the effect that existing French law tends to sanction housing discrimination, in fact, against foreign workers.

Pilot studies, used as a control device by the research teams, tended to confirm the finding that in the three receiving countries of Germany, France and Belgium foreign workers had little opportunity for access to public housing. Therefore, the three national reports were in agreement that such access should be assured by more adequate remedies and fuller information published in the languages of the migrants.

To this end the German report urged control of lodging facilities by a German-Italian Commission before work contracts began and the voiding of work contracts in cases where there was grave inadequacy in housing. Another proposal in the German report suggested that Italian workers be permitted to change their place of employment if adequate housing was not forthcoming. The French research study recommended a special bi-state financial organization to grant monetary aid to Italian families so they could obtain adequate housing.

The summary report for the three countries put stress on strict control over sanitary conditions and on the number of people in a housing unit, especially for group settlements so that minimum comfort would be assured. In no instance, stated the report, should the existence of unhealthful barracks or other types of provisory lodgings be permitted. A recommendation was included which urged cooperation among public bodies, private enterprise, municipalities and social service groups. In this fashion it was hoped initiative would be taken so that migrant workers would be able to obtain normal housing accommodations.

In terms of economic and regional development, it was proposed that pre-planning of immigration should coincide with pre-planning of housing construction for workers. Emphasis was also put on the need for provisions in collective bargaining contracts which would respect the liberty and private life of workers. Moreover, the report proposed that in or near worker housing developments, facilities should be available which would be conducive to the leisure and well-being of migrant workers.[5]

ACTION PROGRAM—SECOND STAGE

In the action program of the Economic Community for the Second State, beginning in 1962, one of the objectives listed was the fulfillment of housing needs in the Community, especially in the area of low-cost housing. Recognition was given to the necessity for improving the quality of housing, in particular for migrant workers. The action program resolved to encourage financial cooperation among the member countries to provide housing for workers who had moved to new locations within the Community. Specifically in paragraph 82 in the action program reference was made to the need to formulate views and proposals on housing problems from a qualitative aspect and with special application to the needs of migrant workers.[6]

To meet this objective the Commission drafted a recommendation to the member states relating to housing for workers moving from one member country to another. Discussion took place on the proposal at two sessions for representatives from employer and worker organizations, government experts and representatives of the International Union of Family Organizations. A large measure of support was given the recommendation in terms of both necessity and objectives.[7]

As another method of implementing this general policy in the action program, the Commission held a symposium in Brussels on low cost housing from December 16 to 19, 1963. Among the subjects discussed were methods for determining housing requirements, demand and ability to pay and qualifications for tenancy. Delegates to the symposium were appointed by governments, employers' and workers' organizations and the International Union of Family Organizations. Six representatives of the Commission were also present. In addition, observers were present from the European Parliament's Social Committee, the Economic and Social Committee and the International Labor Organization. The housing committee for the United Nations' Economic Commission for Europe was also represented at this symposium.[8]

SUMMARY REPORTS—1963 HOUSING SYMPOSIUM

Concerning the first summary report from the symposium, dealing with housing needs and the methods of determining them, attention was given to both actual deficits and future needs. It was the conclusion of this report that the current evaluation of needs and deficits in housing tended strongly towards an underestimation of the quantitative importance of this problem. The report indicated that the methodology used in making estimates was partly responsible for this deficiency. However, the norms and hypotheses on which the evaluations were based also contributed to the bias toward understatement.

With this inaccuracy present in a whole series of evaluations, the report declared that a veritable cascade of underestimations could result. As a consequence there was a natural tendency to delay measures which would bring a solution to the actual volume of housing shortage. Meanwhile, the report noted, the problem of those workers confronted with inadequate housing will become steadily worse. Thus in a period of growing prosperity for others, the contrast will be more striking for the many who have not been able to obtain better housing. Yet the report noted that it is the attainment of such a goal which ought to be regarded as a true index of social progress. The report concluded with the warning that every effort should be made to avoid the countless risks toward underestimation in the evaluation of housing needs and deficits.[9]

In the second summary report of the symposium, bearing on the demand for housing and its solution, the observation was made that in such a synthesis of the three national reports there can be only an imperfect review of the concepts and empirical material relating to housing developments in the member countries. The selection which has been included in the synthesis may therefore appear to be an arbitrary one. In any event, from the Belgian report, for example, attention is given to raising funds for housing and actual housing production. Note was taken of the level of rents and the cost of credit. Attention was likewise given to the relation between the volume of new housing built and the accumulation of savings.

The second summary report pointed out that despite divergence of housing problems, the member countries have in common numerous basic approaches to their solution. Such indications were found in the research methods used and in the technique of interrogation for determining the demand for housing. All of the countries had an abundant source of statistical, sociological and economic studies at their disposal to determine housing policy. Mutual exchanges of experiences were advocated in the second report, as well as closer agreement on methods of research. In this fashion comparison of findings obtained in the different member countries would permit the gaps in data, still existing, to be narrowed somewhat.[10]

In the third summary report relating to conditions affecting leasing of public housing designed for rental only, note is made that because of the destruction caused by World War II, scarcity of housing is especially acute. Moreover, the almost complete cessation of housing construction during the war, and the recent demographic expansion have tended to aggravate the crisis. These circumstances tend to explain the growing influence of the public authority in housing policy and particularly on public housing developments.

Further, the report observed that inadequate resources in lower income groups made it evident that decent and adequate housing will only be within their reach if government subsidies, directly or indirectly, are made available to them. As a consequence, the third summary report noted, budgetary items dependent on governments, in the domain of housing, have taken on considerable proportions. Recognition was given that care must be taken to award these government subsidies to those families which are in greatest need of such assistance. By the same token the third summary report acknowledged that the legislatures of the Six have endeavored to set up a policy and a body of rules which will insure a priority to low income groups with respect to the rental of public housing.[11]

Among the conclusions of this summary report concerning general rental policy was the belief that member states have endeavored to achieve a progressive liberalization of the rental market in hopes of lessening somewhat the scarcity problem. Nevertheless, it was acknowledged that this goal still is remote. The report, in regard to the rental market for public housing, considered the continuance of governmental regulation indispensable to assure an equitable sharing of the subsidies attached to rented public housing. Here the report found that in the member countries of the Community the very term "public housing" carried with it the concept of lodging provided at low rent with priority for those of greatest need and least able to pay the rental rates prevailing on the private market.

Even on the criteria determining eligibility for occupancy a marked similarity of tests was found in the member countries; these emphasized inadequate housing presently occupied by the applicant, the size and condition of his family and modest financial resources. Nevertheless, the report observed that certain areas of public housing do not offer sufficient variation in space so that the needs of applicants with large families may still go unsatisfied. It was recommended that new programs of construction take this need for variation into account. The report also urged that foreign workers should be given greater opportunity to rent public housing units.[12]

FUTURE OUTLOOK FOR PUBLIC HOUSING

Reviewing developments in public housing for 1963, the Economic Community noted that the total number of public housing units constructed in that year exceeded the figure of 1,400,000 for the first time despite a slight recession in Belgium and Germany. With upward of 570,000 housing units built in 1963, Germany still maintained the lead for the Six both in absolute figures and for the number of lodgings built for each 1,000 inhabitants. Next came Italy, which in 1963 constructed about 400,000 units.

But the high cost of building sites as well as of construction has affected plans for public housing developments by upsetting financial calculations. There has also been some fear of the consequences for national public housing programs from the restrictive economic and financial policies designed to combat the threat of inflation.

On the positive side, the Economic Community noted an enlarged perspective for social policy relating to housing insofar as consideration of kindred problems—such as urban renewal, regional management and community development—were being integrated with plans for public housing. Thus, besides the usual financial measures designed to provide adequate housing for low income families there has also been considerable preoccupation with problems of air pollution, noise control and research programs on all the economic and human aspects of housing.

The Economic Community, in a 1964 report, also recalled the recommendation of its Commission which was adopted by the Council April 15, 1964. This proposal invited the member states to take particular measures designed to curb the demand for construction in areas where existing resources could not supply the market. Nevertheless, the Commission urged in its recommendation that for regions where there was a dearth of schools, hospitals or housing designed for low income groups, construction in these categories should not be reduced or made more difficult.

Despite this safeguarding clause, the Economic Community found it regrettable that in some countries certain measures looking to economic stabilization have had unfortunate impacts on policies for public housing. Vigilance was urged to prevent new setbacks. Some concern was expressed that there is an increasing trend to remove rent controls as a means of favoring private investment in the construction industry. Admission was made, nevertheless, that here and there suitable measures have been taken to cut excessive rents or protect tenants with low income.

However, indexes from 1959 to 1963 were cited to show that in West Germany there was a notable increase in rental charges, going from 102 in 1959 to 134 in January, 1964. For the same period, the index in France climbed from 114 to 189. In Italy there was an increase from 114 to 172. By contrast, in Holland the index only progressed from 100 to 124.[13]

THE EUROPEAN COAL AND STEEL COMMUNITY

Improvement of housing conditions for workers and their families has always been considered a major responsibility of the High Authority by reason of Article 3(e) of the Treaty of Paris which directs the Community to advance measures conducive to raising the standards of living and working conditions in a coordinated fashion for the labor force in each of the industries under its jurisdiction.[14]

HOUSING AND WORKER MOBILITY

As early as 1956 a study on mobility and readaptation of workers, published by the Community, declared that housing constituted one of the gravest material obstacles to free movement of workers, both in terms of frequency of citation and from evidence at hand. The report stated emphatically that a significant transfer of workers to a new location cannot be expected if housing is not adequate there to receive them. Moreover, it was acknowledged that the presence of new housing often plays a key role in persuading workers to move to different locations, especially if the rental charges are less than at their previous places of residence. Just the opposite response is often encountered if it is learned that the new job opportunity would require the worker, because of inadequate housing, to be absent from his family on a weekly or seasonal basis.[15]

The 1956 study also pointed out that the adaptation of a migrant worker to a new environment necessarily supposed that suitable housing would be at his disposal. In contrast it was found that bad housing conditions not only made the life of the worker and his family cramped and irritating, but actually helped develop an inferiority complex blocking progress toward adaptation.

Despite these foreseeable consequences, the research study noted that the accommodation of foreign workers newly arrived in another country of the Community is often far from satisfactory. In actuality it was found that many immigrants were housed in barracks, camps and hotels for bachelors. As an example, the report declared that adaptation of Polish workers, installed in Dutch mines, was made almost impossible because of the makeshift housing facilities allotted to them. Even in the case of internal migration, the Bureau of Statistics in The Netherlands attributed its declining volume to inadequate housing and to regulations which prevent a worker from living where he wishes and from choosing his own type of lodging.

Some difficult questions have faced regional housing committees cooperating with the Coal and Steel Community concerning the suitability of favoring access to home ownership for migrant workers; pertinent is the issue as to whether they should have priority over native residents. Moreover, the question has been raised in regard to grouping migrant workers in residence areas according to country of origin, as contrasted to dispersing them among other nationalities.

Far from encouraging readaptation, it was acknowledged that migrants who are obliged to live apart from native residents tend to cling to their own customs and mode of life. While certain common problems of adjustment may thus be settled speedily, there is great risk that such segregation will be a handicap if a migrant becomes a permanent resident.

The 1956 research report on mobility acknowledged, however, that in recent years considerable effort has been taken to improve housing conditions. Nevertheless, in some instances certain immigrants refused to avail themselves of the better accommodations, preferring to stay in the low rent barracks in order to use more of their wages as they saw fit.[16]

THE 1958 HOUSING SURVEY

At the request of the Commission for Social Affairs of the European Parliament, the High Authority undertook a full-scale investigation of housing conditions for workers in 1958. The objective of the study was to gather comprehensive data on the standards of comfort in housing, and especially on the prevalence of barracks and other makeshift lodging in the Community.

This housing study was the first of its kind ever undertaken on an international level, and covered 40,000 workers selected at random from the 1,500,000 in the work force of the Community. Of this work force, 966,000 were in coal production, 450,000 in the steel industry and 52,000 in ore mines. Each worker was visited personally in his home by a trained investigator to obtain responses to a questionnaire standardized for use in the Six.

For the work force as a whole, it was concluded from the study that while 90 per cent of the workers lived in dwellings of a normal type, at least 45,000 workers and their families in Germany, France and Belgium were housed in barracks or some other type of structure not originally designed for family residence. Moreover, though a relatively high proportion (32 per cent) of the housing units had been built after World War II, it was estimated that 40 per cent of the dwellings in the Community had been built before 1918.

At least 118,000 workers were without running water in their places of residence. Moreover, a large number of housing units were found to be too small. Thus over 550,000 housing units contained one or two rooms and a kitchen, though the average number of occupants was between three and four persons. Further, 132,000 workers shared their homes with another family, predominantly in Germany and to a lesser degree in Belgium and France and the other countries.

The study also revealed that about 73,000 workers (5 per cent) were living apart from their families in other households or in establishments for roomers. In Germany there are such institutions which are maintained almost exclusively for foreign workers. For the Community as a whole it was found that about 74 per cent of the workers were married and this percentage remained rather constant from one occupation to another.

The great preponderance of workers in the Community, as indicated by the 1958 study, were living in private homes, either single family or multifamily structures, though it was concluded that in about 13 per cent of such dwellings there was more than one worker. Note was taken, however, that about 70,000 lodgings were merely furnished or unfurnished rooms. In 1958 it was estimated that 30,000 workers and their families were living in barracks and about 15,000 were lodged in merely makeshift accommodations.

In terms of data of construction the Community housing study disclosed that 40 per cent of the worker housing units had been built prior to 1918, 26 per cent between the years 1918 and 1944, and 25 per cent since 1950. Surprisingly enough, coal miners appeared to be living in more recently constructed dwellings than workers in other industries. However, for workers in the Italian ore mines it was found that the percentage of lodgings built before 1918 was particularly high, over 62 per cent. Nevertheless, for Belgian and French steelworkers, 60 per cent of their dwellings were also built about the same time. The portion of housing units built since 1950 is relatively of greatest significance in Germany and The Netherlands.

For the Community as a whole, 80 per cent of the units had water available inside the home. Yet occupants of 8 per cent of the housing units had to obtain water either at a nearby outside pump or from a more distant public fountain. In effect, 118,000 workers were obliged to leave their homes to obtain water. Seventy per cent of the dwellings had no plumbing for a wash bowl, bath or shower. For about

40 per cent of the lodgings, modern toilet facilities were installed. Nevertheless, in France and Belgium there was a very great number of workers' homes, about 400,000 (32 per cent) which depended on outside toilets. By way of contrast practically all worker homes in the Community were equipped with electricity.

For workers in the three industries of the Community, the average number of persons per household was 3.8. Housing units with above average occupancy were found in the Italian coal mine areas (5.4 persons) and in The Netherlands for both coal miners and steel workers (4.5 persons). For the Community as a whole it might appear that there was an average of one person per room. However, the report stressed that such was really too favorable an impression since the kitchen is included in the number of rooms. In actuality 17 per cent of the housing units (213,000) consisted of one room plus a kitchen and these were occupied on an average by three persons. In Italy and in the Dutch steel areas the average for such units was four persons.

Ownership of 22 per cent of the dwellings in the Community belonged to the workers themselves or a member of the immediate family. Employers owned 25 per cent of the housing units used by their employees. The proportion of company owned housing was especially high in the coal industry, running about 70 per cent in Italy, 60 per cent in France and 40 per cent in Germany.

For the Community as a whole, the number of workers living in collective dwellings was in the area of 13,000, of which 10,000 were coal miners, particularly in Germany and France. The number of beds per room seems to be a significant index of the density of occupancy in such lodgings. The research report concluded that 34 per cent of the workers in such residences were in rooms with three beds. Twenty-five per cent of the workers lived in rooms with two beds and 20 per cent in rooms with four beds. Only 8 per cent of the workers had the use of a single room.

Concerning distance between residence and place of work for the three industries, 43 per cent of the workers required less than 15 minutes to make a one-way trip to work. For 36 per cent of the employees this travel time required 15 to 30 minutes. For 15 per cent of the work force the one-way trip required 30 minutes to an hour. Only 6 per cent (86,000) had to travel for over one hour to get to their place of work.

At the close of the interview during the Community-wide study of housing in 1958, it was customary to ask the worker if he desired to change his place of residence for any reason. About 30 per cent of the workers living in private homes replied affirmatively and usually gave as their reason that their present dwellings were too small or too old or were lacking conveniences. So far as taking action to fulfill their wishes to move, the report observed that at the time of the investigation in some of the member countries, housing was in such short supply that there would have been little advantage for a worker to enter the market in search of a new residence.

A significant contribution made by the 1958 research study was to throw light on the variety of pressing needs here. The conclusion of the research report drew attention to the number of makeshift lodgings, barracks, and homes too small or old and bereft of even the most elementary types of sanitation. Attention was also called to the number of workers who had to prolong the work day unduly by excessive travel time.[17]

EXPERIMENTAL HOUSING PROGRAMS

On a modest scale the High Authority, as early as 1954, decided to launch an experimental program for housing by granting financial aid as part of its promotion of technical and economic research on the improvement of building methods and cost reduction.[18] Of over 1,000 housing units projected, 350 units had been completed by November 1, 1955. Various research centers were asked to determine comparative building costs on these projects.[19]

A second experimental program, begun in 1958, was largely completed by 1962.[20] To carry out the objectives for this program, the High Authority had invited directors of institutes of research on building methods, along with consulting scientists, to form a committee of experts to visit construction firms in five member countries cooperating in the project. Following these visits of inspection and their independent studies, the members of the committee made known their findings in 1961. The committee report dealt with such matters as the productive capacity of the various contractors, the degree of tolerance to exposure of different building materials and the recent developments in the use of steel in home construction.

When the High Authority decided to sponsor this second experimental program in 1956 it set aside a sum of $4,334,000 for the purpose. A particular objective of the program was to encourage practical experiments which would advance the standardization and coordination of building methods, especially in utilization of both traditional and novel materials in conjunction with steel.[21]

In effect, the first two experimental building programs aided in raising productivity in the building industry by better work planning and standardization. A third research program, underway in 1964, was launched to study operations in the construction of large housing centers and encouraged community development.[22]

ARCHITECTURAL DESIGN AND WORKER HOUSING

In addition to supporting research on costs and methods of production, the High Authority, in 1960, considered it equally necessary to contribute toward improving the architectural design and attractiveness of homes for workers in the Community. Thus, the High Authority sponsored an architectural competition in 1959, inviting participation from architects in the Six.[23]

Housing plans were to be based on requirements which answered the needs of coal and steel workers and also were adaptable to climate and customs in the member countries. For purposes of the contest, designs also had to take into account integration of these model homes within a general plan of modern urban development.

Qualified government officials of the member countries helped conduct the contest. Cooperation was also provided by the International Union of Architects. Within the date set for submitting designs, 250 architects had entered the contest. Upon completion of its study of the exhibits, the jury for the contest noted in December, 1959, that the contestants had zealously devoted themselves to the actual problems of housing for workers.

It was evident that the basic architectural problems could be resolved by different methods in accordance with climate, customs and advancement of building techniques. The jury observed that, despite a great variety of designs, two basic tendencies were apparent: good adaptability to the terrain and a common will on the part of the architects to develop and improve housing standards. In agreement with construction firms and participating governments, the High Authority proposed to adopt the prize-winning designs for use in its housing programs.[24]

FINANCIAL AID FOR HOUSING PROGRAMS

In 1955 the High Authority had already initiated the first of several regular financing programs to encourage construction of worker housing units by loans for 25 to 50 per cent of the building cost. Through credit totaling over $18,000,000—obtained from banking institutions in the member countries—the High Authority of the Community was able to help finance the construction of over 12,000 housing units in

1955, of which 10,000 were planned for Germany. As in the case of much larger financing operations later, the determination as to how this financing would be allocated was by discussion between the High Authority and regional committees representing employer and worker organizations in the different producing areas. Representatives of the national and regional authorities also participated in the discussions.[25]

By 1956, the sum for housing development which the Coal and Steel Community had acquired through loans in the member countries had reached the figure of $23,600,000 and had been used to help finance the construction of 14,145 housing units. As of January 1, 1962, 13,854 of these units had been completed.[26]

For its second financing program the High Authority, in 1956, decided to use funds from a special reserve, built up from interest on investments. A sum of $16,870,000 was thus made available for worker housing, which was supplemented by $22,900,000 obtained from the capital markets of the member countries. Social security administrations and insurance companies also provided credit for this supplementary fund.

Loans for building purposes, authorized from the High Authority's special reserve, carried an interest rate of only about 1 per cent in most cases. Though the interest on funds from the capital markets was put at a much higher rate, the combination of the two rates actually placed housing loans at a level of interest which could be sustained by the purchasing power of the workers in the Community. The total fund from the two sources assured the financing of 19,348 housing units. From the second credit program, 17,471 lodgings had been completed by January 1, 1962; the remaining units were either under construction or in a preliminary stage.

In 1958 the High Authority launched a third program of loans to promote housing construction for workers by using a base sum of $15,000,000 from a special reserve fund. In addition to the $8,350,-000 which the High Authority had designated for Germany, another sum of $21,900,000 had been raised in the capital markets of that country. For Germany the total sum of $30,250,000 was available to help finance the construction of 16,216 housing units. By January 1, 1962, the Community reported that 9,313 of these dwellings had been completed. Through additional credit operations the High Authority provided loans for housing construction in France, Luxembourg, The Netherlands and Belgium during the third credit program.

To encourage the construction of more housing units the High

Authority, March 29, 1961, initiated a fourth credit program. As in the earlier measures for this purpose, the fourth program made funds available to building associations or financial institutions. For this purpose the High Authority established a sum of $45,000,000 of which $15,000,000 came from a special reserve and $30,000,000 from the capital markets of the Six. It was expected that such financing would contribute to the construction of 20,000 housing units. Again the overall rate of interest paid by the home buyer was considerably less than the going rate, because of the almost nominal interest charge imposed for the direct loan of $15,000,000 from a special reserve of the High Authority.

A particular objective assigned to the fourth credit program was to accommodate the housing needs revealed by the extensive research in worker housing in 1958. Accordingly, special effort was planned to replace barracks and other types of makeshift lodging by normal housing construction designed to meet modern needs for sanitation, convenience and comfort.

Another objective of the fourth program was to facilitate the rehousing of miners who were being relocated in this industry because of mine closings in the Community. The program also was designed to provide housing for workers who were being hired for steel mills recently built or expanded. In effect, this redevelopment in the steel industry was considered justification for vast additional construction of worker housing projects.[27]

With three housing programs practically completed and the fourth program well advanced in 1962, the High Authority was still determined to maintain its policy of encouraging construction designed to meet the needs of coal and steel workers. Though the four previous credit programs had helped toward financing about 75,500 housing units for workers—at a cost of $583,000,000 of which over 25 per cent had been direct loans by the High Authority—housing needs were still awesome. An inquiry made by the Statistical Office of the European Communities had indicated that 280,000 more housing units were required to meet actual needs.

In light of this situation the High Authority, May 23, 1962, set aside $25,000,000 from a special reserve to begin the fifth credit program for construction of worker housing; it was to be completed within three years. The High Authority stated it would supplement its own fund with an additional sum of $50,000,000 to be raised in the capital markets.[28]

By November, 1964, the European Coal and Steel Community

had seen over 60,000 worker homes completed which were financed in part by Community credit. Current plans included rapid completion of additional homes to bring the total to 85,000.[29] Upon the termination of the 1964 housing program it was estimated that the entire number of houses thus built, with financial aid from the Community, would be equivalent to a city the size of Boston proper. The entire expenditure for the first 75,000 homes was estimated at $750,000,000, of which the Community had provided over $200,000,000. Over one-third of the coal and steel workers living in these homes at present own them.[30]

On June 7, 1964, on the completion of the sixty thousandth worker home, M. Dino Del Bo, president of the High Authority, declared that as the result of further credit obtained construction of 100,000 housing units would ultimately take place in the six member states with financing in part by the Community.[31]

WORKER HOUSING IN AMERICA

Through cursory comparison of efforts to meet worker housing needs in the United States with the programs in the European Community, the impression develops that (proportionately) our record has not been too impressive.

It is true that the Federal Housing Act of 1949 authorized the construction of 810,000 units of low-cost housing by the end of 1953. Yet in 1961, 12 years later, the AFL-CIO made the proposal that a new housing act should require the construction of 400,000 such housing units, merely to complete the total authorized in the 1949 Act. Nevertheless, the administration bill in 1961 only specified 100,000 new units.

It has been said that failure to meet our low-cost housing needs has been "one of the greatest single domestic scandals of post-war America."[32] Despite carefully evaluated surveys of the existent housing problem and the repeated forecasts of urban congestion in the next two decades, poor and inadequate housing for low income families is unabated in this country.

From preliminary figures of the 1960 census, it was estimated that 15,600,000 (27 per cent) of the 58,000,000 occupied dwelling units in the United States were below normal standards. Recalling the barracks and makeshift shelters in Common Market countries, it was estimated that 3,000,000 of our substandard housing units were tenements, shacks and hovels. Moreover, another 8,300,000 housing units of the substandard group were in a state of deterioration. While 4,300,000 units were called structurally sound, they were lacking in some or all necessary plumbing equipment. Unlike the research data on housing in the European Coal and Steel Community, the United States census figures did not take into account supposedly sound housing which was subject to excess density of occupation.[33]

As is painfully apparent, the vexing problem of discrimination in housing is not peculiar to European countries. Harrington finds that suburbs in the United States have become a barrier which excludes low-cost housing developments and thus locks the poverty groups within the deteriorating central sectors of American cities. While many believe that provision for low-cost housing units in urban areas is being met by widespread slum clearance projects, the reality seems to point to more frustration. The hard facts indicate that the number of new housing units built after such slum clearances fails to equal the number which were razed. The dispossessed families are often either packed even more densely into remaining slum housing or leave the area without a trace.[34]

Another observer of the American scene, Gunnar Myrdal, concludes that attempts at slum clearance in our cities have chiefly been of advantage to middle-income tenants who can afford to pay the rents in the new dwellings; only a few of these actually have been low-cost housing.[35]

In an effort to refute the frequent charges that urban renewal has largely failed to cope with its rehousing obligations for those it displaces, Robert C. Weaver, the Federal Housing Agency administrator, stated on March 17, 1965, that in actuality the re-housing record shows a high degree of proficiency. On this occasion the Housing and Home Finance Agency made public a Census Bureau survey of 2,275 relocated families which indicated that 94 per cent of the sample had found "standard" accommodations elsewhere. *The New York Times* remarked, however, that the census omitted reports on 540 other families, displaced from the same urban renewal projects in 130 cities, which had left the areas and either could not be located or were unavailable for interviews.

Even for relocated families included in the survey, half of them reported that their new homes were only about as conveniently located as their old slum quarters, and the other half found their new homes decidedly less convenient. Thirty-seven per cent indicated that much more time was now required to travel to work. About the same proportion found shopping areas much less available.

Of the relocated families interviewed in the summer of 1964, it was found they were generally paying higher rent than formerly. Moreover, the great majority of the rehoused families were in a low-income bracket.[36]

The magnitude of the problem to provide adequate low-cost housing for millions of American citizens is startling when the required expenditure is measured. An estimate in 1955 by Joseph P. McMurray, then State Housing Commissioner of New York, given before a House Subcommittee on Housing, was $125,000,000,000 in both public and private investment over a period of 25 years. In Mr. McMurray's estimation, such a program would require Government participation five times greater than current Government outlays.[37]

Yet, in the face of a national housing problem which is assuming alarming proportions, inaction or inadequate action seems the hallmark of those in position to take remedial steps. In a recent message to Congress, President Johnson declared that for the next 15 years 30,000,000 people would be added to our cities. He acknowledged that by 1975 we shall need over 2,000,000 new homes each year.

Despite the admission in the President's message to Congress that the efforts by city officials to meet these crises are frustrated by inadequate resources, insufficient authority and paucity of trained personnel, the point was made that the federal government will only be able to assume a small part of the task required to cope with the emergency.

Among the proposals in the President's message was a recommendation for federally insured private loans to finance the purchase and development of land for new communities and subdivisions. To stimulate a large increase in the number of housing units for low and moderate income families, federal rent subsidies were recommended. Again, urban renewal and public housing funds were suggested to recondition existing housing for low and moderate income groups. A proposal was also made to increase funds for urban renewal to a level of $750,000,000 annually by 1968. Continuation of purchase of housing mortgages for 40,000 units at below market interest rates was also requested of Congress for the year 1966.[38]

Commenting on the President's message on housing, William Reid, chairman of the New York City Housing Authority, pointed out that an allocation of funds had been proposed the previous year for the building of 100,000 low-rent housing units annually throughout the nation. Reid observed that proposals in the President's message of March 2, 1965, called for funds to build only 35,000 low-rent housing units a year. On a prorated basis he found it would amount to merely 3,000 new units for New York City in the face of 100,000 applications a year for low-rent apartments there.

Another critic of the new federal housing proposals stated that they evaded the whole problem of the need for low-rent housing. Instead, it has been claimed, the administration housing bill mainly provides a large-scale rent subsidy program for moderate income families receiving from $4,000 to $6,500 per year.[39]

Editorially *The New York Times* commented that the measures proposed in the President's housing message are not "going to enable the nation at this late date to master or even come abreast of the needs of its cities."[40] Recalling that in the Six, for 1963 alone 1,400,-000 public housing units were constructed, it seems not unlikely that the European Communities will have overcome their housing problem long before we achieve that same goal.

Advancement of Regional
Labor Programs

REGARD FOR REGIONAL DEVELOPMENT IS, IN THE ESTIMATION of the president of the Commission, Walter Hallstein, a principal responsibility of the European Economic Community by virtue of the Treaty of Rome.[1] He finds Article 2, cited above in Chapter One, affirming that the Community should encourage the harmonious economic development of the member states.[2] Hallstein notes that this mandate will have to be realized sector by sector, in accordance with the different economic areas through regional planning.

CONFERENCE ON REGIONAL POLICY

In his opening address for the 1961 Conference on Regional Economies in Brussels, sponsored by the Economic Community, Hallstein emphasized that every economic and social policy naturally relates to man as a social being who lives with and depends on other men.[3] Hallstein noted that a perplexing problem of regional policy stems from the concentration of industries in certain regions while other areas become depopulated. To overcome this frustrating problem, he stressed that enlightened action by governments is required on transportation policies, schools, housing and social issues. In effect, Hallstein observed that whenever an economic and social policy is deter-

171

mined, inevitably a regional policy is fashioned also, consciously or otherwise.

Nevertheless, Hallstein emphasized that economic growth should not be gained at the price of causing millions of men to leave their places of origin and break all social ties to seek a livelihood in some burgeoning zone of industrial concentration. Accordingly, he noted that the regional policies of the Community are designed to avoid such hazards by extending potential technical and financial resources to critical regions of unemployment in a degree never before known.

Hallstein urged that member states adopt general policies on the national level which do not contradict the aims of the Community's regional policies, but rather effectively promote these objectives. Accordingly, he stressed that national and regional policies should serve to improve economically weak areas by inducing enterprises to establish new plants, thus encouraging an economic movement which, after revitalizing a region, will enable the area to continue its own development.[4]

Attending this Conference on Regional Economies were representatives from governments of the member countries, professional organizations, employer and union members of various economic and social councils and representatives of organizations in charge of regional development.[5]

In the principal address given at the Conference, Robert Marjolin, vice-president of the Commission, pointed out that in order for overall Community productivity to increase at a desirable rate it would be necessary to put more vitality in the populations remaining at the margins of industrial expansion and in agricultural areas. Not mere abstract economic considerations, but the human problem must preoccupy those having responsibility for policy, he noted.

Marjolin emphatically stated it was not the regions which concern the policy makers, but the people who live in them. He would regard it as intolerable that our era, in which industrial, agricultural, economic and administrative techniques offer limitless possibilities for action, should see the continuance of a mediocre existence for millions of workers in the Community, workers bereft of opportunity for self-development or for notable improvement of their living conditions. It would be even more intolerable, in his estimation, if youth should grow to adulthood and not see the same opportunities their more favored contemporaries face in prosperous industrial or agricultural regions opening before them.

In other words he stressed that the Common Market, at the same time it brings on a commercial revival, should take significant steps to the same degree in the social progress of the peoples within its borders. To this end he saw, as a necessary complement to a liberal commercial policy, an active, systematic and extended policy of regional development, a massive and continued program of vocational training and retraining, as well as reconversion policies for enterprises and regions in economic difficulties. In this fashion Marjolin believed the promise of the Common Market, that all groups of the Community should have an equal opportunity to share in its rapid development, could be fulfilled.[6]

In support of Marjolin's position, J. Milhau, president of the Regional Center on Productivity and Economic Studies at Montpelier, France, stressed before the Conference that correction of regional imbalances must be sought in a wider context than merely locally applied remedies. For him the true context was an accelerated general expansion of the economy. He did not deny that it would be necessary, however, to intervene within certain zones which are in need of more rapid reconversion or industrialization. Nevertheless, the predominant objective should be a harmonious growth of a nation's economy as a whole.

Milhau noted that since World War II a policy of regional development has gained acceptance in most of the European nations; it has been spurred on by the presence and aggravation of interregional imbalances which were capable of hindering national economic growth. The example of France was cited. There a long-established policy of political centralization had tended to amplify regional distortion, causing a contrast today between enormous capital funds in one area and the vast depopulated and underdeveloped regions elsewhere in France.

While France established a juridical basis for programs of regional development in 1951, other countries such as Italy, Spain, Greece and Turkey have also been active in launching regional programs of spectacular dimensions. Nevertheless Milhau acknowledged that there were earlier outstanding precedents such as the Tennessee Valley Authority in the United States and the decision of 1918 to drain the Zuiderzee in The Netherlands.[7]

Turning to particular regions in the Community, an Italian report at the Conference on the southern region of that country referred to the stereotype image which pictures Italy as a country poor in resources, poor in capital, but with an abundance of manpower which exceeds the possibilities of absorption, even though gifted with remarkable intelligence.

To overcome this cliche, the Italian report took note of discoveries in the subsoil there of both mineral and power resources. Moreover, hitherto inadequately used monetary resources of considerable importance have now been activated. With increasing economic activity, the report noted that in a number of regions in Italy there is a scarcity of manpower. There was no denial, however, that partial unemployment and total unemployment in other regions of Italy were far from disappearing and that before this problem could be solved extensive vocational training would be necessary to raise the qualifications of the Italian labor supply.[8]

Regret was expressed that, even at present, industrial promotion in Italy has not progressed much beyond the stage of advancing credit and other financial aid toward studies of a region or of a specific project. Emphasis was placed on the need to develop an infrastructure within a region which will assure adequate economic and technical resources there to attract industry.[9]

Acknowledging that the problem in southern Italy of surplus farm workers can also be found elsewhere in the Community, Sicco Mansholt, vice-president of the Commission, posed the basic policy question whether such workers should be moved to new industrial centers, or whether industrial investment should be brought to workers in their native regions. Mindful of difficulties that will arise, Mansholt nevertheless urged that industrial centers be established in the regions of surplus labor, the less developed areas. He noted that the Commission was concerned over the effects of a large-scale program of vocational training in southern Italy which might result only in speeding up the migration of Italian workers to northern Italy, Germany or elsewhere and thus seriously impoverish the native regions by despoiling them of their best manpower, and blocking efforts to develop such areas.[10]

One of the study committees during the Conference considered the concrete problem of judiciously directing the labor supply for the industrial market in such a manner that surplus population does not migrate toward other, already overconcentrated zones. It was suggested that employment policies should have the advance approval of those who are directly interested and who hope to benefit from their execution.

The point was made that while there are acknowledged advantages in the development of productivity and competition within the Community, such purely economic factors should not permit losing sight of the more important goal of the Community, namely, its contribution to the establishment of a social, cultural and political life in keeping with the ideals of western society.[11] Accordingly it was stressed that a program of regional development should take into account social and cultural factors, as well as economic. Care should thus be exercised by public authorities to develop a cultural infrastructure, including not only schools, but universities as well.[12] Moreover, an infrastructure of this width and depth was considered necessary to attract new industrial enterprise to the less developed areas.

Stressing the second objective of the Treaty—social progress— M. B. Motte, a member of the National Assembly in France, noted that the Treaty had created specialized instruments to assure social progress by improving standards of living. Among such measures, he observed, was the Social Fund. He suggested that the Fund might consider establishing a special organizational structure to assure social advancement for regional development.[13]

Referring to the Community's policy on employment, M. J. Kulakowski, Secretary-General of the European Organization of the International Christian Trade Unions, pointed out that in addition to a quantitative policy of employment it is necessary to be mindful of the importance of a qualitative policy, the establishing of optimal working conditions for all members of the labor force in regions which the Community is seeking to develop.

He urged that such a policy be closely allied with the program of vocational training. Even though methods of such training may differ somewhat in various geographical sectors, Kulakowski stressed that a certain number of general principles should be retained in common, especially on optimum working conditions.[14] Here he referred to Article 128 which states that the Commission for the Community should advance "general principles for the implementation of a common policy of occupational training capable of contributing to the harmonious development both of national economies and of the Common Market."[15]

In his concluding remarks at the Conference on Regional Economies, vice-president Marjolin put special emphasis on the growing importance which must be accorded social and cultural infrastructures in any program of regional development. Nevertheless, he found that too little recognition thus far had been given this factor. He observed that problems of housing, schools, facilities for recreation and social life as a whole in regions undergoing development are basic to any plan for a regional economy. Marjolin stressed that men are not pawns to be moved on an economic chess board at the will of a policy conceived in abstract fashion by remote government bureaus. He noted that men will not remain, or even enter, regions lacking not only in proper conditions of work, but also in satisfactory conditions of living.

Marjolin pointed out that in peripheral areas of the Community there are men who are still unemployed or under-employed. He recommended that inducements be proposed to persuade industry to move from the central areas of full employment and surplus employment to these peripheral zones. Heads of corporations should be shown the potential advantage of building new plants in regions where manpower is abundant and where annoying conditions of work, now characteristic in zones of excess concentration, do not exist. He noted that this concept of diversion of industry from the over-concentrated central bloc to the border regions is gaining acceptance. Governments and industrial associations are now giving it study and are becoming aware that it would redound to their advantage.

In keeping with the objective stressed during this Conference of not depopulating peripheral regions by drawing workers to already congested central areas, Marjolin took note of the essential difference between mobility of labor and migration of labor. For the interior of the same region or within a circle geographically limited, workers must be able to transfer readily from one firm to another in accordance with their needs or preferences. To achieve this labor mobility Marjolin regarded it as necessary that facilities be available to give workers an adequately rounded vocational training. He declared, however, there is a profound difference between the necessary mobility in a limited area and migration of workers from region to region or from country to country. While such migrations are at times still necessary, they are accompanied by unfavorable sociological, political and psychological phenomena. Accordingly, Marjolin stressed that wherever possible industry should be moved toward the workers rather than the reverse.[16]

COMMUNITY STUDIES ON REGIONAL DEVELOPMENT

Dissatisfaction over certain aspects of regional development in the Community was also expressed at the close of 1961 based on the Community's study of social activity during that year.[17] It was found that generally the more heavily industrialized sectors had enjoyed the greatest benefits from regional programs. This observation had particular application in Italy, where in 1960 the northwestern and, to a lesser extent, the northeastern and central areas made notable advances though the south still lagged.

On a similar basis, the center and southwest of France was behind the rest of the country in economic progress. Anxiety was expressed that the chronic persistence of these regional imbalances would have a dragging effect on the overall economic equilibrium of the Community. Far from holding to a belief that this problem would find its own solution in the natural course of events, measures were urged to aid retarded areas by every means the Treaty makes available. While not wishing to hamper the influence of free competition in advancing common progress, belief was expressed that the social development of the Community made indispensable a more coordinated program of harmonization for the member states.[18]

By 1963 coordinated studies were being made by the Commission to devise future Community programs relating to regional development. The largest regional study at that time dealt with the industrialization of the Taranto-Bari region of southern Italy, at the heel of the peninsula. Here several steel companies have been located. The area is sufficiently restricted for a compact study; there are adequate resources in manpower and material to sustain a substantial industrial complex. Both the Commission and the High Authority were engaged during 1963 in determining the proper level of investment necessary to make the region self-sufficient economically.

Another regional study, sponsored by the Commission during 1963, involved the common problems of two sectors divided by a political frontier, namely the border regions of France and Belgium. Their mutual concern over water supply, vocational training and inducement of new capital investment had been alleviated by 1963 through improved cooperation of the public authorities on both sides of the frontier. The Commission had succeeded in encouraging and directing this cooperation toward a solution of the common difficulties facing the two countries.[19]

REGIONAL REPORTS BY STUDY GROUPS

During the conference on Regional Economies, held in Brussels in December, 1961, the Commission decided to request study groups, made up of experts in the field, to examine methods capable of being employed in each member state to speed up the development of less economically favored areas. One of the reports from these study groups, presented to the Commission in 1964, dealt with the objectives and methods of regional policy in the Economic Community.[20]

Referring to the long-standing industrial zones in the Community, notably the Ruhr, the north of France, Luxembourg, the Saar and

Lorraine, the report notes that economic development began in these regions on a large scale in the last century, and has continued since because of the presence of coal and iron ore. Steel, the basic industry of that time, necessarily located in these areas of raw material because of difficulty in transporting coal and ore out of this region. In their turn the steel mills have since attracted the fabricating industries in a cumulative fashion.

At present, however, these industrial regions are undergoing rapid transformation, with particular repercussions on the labor force. In the coal mining industry the demand for manpower has greatly decreased from the double effect of improved methods of production and a decrease in the use of coal as a source of energy.

Fortunately the manufacturing industries provide a large market for highly qualified manpower. Moreover, because of rapid expansion in these industries, even unskilled labor, available in these older industrial regions, has been absorbed.[21] Further, while the technical imperatives of a previous epoch which drew industry into the coal basins of Europe no longer have their former significance, the newer industries on which the future standard of living will depend necessarily maintain the past patterns of industrial concentration.

The report on regional policy acknowledged that general prosperity warrants notable differences in types of economic activity among different regions. Admission was also made that though modern farming methods had greatly reduced the need for agricultural workers, those who remained in this activity were now able to obtain suitable income. Nevertheless, it was pointed out that modern economic developments had brought about regional imbalances which could cause grave human loss, especially among the young in blighted regions where the decline in educational standards prevents even gifted youths from completing their studies, who would provide the economy with the educated personnel requisite for prosperity. It was noted that in the underdeveloped regions the number of diplomas denoting advanced study has been particularly small.

In such less-favored regions of the Community, therefore, a factor which discourages the entrance of new industrial development is the lack of adequately trained manpower and the dearth of executive personnel with sufficiently advanced education. Moreover, the realization of this regional deficiency causes the more alert members of the population to travel to more promising areas in search of employment, thus intensifying the spiral of economic decline in their native regions.

COMMUNITY REGIONAL POLICY

The objective for the Community's regional policy is the elimination of excessive imbalances among economic regions, first within each member state and then progressively throughout the Community. Yet there is no intention to thwart tendencies to industrial concentration where they are economically justified, or to hold back the growth of more richly endowed sectors. Rather, the Community regional policy seeks to avoid extreme economic changes and the resulting upheavals, especially for regions where income may decline to a less than acceptable minimum politically and socially. In pursuit of this objective efforts also will be made to institute measures to reduce excessive industrial concentration in certain zones where, as a result, the population may be put to grave inconvenience. This regional policy will take on different forms in particular regions in accordance with the problems present there.[22] In every instance, nevertheless, effort will be made to persuade members of the work force in the different regions to contribute most effectively toward the prosperity of the economy, first nationally and then in terms of the Community.

The Community report of 1964 on aims and methods for regional policy emphasized that, before all else, regional development involves the creation of costly infrastructures which will bring no appreciable regional growth for such a long time that local public opinion has little enthusiasm for their creation.

These infrastructures were designated as public resources which make up the framework of economic life under three headings. First, there is the formative infrastructure or the entire system of general education and vocational training on which depends the quality of the potential work force for the region. Second, there are the socio-cultural infrastructures which comprise housing, sanitary facilities, and provision for cultural and recreational pursuits. It was pointed out that when these are of high quality they are a positive influence toward attracting both manpower and new enterprise. On the contrary, if they are of low standards as in poorly developed regions, the depressing living conditions which result actually accelerate the emigration of the work force.

A third type of infrastructure was designated as of the strictly economic type, namely industrial zones with adequate resources in energy and rapid communication. These latter requirements were regarded as taking an increasing importance today in the modern economy because of specialized units of production and greater interdependence among industrial complexes.

It was pointed out that industrial concentration and the density of population which follows require governments to expand infrastructures in the regions affected. In addition, to such material requirements as highways and water supply, conditions must be fostered which will cope with industrial expansion and thus assure growth in public revenue. Moreover, there is need to construct schools, hospitals, as well as social and cultural centers.

Moreover the report conceded that an economic upsurge and the density of population which accompanies it will not take place without social tensions and conflicts in Europe. Such a consequence is inevitable since from this type of economic expansion the average income in zones of industrial concentration is now notably higher than in other regions of Europe.[23]

METHODS TO IMPLEMENT REGIONAL POLICY

Another report presented to the Commission in 1964 dealt with methods for applying regional policy; stress was placed on vocational training and retraining.[24] It was pointed out that to understand the role of training and retraining in terms of regional development, one had to be aware of the actual trends in specialization and automation which have in consequence put heavier demands on the institutes for vocational training. Industrial units which move into the less favored regions should be able to take for granted they will find a work force already possessing basic vocational training and institutes suitably equipped to adapt this manpower to the needs of the new plants.

Noting that regional policy has a special significance for areas characterized by acute or anticipated unemployment or under-employment, appropriate financial aid must be accorded such regions. The report of the study group on methods stressed that experience in the member countries clearly showed that this financial aid ought not to be placed necessarily where the unemployment is localized, but where the likelihood of creating employment is most promising, first of all in the primary industrial centers and then in secondary industrial centers.

For the larger regions there may even be required some population movement, but wherever possible it should be only within the boundaries of the region itself. One example cited referred to migration of workers from the interior provinces of Sicily toward the coast.

In the smaller regions the distance between a worker's home and his new place of work should be easy to traverse daily.

The report warned that there was no basis for expecting the goal of adequate employment to be attained by permanently subsidizing enterprises unable to meet competition. Instead it was pointed out that the problems of creating employment in less favored regions can only be solved by establishing healthy and stable enterprise.[25]

REGIONAL RECONVERSION

In a third study report dealing with readaptation of older industrialized regions, it was stressed that a more obvious indication of present lack of adaptability of an area to economic change is the closing of plants or reduction of their output, with the consequent laying off of workers who have no hope of reemployment. The report did acknowledge that economic progress at times demands that certain industries decline in order to make room for new enterprise which is more productive and adaptable to changes in the economy. On this point note was made that between 1958 and 1962 the rates of employment had changed considerably in several industries of the Community. On the negative side, coal mining had sustained a drop of 28 per cent in volume of employment. Agricultural employment had also declined, but not as drastically. A moderate growth in employment had taken place in steel, but in business and services the upward trend had been much more pronounced.[26] A finding of the report on regional readaptation indicated that a high proportion of the work force in a declining industry is often in older age groups; these are also the most difficult to retrain.

It might appear that emigration of the laid-off workers would be the solution rather than an attempt to readapt them for different work in their native region. On a commuting basis this remedy would be practicable only if the neighboring regions of employment were within a reasonable distance of the worker's place of residence. In any event, his native region tends to lose part of the income derived from such a worker when he is no longer a full-time resident. As one instance, service activities show marked decline in an area where a large part of the work force begins to commute daily to another region for a livelihood.

If such emigration also involves a change of residence it may mean the permanent loss of younger and more qualified members of the community; adaptability of the region to new economic activities thus becomes all the more difficult because of the disproportionate number of older workers left in the region.

The older unemployed workers remaining in a declining economic region are reluctant to accept employment in a lower classification than their former jobs and with a corresponding lower rate of pay. Manifestations of this condition have been found even in prosperous West Germany in the regions bordering on East Germany where whole towns and districts have been shorn of their natural trade zones. Between 1950 and 1960, 10 per cent of the population in this area (600,000) moved into other sectors of West Germany.[27]

The report on older industrial regions recognized that centers for vocational retraining would have to be supported by governments, either by direct operation or through subsidies for centers maintained by groups of employers. The actual amount of government aid would be dependent on the duration of the retraining period, the complexity of the program involved and the kind of organization conducting the training institutes. It was noted that government subsidies would have to include wages and other expenses for trainees and their instructors, cost of supplies and maintenance, and even the cost of training the instructors themselves.

The European Economic Community has provided financial help for operation of vocational retraining programs through the European Social Fund which, up to the end of 1963, had made grants of $20,000,000 for this purpose. The retraining programs thus subsidized were carried on in all the member countries except Luxembourg and included 263,000 workers. The two countries with the largest number of workers thus retrained were Italy (167,501) and Germany (73,989). It must be noted that the subsidy from the Fund, as required by the Treaty, matched the funds made available from government sources.[28]

In terms of synchronizing the termination of one type of industrial activity with the creation of new forms of manufacturing, the study group on older industrial regions urged that retraining programs should anticipate the date for beginning new operations. By this arrangement interruption of regular employment can be greatly reduced or even eliminated. In effect it was proposed that retraining for the new jobs should take place in the old plants under existing work contracts. Where unions are present in industry, their participation in the retraining program was regarded as essential for success.[29]

In the Fall, 1964, the EEC Commission prepared proposals for the Council relating to a common regional policy designed to extend prosperity to the "poverty pockets" still present in the Community. While consultation took place in advance of these draft proposals with government officials in the member countries responsible for regional policies, considerable use was made of the recommendations of the three reports (just referred to) which examined regional economic problems.[30] The document containing these recommendations was forwarded to the Council on May 11, 1965.[31]

THE EUROPEAN COAL AND STEEL COMMUNITY

In the original text of the Treaty of Paris, the European Coal and Steel Community was authorized to encourage regional economic policies by virtue of Article 46 (4) which states that the High Authority shall:

> at the request of the interested governments, participate in the study of the possibilities of re-employing, either in existing industries or through the creation of new activities, workers unemployed by reason of the development of the market or technical changes.[32]

In line with this directive the Community, by 1956, had worked on several studies on regional possibilities for employment in cooperation with national experts. In that year it reported some of its findings on different economic and geographic factors that prompted establishment of new enterprises or the relocation of existing industrial activities. As one instance, it was noted that in 1956 Italian steel plants were being built close to seaports which received shipments of iron ore and coke. The new sites for steel plants were also determined by taking proximity to sources of methane gas into account. Usually the steel plants at these new locations drew their work forces from the local labor supply. Only a portion of the personnel was made up of the original manpower from other regions of the country where the old plants had been located.

Factors accounting for the depression of an economic region dependent on a basic industry were traced to such causes as new programs of industrial rationalization, or gradual exhaustion of coal deposits. As a consequence, such regions were beset with unemployment. Moreover, even if there was assurance of sufficient jobs for the present work force, the depressing realization spread that there would be no escaping an acute regional employment problem for the next generation. Regions in 1956 facing such an economic crisis in more or less degree were in certain coal fields in south central France, the Sardinian coal area, and the region around Borinage, Belgium.[33]

DEVELOPING NEW SOURCES OF EMPLOYMENT

As early as 1957, Rene Mayer, the president of the High Authority, declared that the Community was deeply aware that the true solution for problems of readjustment caused by the existence and development of the Common Market was to be found in the on-the-spot development of opportunities for reemployment of laid-off manpower. To be prepared before hand, the High Authority had for some time been organizing relevant data on regions where it appeared that normal future growth of employment in the coal and steel industries was in doubt.

This data on regional labor markets was useful in drafting relevant measures for assuring normal employment conditions. In this fashion imbalances could be foreseen, or at least their effects could be softened, by evaluating in advance the manpower needs and resources, considering the general trends of the population, and noting the outlook for a regional economy as influenced by its basic industrial activities. Over the years the experts employed in these regional studies by the High Authority have developed a formula for diagnosing the status of a region's employment potential and for determining suitable measures to realize its development.

One of the Community's first regional studies on employment dealt with the two coal basins of Auvergne and Aquitaine of south central France. It was directed by J. F. Gravier, a member of the French National Committee on Economic Orientation.

Earlier the French government had requested financial aid from the High Authority for the retraining or transfer of miners in the south central region of France. Nevertheless, the deep attachment of these miners to their own countryside and their lifelong associates, as well as a repugnance toward transfer persuaded the High Authority all the more to seek regional solutions to regional problems of employment.[34]

The conclusion of the Auvergne-Aquitaine study observed that Aquitaine in the very near future would be threatened with the loss of a large part of its coal market because of methane gas. The threat was made even more certain by the action of the French government in reducing the price of natural gas to be purchased by approved companies in 16 departments of southwest France. It was predicted that the problem of employment would rapidly become tragic in this region of Decazeville, if prompt action were not taken to attract light industries, not only in the coal basin as such, but also in neighboring zones where conditions were less ominous.[35]

In addition to encouraging studies on regional employment, the original text of Article 56 permitted the High Authority to give financial aid toward retraining of workers, within narrow limitations, where it appeared that new technical processes or equipment might lead to an unusually large reduction in labor needs for the coal or steel industries.[36]

Desirous of putting as much of the work force as possible under the Treaty's article providing for retraining, the High Authority, in 1959, supported the expressed objective of the European Parliamentary Assembly, as well as of different professional groups, by requesting an expansion of Article 56 in the Treaty.

On March 29, 1960, the enlarged text of Article 56 was approved and in effect. Historically, it denoted the first legislative act undertaken by the European Parliament. A vast new field of retraining was thus opened for the High Authority. Among other aspects, it meant the possibility of participating more extensively in the actual development of new economic activities which would be conducive to assuring productive reemployment of manpower.

The second paragraph, which was added to the original provision in Article 56, in part states:

> should profound changes in the marketing conditions of the coal mining or of the iron and steel industry, not directly connected with the introduction of the Common Market, make it necessary for certain enterprises permanently to discontinue, curtail or change their activities, the High Authority, at the request of the interested Governments, . . .

might give aid toward financing programs in the coal and steel industries (or with the consent of the Council in any other industry) designed to develop new economic activities or convert existing enterprises to assure productive reemployment of workers. Financing of retraining programs for such workers was also provided for in the supplement to Article 56.[37]

Authorities on the Treaty have regarded the expansion of Article 56 profoundly significant in view of the structural changes which have been taking place in the coal market and the consequent widespread closing of coal mines, particularly in Belgium. Industrial reconversion has become imperative in such coal regions, and now Article 56 enables the Community to exercise broad discretion in the development of new economic activities.

CONFERENCE ON REGIONAL CONVERSION

By June, 1961, the High Authority, with the approval of the Council, had begun to organize an intergovernmental conference on problems of regional reconversion to exchange experiences and appraise measures of the member countries. No such study on a European level had ever been undertaken before. Particular attention in the agenda for the conference was given to the financing of new industrial operations in areas where coal mining had to be reduced. The High Authority was prepared to render financial aid toward this objective, as provided for under Article 56.

It was acknowledged by Piero Malvestiti, president of the High Authority in 1961, that the actual plans for reconversion and their execution would have to be carried out under the auspices of the member countries themselves. In addition to financial help, however, the High Authority would participate actively in studies on the complex problems enmeshed with programs of reconversion. Nevertheless, it was pointed out that the Community could not inject itself in a responsibility proper to a national government, especially so when the new industrial activity planned might be outside the scope of coal and steel.

Expectation was expressed that in the projected conference there would be participation by the EEC Commission to encourage fruitful cooperation between the Communities toward harmonious construction of the new Europe.[38] In preparation for the conference a study group was appointed with representatives from the member governments, the High Authority, the Commission and the European Bank of Investment. Two technical commissions also took part in the planning stages.

One commission, under the title of Methods of Intervention, examined the most effective measures available for the purpose of promoting industrialization and industrial reconversion. For its consideration the High Authority sponsored a special study project, Conditions Which Facilitate the Creation of New Activities. In this study, stress was placed on a classification of juridical and financial measures in the member countries which had been most effective for industrial development.

Another commission, with the title Experiences of Reconversion, gave attention to obstacles encountered in the course of executing the different stages of reconversion, as well as the results which were obtained.

It was believed that the reports of the two commissions would enable those attending the Conference to determine the relative effectiveness of different methods of reconversion so that they might obtain satisfactory results in their own situations.[39]

After this preparation the three day intergovernmental conference on industrial reconversion for regions affected by the closing of coal mines was called into session at Luxembourg on September 27, 1960. In addition to government representatives, delegates were also present from employer and worker organizations.

During the sessions of the conference the High Authority put special stress on regional studies it could pursue in accordance with Articles 46 and 55 relating to new industrial activities for the reemployment of former coal miners.

As an evaluation of the Conference, it appeared that the objective was fully achieved. The members reached a vast confrontation relating to methods used, results accomplished, and means of cooperation available between member governments and the European Communities for the purpose of promoting reconversion. Since the practical initiative in reconversion programs would have to come from the member governments, providing the massive confrontation of all the various possibilities was as much as the European Communities could do directly to influence the member countries.

Subsequent to the Conference a synthesis was drafted of the conclusions. It was compiled by the same committee which originally had planned the conference. In turn, the High Authority, in cooperation with the other European Communities, decided upon a number of propositions bearing on regional reconversion which seemed conducive to rapid accomplishment of positive results.[40]

The synthesis of conference findings was made available to the Council and to the Consultative Committee of the European Coal and Steel Community in September, 1961. Bearing the title Lines of Direction for Solving Problems Posed by Industrial Reconversion in Regions Affected by the Closing of Coal Mines, the synthesis was regarded as a likely basis for future Community action.[41]

This document grew out of the cooperation of the High Authority, the Commission and the Bank for European Investments. Additional proposals sent to the Council were designed to complete, on the practical side, the synthesis of the proceedings from the intergovernmental conference.

The policy on reconversion which was sent to the Council distinguishes two phases of development. First is the relatively simple case where it suffices to aid in financing a new plant or extending an existing enterprise. At the other extreme, it is appropriate to launch a vast program of reconversion by persuading industry to locate in a region where mining activities have declined.

This document on policy emphasized, however, that the primary responsibility for facilitating economic recovery devolved upon governments by means of their financial reserves and other resources conducive to recovery programs. The European Communities are disposed, within their legal powers, to utilize the possibilities of intervention, but not in the sense of considering them as basic objectives set down by the Treaties.

CENTERS FOR INDUSTRIAL DEVELOPMENT

The synthesis on policy for reconversion considers that the most effective approach is to encourage the creation of "centers of impulsion" which will be conducive to effective regional development because of the actual responsibility entrusted to these centers.

Among the responsibilities they incur is the duty to define the goals of reconversion, taking into account long term perspectives and especially new economic horizons resulting from the establishment of the Common Market. The centers are to mobilize financial resources and create zones to encourage vigorous industrial development based on both the polar and axial concept. For these zones the centers for development are to provide infrastructure and public services.

Another function entrusted to the centers is to seek out, in accordance with modern methods of publicity, industries likely to locate plants in the regions of a particular planning center. Moreover, the centers will be expected to construct the industrial plants in accordance with the preference of the firms which are to rent or purchase the structures.

Even after the new plants are erected, the centers for development are expected to look after their maintenance, if necessary, and provide public services for the industrial zones. Underlying the program of action for the centers is the goal of making the industrial sites as attractive as possible to fulfill ultimately the social and cultural needs of the population in the industrial zones.[42]

RECONVERSION IN PRACTICE

Practical application of the measures for reconversion, discussed above, were put into effect for the first time after the closings of coal mines in Belgium, especially in the area of Borinage. It became necessary there to establish new industrial activities in order to provide employment for displaced coal miners.

Hoping to find the most effective solution to the problem the Belgian government requested the High Authority, by virtue of Article 46 (section 4), to take part in a study of the Borinage area. The objective was to devise a program of reconversion capable of integrating the Borinage region into the Common Market especially in harmony with the industrial development in the north of France.

Even as early as 1959 the Belgian government had enacted legislation to facilitate the creation of new industrial activities in regions where economic growth had been judged inadequate. Borinage, the Centre, and the Liege basin had been designated as zones for development.[43]

Also in 1959 the High Authority had commissioned the Institute of Economic Sciences of the Catholic University of Milan to undertake a study on the economic progress of the steel industry and the status of employment in the regions of Brescia and Udine. The High Authority had likewise agreed to cooperate on a study of the region of Umbria where a steel center is located.[44]

The first of these studies, completed in 1961, pointed out that the regions of Brescia and Udine had such a low standard of living that by themselves the areas were unable to attract new industrial activities. The stagnant economy there was said to be caught in a vicious circle of poverty. Income was slight and volume of new investment at the lowest level. Unemployment was at a very high rate.[45]

Nevertheless, the study foresaw the possibility of new economic development for the steel industry in this region sufficient to resolve the local problems of structural unemployment.[46] By such industrial changes—if undertaken immediately—as integration, concentration and modernization it was believed that competitive disadvantage could be overcome in the steel industry so that a satisfactory employment rate could be maintained.[47]

In July, 1961, the High Authority acted favorably in regard to two projects proposed by the Belgian government for the Liege basin. As an indication of the impact on employment because of mine closings, from 1953 to 1960, the number of active mining sites in this coal basin had dropped from 34 to 18 and employment had fallen from 30,000 to 18,000.

To encourage reconversion, the High Authority decided to grant a loan of $2,300,000 to the Provincial Corporation of Industrialization at Liege. The PCI had been established in 1961 under a 1959 law which set up special measures to promote economic expansion and new industries. In effect the PCI is an intercommunity organization the purpose of which is to make industrial sites available. It also maintains connections with investors in order to encourage economic revival in the Liege province.

Further, the High Authority—by reason of Article 54 which authorizes the Community to grant loans to industry under its investment program—extended credit of $1,800,000 to a steel company in the Liege region which had agreed to employ a certain number of older miners in its new installations.[48]

The first measures undertaken by the PCI in the Belgian Province of Liege, was to locate three enterprises in the area of Herve and Battice. In the contracts, signed by the Provincial Corporation with firms establishing plants on sites under the jurisdiction of the PCI, there is a clause which provides for the employment of workers displaced because of the closing of the coal mines.[49]

IMPORTANCE OF RAPID INDUSTRIAL TRANSITION

Of particular significance for the High Authority and the member governments active in industrial reconversion has been the new section in Article 56, especially the clause which permits the High Authority to facilitate the financing of new, economically sound activities which will assure reemployment to workers displaced from other industries.

This new provision in Article 56 has been most welcome because of the keen awareness of the necessity to avoid a delay between a mine closing and the operation of new industrial activities. There is realization that if there is a delay at such a critical juncture, the new industry only partially will be able to hire the most efficient members of the local work force; during the hiatus many in this category would be drawn to other local firms or would quit the region entirely. It has been found that delayed entrance of new firms may mean the necessity of recruiting too many ex-miners who are in upper years or physically handicapped. Even to persuade the newly arrived companies to employ miners as such, who would likely be less productive than experienced factory workers, it is necessary for the Community to offer those firms greater advantages, such as preliminary market research, than would be necessary under normal conditions.[50]

Even before the 1960 revision of Article 56 the increasing competition of fuel oil had forced the sudden closing of an important part of the Belgian coal mines by 1958. In the region of Borinage and the Centre, coal production was cut in half. In the face of this crisis the Belgian government announced its intention to promote a policy of reconversion. A cooperative society was created March 13, 1959, with the designation S.O.C.O.R.E.C. These letters indicated the purpose of the society: to do research and provide assistance toward the economic reconversion of regions affected by the closing of coal mines. Immediately upon its creation the S.O.C.O.R.E.C. was preoccupied with launching an overall study intending to draw up a spaced action program on a long term basis. The regions chosen were the Centre, Charleroi and Borinage.

Because of its interest in this study, the High Authority agreed to pay one-half the cost for the research. A directing committee was set up comprising representatives from the Belgian government, the Community and the cooperative, S.O.C.O.R.E.C. The resulting study, taking a year and one-half, comprised about 3,000 pages and constituted an almost complete inventory of the conditions and problems in these regions on the industrial level. Avoiding any superficial approach, the directors of the study endeavored to draw up an action program in hopes it would gain the attention of all responsible interests—the government, the European Community, the industrial fraternity and local governments.

In a true European context, the regional study drew upon the resources of the Society of Economics and Applied Mathematics in Paris and a similar society in Belgium. The Institute of Economic Research of Hainaut and the Institute of Sociology at Solvay also participated in the study, as did the Institute of Economic and Social Research at Louvain. Particular stress was given to the perspectives of development as they involved inter-regional relations between the north of France and the western part of the Hainaut province of Belgium.

In 1962 S.O.C.O.R.E.C. was prepared to propose an action program to improve all segments of the three Belgian regions on parallel lines. Among the essential elements of the program were the following:

1. By 1965 to maintain the employment level of 1961 in the industrial region of the Hainaut province. This goal acknowledged that because of the decline in coal production the stabilized new level of employment would be 10 per cent less than in 1957.

2. For the time it was frankly acknowledged as impossible to create the new industrial employment necessary for full employment each year. Recognition was given to the necessary dependence of industrial expansion on adequate infrastructures, housing, public services and facilities to encourage industrial development.

3. It was noted that a vast housing program would progressively attract a more desirable worker to the region. In effect there would thus be recuperation from the loss of foreign manpower (which left the region because of the closing of mines) by attracting a new type of

worker versed in metal fabrication, ceramics, and electrical equipment.

4. To this end a decision to double the rate of development for infrastructure and to increase housing construction to 15 per cent of the national total was reached. In regard to new industry as such, care was given to selecting sites for industrial parks and providing them with facilities to make them attractive to investors. Moreover, sites for housing projects were to be chosen which were convenient to the industrial parks.

5. Stress was placed on the fact that a broad program for reconversion of this type depends on the coordination of policy and action of all action programs in the region.

The president of S.O.C.O.R.E.C. in 1962, Pierre Van Der Rest, expressed satisfaction in the decision taken by the Belgian government to accept the findings of this study and put them in effect.

In the same year the High Authority published a synthesis of the findings on the study outlined above.[51] It marked the first volume in the series of researches on development and reconversion guided by the High Authority, or with its participation, in such countries as Belgium, France and Italy.[52]

As another step to encourage the development of new economic activities, in 1962 the High Authority published a revised looseleaf edition of its digest of financial and legal arrangements in the member countries and the United Kingdom, thus aiding the establishment of new economic activities. Following a uniform layout and classification, the digest provides briefings on the different means of action available in each country for the promotion of industrialization and industrial redevelopment. Note is taken of financial and fiscal concessions permitted by the various countries, as well as rate differentials, indirect aid to enterprises and benefits available to workers.

As an introduction for the digest of reconversion arrangements for each member country, an excellent summary of government policy is set forth for such matters as full employment, reemployment and regional development.[53]

RECONVERSION PROGRAMS IN THE UNITED STATES

The employment crisis experienced in certain provinces of Belgium because of the closing of coal mines in the late 1950's brings to mind the much more chronic situation which has been plaguing the Appalachian region for many years. This mountainous area covers most of Pennsylvania, all of West Virginia, a small section of Maryland, the southern tip of Ohio, eastern Kentucky and Tennessee. It also includes the western parts of Virginia and North Carolina, northern Georgia and the northern portion of Alabama.[54]

Drastic reduction in employment took place in this region since World War II with the trend toward mechanization of coal mining and the replacing of coal by oil and natural gas. Declining employment in agriculture also added to the general problem. In May, 1963, Appalachia had over 11 per cent of the country's unemployment, but only 5 per cent of the nation's labor force. Its rate of unemployment then was 12.5 per cent, or more than double the average rate for the country. In terms of all the areas in the United States eligible for aid toward redevelopment under the Area Redevelopment Act of 1961, Appalachia accounted for 35 per cent of all the unemployment involved in 1963.[55]

APPALACHIAN REDEVELOPMENT

In 1963, President Kennedy established a joint federal-state committee on Appalachia within the Department of Commerce. As a comprehensive program for the economic development of Appalachia, it was proposed that facilities should be improved for all types of passenger and freight transportation in the area. There were also proposals for expansion of facilities in education, research, training and the development of water, mineral and forest resources. Promotion of tourism was also slated for attention.[56]

To aid in development of the Appalachian region, the government has been lending funds at an annual rate of $18,500,000 for housing construction and repair. It is hoped that these initial funds will generate much more private lending for the same purpose.[57]

In keeping with the federal-state structure for Appalachian development, a policy was established to work closely with state officials and university heads in the Appalachian region for the purpose of founding an "Appalachian institute" to study long-run needs relating to economic development in the area.[58]

To counteract the declining competitive status of coal and increase employment for miners it has been proposed to build a large number of electric power generator stations at the mine mouths and avoid heavy transportation costs for coal shipments. It is now cheaper to transmit electricity by wire to the power load center than to ship a coal supply to a generating station located at a distant point.[59]

THE AREA REDEVELOPMENT ACT

Though Appalachia is the most prominent of the depressed regions in the United States, the large number of such areas prompted Congress to enact the Area Redevelopment Act in 1961. Under this legislation, administered within the Department of Commerce, initiative for redevelopment has to come from a depressed area itself and it must draft its own economic development program. Moreover, it is required that major financing for redevelopment must come from private sources. ARA is authorized to assist both urban industrial areas and low income, rural areas of underemployment by means of long-term, low-interest loans to encourage the entry of private enterprise, and assist existing industry to expand production and employment.

In technical assistance, ARA finances research and industrial studies by private firms, universities or government agencies to enable redevelopment areas to find solutions for economic problems. Subsistence payments are also provided by ARA to permit jobless workers to follow retraining programs to qualify for newly created jobs in an area.[60]

For some time there has been criticism of the ARA approach to the effect that the size of the areas designated for development have been too small and too numerous for administrative feasibility and economic potential. On December, 1964, the ARA program had 1,034 areas on its eligibility list for Federal Aid.[61]

As the administrator of ARA, William L. Batt, Jr., has acknowledged, in the United States the term "depressed area" has customarily been associated with the "commuting pattern of people" in relation to their work. Similarly, statistics on the rate of unemployment have been based on this type of labor area. Where annual rates for unemployment were found to be steadily higher than the national average it has become the habit to refer to such areas as "depressed."[62]

Unfortunately the Area Redevelopment Act has been fashioned to deal with these statistical areas as if they were economic units. In effect the county unit has been often designated as an "economic unit" for purposes of development since it provides ready data both on unemployment and on income levels. But many economists now express doubt that the county should be regarded as the administrative unit for purposes of economic development. Instead they put emphasis on the need for regarding groups of counties as part of economically similar areas. In fact, in such a region as Appalachia it is held that economic development might well be geared to an interstate regional organization.

Actually, the belief is quite general today that the ARA program has spread its limited resources and facilities over far too many redevelopment areas; these are both administratively and economically too small for effective results. In other words projects relating to water sheds, sewage disposal, vocational training, education facilities and highways must be associated realistically with regional planning on a multi-county or even multi-state basis.[63]

Fortunately—though belatedly—President Johnson in a special message to Congress March 25, 1965, urged that economic aid to depressed areas should give stress to regional redevelopment rather than to individual cities or counties in the future. Request was also made of Congress at this time to authorize the federal government to make loans available in the annual amount of $510,000,000 to areas with high unemployment and low income on a permanent basis. The new request for funds was about double the annual outlay permitted in the then current area redevelopment program.[64]

THE APPALACHIAN REDEVELOPMENT ACT

In actuality the Appalachian Regional Redevelopment Act of 1965, which President Johnson signed into law March 9, 1965, takes into account the multi-county and multi-state approach. The largest expenditure under the Act will be for a 3,350-mile system of development highways and access roads. Other programs relate to matching funds for land stabilization and erosion control, development of timber resources and a water resource survey. Efforts will be given to reclaiming strip mine areas, construction of vocational schools and regional health centers. For communities in Appalachia which have had difficulty in providing matching funds for development programs, there is now authorization of supplemental federal grants-in-aid.

The 1965 Act provides for the creation of an Appalachian Regional Commission as a joint federal-state body to administer and coordinate all programs of economic development in Appalachia.[65]

The Appalachian Regional Redevelopment Act of 1965 shows a partial similarity to the underlying concept of the Tennessee Valley Authority. Recognition is given to economic redevelopment as basically a regional problem, rather than a task within the particular scope of each community or county. Nevertheless, there is no indication of any independent governmental authority which would be responsible for the economic development of the Appalachian region as such. Authority continues divided among more than a score of Federal, state, and local agencies; it remains to be seen how effective action can be mobilized to resolve the many and difficult administrative problems involved in expanding the regional economy of Appalachia.

THE TENNESSEE VALLEY AUTHORITY

Appalachia includes some of the area under TVA. However, TVA is coordinated with a river valley, rather than a mountain range. Moreover, the objectives set down by Congress for TVA in 1933 were not identical to the aims of the 1965 Regional Redevelopment Act for Appalachia. TVA includes all of Tennessee, the southern region of Kentucky, the extreme western part of Virginia, much of Mississippi and some northern counties in Alabama and Georgia.[66]

As contrasted with the Regional Redevelopment Act, TVA was charged with the responsibility of promoting the multiple use of the Tennessee River system, involving flood control, navigation and the generation and sale of electricity. In addition, TVA was entrusted with the establishment of industry, the extension and development of recreational facilities (which include fish and wild life resources). Land and forestry conservation are also responsibilities of TVA.

Though TVA is an independent governmental agency with headquarters in Knoxville, Tennessee, it has successfully enlisted the initiative and vigorous cooperation of state agencies, counties, municipalities, educational organizations, cooperatives and private enterprise.[67] In terms of employment the 200-county Tennessee Valley has enjoyed notable growth in manufacturing employment since the depression of the 1930's when TVA was created. While only 12 per cent of total employment in the region was attributed to manufacturing in the early 1930's it had risen to 38 per cent by 1963, which was a slightly higher proportion of the work force than for the United States as a whole.[68] Total manufacturing employment in the Tennessee Valley region rose about 15 per cent between 1959 and 1963. For the whole country the increase was less than 3 per cent.[69] Though, as noted earlier, the Appalachian region had an overall unemployment rate of 12.5 per cent in May, 1963, Tennessee— the only State fully within the TVA area—had an unemployment rate for the year 1962 of 5.9 per cent.[70] Nevertheless, since one-third of industrial employment in the Tennessee Valley area was in the moderate paying apparel and textile industries (as against only 13 per cent for the country in general) average earnings of manufacturing workers in the Tennessee Valley were lower than for the nation.[71]

In other parts of the world, when the subject of regional development is associated with the United States, it is the TVA program which immediately comes to mind. Foreigners continue to visit TVA headquarters at Knoxville in large numbers. In 1964, 2,400 persons from 107 countries examined activities there relating to unified re-source development. Toward the end of the fiscal year 1964, the seventh seminar was held since 1961 on economic and resource development. In attendance were 32 government officials, engineers, technicians, economists and military officers from 16 countries. Coop-erating with TVA in conducting the project were both the University of Tennessee and the Agency for International Development.[72]

10.

Industrial Relations in the
Member States

IN COLLECTIVE BARGAINING AND THE DAY-TO-DAY RELATIONS
between employers and worker representatives, the treaties for both
the European Economic Community and the European Coal and
Steel Community provide no jurisdiction on the part of the governing
bodies. Nevertheless, Article 118 of the Treaty of Rome allows the
EEC Commission to collaborate closely with the member states
through studies, opinions and organizing consultations on such matters as the law on "trade unions, and collective bargaining between
employers and workers."[1] Similarly, Article 46 of the Treaty of Paris
has been understood to permit the European Coal and Steel Community to sponsor studies in the field of industrial relations by reason of
Section 5 which states that the High Authority may:

> gather any information required to assess the possibilities of improving
> the living and working conditions of the labour force in the industries
> under its jurisdiction, and the risks menacing their living conditions.[2]

It has been observed by Paul Finet, the late member of the High
Authority and its one time President, that a study of the basic aspects
of labor law in the Six relates precisely to the area of general knowledge which the High Authority should make available. Finet stressed

that through the understanding and comparison of the diverse legislation now existent, as well as of the theories and doctrines underlying such laws, a foundation can be established for mobilizing efforts to achieve a harmonization of working conditions in the member countries.

To this end, a series of studies was instituted by the High Authority on comparative labor law. The program of research was entrusted to a committee of jurists from the member countries. Also cooperating were representatives from the Economic Community and the International Labor Office in Geneva.[3]

THE INDUSTRIAL PARTIES AT THE LEVEL OF THE FIRM

As Gerhard Boldt indicates in the study on sources of labor law, toward the beginning of the twentieth century it became apparent in the member countries that definite forms of worker representation were arising, which in spite of their casual character pointed to the presence of an objective need that was closely related to the general political and economic development of the times and especially to the growing industrial pattern.[4]

One situation prompting recourse to worker representation was the desire by both employers and workers to utilize rules for safety and health more effectually because of the anxiety of workers to avoid the ill effects an accelerated rhythm of production brought on through such innovations as the assembly line. Another proximate cause was the astuteness of certain employers who, conscious that familial management was being replaced by large, impersonal enterprise, felt the need for organic worker representation as a substitute for the fast-disappearing personal contact between worker and employer. Growing social tension in industrial plants has also been considered a contributory cause to the development of worker representation.

In the period immediately following World War I employee committees at the level of the firm had become rather general in most of the countries of the Common Market. Moreover, representation beyond the individual firm was also becoming manifest. Inevitably, the economic problems relating to industrial reconversion after the War and the social and political agitation of the times prompted even public authorities to take a more active part in the control of relationships between employers and workers. Accordingly, in several member countries, legislation was enacted which supported the principle of worker representation, especially at the level of the firm, and also contained specific regulations to that end—some of purely legislative origin and some from agreements by the parties themselves.

Nevertheless, the trend toward the development of industrial democracy was later abandoned in certain member countries such as Germany and Italy, because of an abrupt change in the political climate. In other countries, such as France, the consequences of the great economic depression of the 1930's encouraged additional worker demands which led to even newer forms of industrial representation, including the institution of worker delegates.

By the end of World War II, the parallel development of the trend toward industrial democracy had once more been resumed in all the member countries especially at the level of the firm. Further, the growing complexity of industrial structure and changes in systems of production necessitated more sophisticated worker representation. Another complicating factor was the continuing legislative intervention by all member governments, with the exception of Italy. In that country, regulation of worker representation was left entirely in the domain of collective bargaining.[5]

The institutions for collaboration between employers and workers carry different designations, according to the particular country of the Community. In Germany, Belgium and The Netherlands, the term commonly used for them is Council of the Enterprise; in France, Committee of the Enterprise; in Italy, Internal Commission of the Enterprise; Worker Delegation is used in Luxembourg.[6]

Moreover, the structures of these groups vary considerably from one member country to another. For such countries as Germany, Italy and Luxembourg they are composed exclusively of worker members, and negotiations with the employer usually take place in separate sessions from the meetings of the worker groups. However, in Belgium, France and The Netherlands, these organizations are of a mixed character; the employer is also a member and serves as chairman. In Belgium the employer may have more than one representative, though their number is not permitted to be greater than the number of worker representatives. For these committees the worker delegates are elected according to proportional representation. The trade unions do not determine the nomination of candidates except in Belgium and France. Yet even in France such union control ceases after the first ballot.[7]

Several different objectives have been apparent in the promotion of worker representation. For example, there is an endeavor to assure the observance of rights relating directly to the worker's place of employment, the domain of collective bargaining. As another instance, worker representation is sought to promote cooperation between employer and workers to assure the latter an effective role in directing the economy in general and the enterprise in particular—the role of co-management.

This evolution in relationship between worker and employer marks a basic change from the traditional sole proprietor of the enterprise who hired employees on the basis of an individual contract with terms of employment left to the discretion of the employer. In the new version, management is no longer exclusively responsible to the investors, but also must take into account the labor community within the firm. It has been said that this modification of the power base marks the transition from the traditional type of enterprise, where the worker is only a subordinate employed for the sole interest of the owner, to a more modern type of firm where the worker is an associate in the process of production.

Thus in several countries the trend toward worker representation is part of a general movement supporting a belief that political democracy should logically be supplemented by economic and social democracy. Nevertheless, there are practical difficulties here, as well as open and sharp opposition to such development. These complications have placed the movement in uncertain status characterized by resort to necessarily ambiguous solutions for difficulties encountered.

In applying the very principle of worker representation within the firm, the participants find themselves in the dubious position of endeavoring to reconcile the role of bargaining agent with that of co-operator and co-manager. From sheer procedural necessity, resource has been made to the selection of impartial chairmen for committees of conciliation, or to the appealing of disputes to an impartial arbitrator. It has been said that this predicament makes apparent the embarrassment of the rule maker who is obliged to institutionalize forces still in full evolution; he must seek to reconcile the bargaining function, pressing from the outside, and the desire of workers to share in the responsibilities of economic power from the inside.

Following World War II the right of representation was extended to an ever-wider area of application in about all the member countries, but the chief emphasis remained in the industrial sector. Both the method of regulating worker representatives, and the patterns of representation themselves have been fashioned according to the size of the enterprise involved and the number of workers employed. And among member countries there are notable contrasts in types of worker representation, influenced by the variety of basic concepts between such countries as The Netherlands and West Germany.[8]

Nevertheless, though each member country may use its own approach in applying the concept of co-management and co-determination of policy within a firm, on the essential issues there is a large area of agreement among the six countries.

Here it may be stated that all of the Six are in accord with making the chief objective of programs for worker representation a more facile development of cooperation between employer and workers. There is a belief that the maintenance of good industrial relations and close understanding inside the enterprise will permit production to proceed in an atmosphere of mutual confidence. This objective, which endeavors to offset destructive influences arising from accentuated social tensions within the plant, recognizes the importance of open communication between management and personnel.

Nevertheless, it is acknowledged in all the member countries, with the possible exception of The Netherlands, that the removal of social tensions within a plant does not follow necessarily because of the establishment of worker representation. In practice, such an institution within an enterprise has been known at times to place the actual representatives themselves in a highly sensitive position. So much so, that in about all the member countries it has been found necessary to give guarantees of job security to employees who take the initiative in representing their fellow workers. The Netherlands remains the exception here. Though in that country methods of industrial cooperation are highly developed at all levels of economic and social organization, there is no legislative protection for workers who take upon themselves the task of being spokesmen and bargainers for the work force in the plant.

Another objective commonly assigned to the organs of worker representation within an industry is the task of surveillance over the application of social legislation within the enterprise, presenting worker claims which may arise to the employer and stressing the need for a uniform solution to all such problems. In addition, worker representatives have performed the task of studying certain aspects of production planning with management. In this fashion worker committees participate in regulating labor conditions inside the firm as well as the hours of work and vacation periods.[9]

The Council of the Enterprise in Germany, when there is not a legal determination on the matter, may negotiate an agreement with management setting forth the hours of work, vacation schedules, disciplinary rules in the plant, wage rates and methods of payment.[10] Because of required consultation prior to hiring or layoffs, the Council of the Enterprise may, within closely defined limits, express opposition to such action by management. When hirings or layoffs are to be on a large scale, the employer must discuss the matter with the Council of the Enterprise before requesting authorization from the regional Office of Labor.

In Belgium it actually pertains to the Council of the Enterprise to set the dates for annual vacations, to extend or modify shop rules, and to establish general standards for layoffs or hirings. In France the Committee of the Enterprise exercises a check over medical service and social services within the firm. Moreover, plant physicians and plant counselors may not be appointed or dismissed except with their agreement.[11]

Administration of social services likewise is within the domain of worker representatives. Nevertheless, the degree of actual participation by workers varies notably from country to country. In Italy the role of the worker committees is confined to drafting rules for such services and cooperation in application. Yet in other countries, such as France, worker representatives actually take part in the administration of social services. Moreover they share in the administration of insurance funds, retirement programs and centers for vocational training.

Nevertheless, there are even more notable differences among the member countries on the degree of responsibility assigned to worker committees on matters relating to strictly economic and technical administration within an enterprise. Such issues were presented anew, and in sharp focus, after World War II. The answers given in this critical area indicate the variety of the several economic structures of the Six, the relative degree of maturity of different systems of production, the varied bargaining relationships between the industrial partners, the level of cooperation between them, and the peculiar political conditions in member countries.[12]

Generally, the worker committees have consultative power exclusively, with a broad exception in Germany. Moreover, this consultative power usually carries with it the right to obtain information, more or less extended, in regard to the economic and financial condition of the firm.

Legislation in Belgium and France specifies the type of information which the employer of a private stock company must make available. In effect the worker committees receive the same documents as are presented to stockholders. Moreover, in France, two members of the Committee of the Enterprise are empowered to take part with consultative voice in the meetings of the Council of Administration.[13] In Belgium, France and Germany worker committees are authorized to make proposals in the technical field, especially in regard to new methods of production. By way of contrast, plant worker committees in Italy are not even qualified to demand information on the economic condition of the firm.[14]

It appears that in Germany the Council of the Enterprise is not merely designed to assure information and representation to workers concerning economic issues of the firm. In actuality, the chairman of the Council of the Enterprise meets regularly with management to discuss the economic status of the firm as well as to report on the activities of the Council of the Enterprise. In Germany—for companies with more than one hundred employees—economic commissions are established, equally represented by management and workers, with the latter selected by the Council of the Enterprise.

These commissions, though having only consultative power, give their opinions to the head of the firm on all manner of essentially economic questions, such as methods of production, programming of work, the economic status of the firm and the condition of the market. Moreover, the head of the firm provides such a commission with the documents necessary for drafting these opinions in precise detail.

In certain instances the German law provides worker representation at the policy-making levels of the company, namely on the council of surveillance and the board of directors. Two main tasks are recognized for the council of surveillance; the appointing and dismissing of members of the board of directors and assuring permanent control over the board's management of the firm.

Nevertheless, workers are differently represented on these two executive committees of the firm, depending on the type of enterprise. In ordinary stock companies the council of surveillance must have one-third of its members from worker representatives and elected by employees. In mining and steel companies, regulated by the law of co-management, the council of surveillance has equal representation between management and workers. In addition it appoints and dismisses the labor director who sits with the board of directors of the firm with rights equal to the other members.[15]

Especially in Germany, the law of co-determination there gives significant importance to worker committees within a company on issues relating to reduction of the work force, plant closings and new methods of production where there would be a notable impact on the personnel of the firm.

Permissive legislation for effective power to share in the management of a firm is at the minimum for workers in Italy and at the maximum in Germany. For the latter country, worker committees have a legal right of co-determination, within defined areas, involving the internal management of a firm, the organization of vocational training and decisions relating to basic changes in production.

With respect to worker participation in the economic and financial management of German firms, the specific legality of such a right was set forth in the law on co-management May 21, 1951, relating to coal and steel enterprises. For these industrial sectors the German legislature conferred rights to workers which no other government among the member countries recognizes in the domain of private industry, that is, the right of co-management of enterprise.

In other words, the German act of May 21, 1951, was not a mere expansion of power normally acknowledged for a worker committee, but actually a structural change in the stock corporation by placing worker representatives on a parity with others in electing members to the board of directors and in its control. The board of directors, by this law, also included a labor director exercising the same rights as other directors; in contrast to the law of July 8, 1956 (for other types of companies) he cannot be elected without the majority vote of the six worker delegates on the board of supervisors.

In such fashion it has been said that in Germany the trend to worker participation associates itself with the movement for reform of corporate law, with the ultimate intention of transforming an institution which is an instrument of modern capitalism into a tool for the control of wealth.[16] There is little indication that this control of wealth has actually taken place.

It must be pointed out that for the most part the powers granted to the worker representatives in a firm are consultative in nature. Yet rather frequently on strictly social issues concerning the worker directly, their representatives have a right of co-decision, and, at least in Germany, even economic issues can be involved. On issues where co-decision is allowed, quite apart from the Council of the Enterprise, workers have representation in policy-making committees of the firms. As one instance, worker representatives in the member countries possess a decisive power to assure that management of social funds will be to the advantage of the company's personnel.[17]

Note should be taken here of the wary attitude of labor unions toward worker representation programs within a firm. The scope of activity of plant worker committees actually covers very similar claims for power being made by European labor unions. Accordingly, action taken by worker representatives within companies constitutes, in practice, an element of competition for the general policy of unions. As a tactical measure, in recent years, unions have sought to establish close-working relationships, both in law and in fact, between programs for worker representation and trade unions. It is acknowledged that because of this circumstance there is a certain degree of risk that employers who have given their support to worker committee programs may seek to remove trade union influence within their enterprises. The degree of influence which unions have been able to exert within a firm varies according to country. It is especially strong in Belgium and in France, where unions dominate the choosing of candidates.[18]

In almost all member countries, labor unions (as distinct from worker representative plans) tend to be organized on a multi-company base; the employer of course, negotiates in collective bargaining from his own unitary base. Still, employers in every industry are generally members of an organization responsible for dealing with a specific list of industrial problems. This situation does not deny that employers are also members of special associations corresponding to diverse orders of interest. However, such employer associations are not used for collective bargaining with unions, except in The Netherlands. By way of contrast, trade unions in every country of the Community—with qualification in Germany—are organized along ideological, political or religious beliefs.

The percentage of all workers in trade unions varies considerably from one country to another. It has been estimated that the proportion is 40 to 50 per cent for Germany, 60 per cent for Belgium, 15 per cent for France, 30 per cent for Luxembourg and 40 per cent for The Netherlands. While trade unions in Italy make a claim of membership equal to 80 per cent of the Italian work force, the claim is regarded as exaggerated.[19]

Caution has been expressed that the percentage of union membership should not be confused with the effective power exerted by union organizations. In actuality, while unions may have a thinner penetration in terms of membership on the national and inter-occupational level, they may be strongly represented in the worker committees for a single firm or even for a particular industry and thus exercise decisive influence. But it cannot be overlooked that the division of effective forces among divergent union movements in Europe tends to weaken union power.

One of the characteristics of European unions in common with

American industrial unions is the organization of workers by particular industry rather than by trade. Accordingly, workers engaged in the metalworking industry, if they are unionized, are affiliated with the metalworking union, regardless of what actual calling they may pursue in a given firm.

COLLECTIVE AGREEMENTS

In the estimation of the research group of scholars appointed by the High Authority to study labor law in the member countries, the development of national legislation to safeguard contracts of employment has been one of the most remarkable trends in modern jurisprudence. Stability of employment has become a basic concept of labor law in the legislation of certain countries. Such a tendency was almost unknown at the beginning of the nineteenth century. Utilization of a contract with a determined duration had been restricted by the circumstances which prevented a wage earner from hiring out for his life time or even for a long period of years.

In the past, therefore, in the rare cases of contracts with a fixed date of expiration, they had been set for only a short period. For the most part labor contracts formerly were of indeterminant expiration and could be cancelled unilaterally at the instigation of either party. But, on occasion advance notice was a consideration extended to the individual who would suffer from the termination of the contract.

Almost imperceptibly a trend developed, with growing industrialization, which has brought about a notable change in the labor contract. A basic factor behind this transition has been an endeavor to assure to workers greater protection against both instability of employment and uncertainty of livelihood. No longer does the concept prevail that labor is an article of commerce, devoid of other considerations. Instead it is recognized that the life of the worker, as well as of his family, depends on a stable work relationship.

In the contemporary scene, as contrasted with the nineteenth century, stable employment is regarded as one of the facets of the broad concern for protection, of which social security is the most striking manifestation. Accordingly, prevalent regulations now safeguarding workers against the hazard of sudden cancellation of their labor contracts do have a relationship with the public recognition given to institutions of social security. In one sense the regard for employment stability has added a new characteristic to the labor contract in some countries, differentiating it from other contractual relationships where both parties are mutually bound to respect the obligations incurred.[20]

Thus, in certain nations, stress on continuous employment has introduced a unilateral aspect to the contract in that workers may be better protected against the hazard of a cancelled work agreement than is the employer.

Again, in the nineteenth century, the juridical status of different types of employment relationships were clearly demarcated one from the other. Thus regulations for laborers notably differed from contracts for civil servants. However, it has been found in contemporary society that developments in different types of occupational activity exert reciprocal influences. Now between both public and private employment, and through an almost imperceptible transition, the private law of labor has taken on a public character. By association with enterprise carried on by moral persons under public law, such as the government corporation, labor law in general has assumed characteristics giving effective assurance to stability of employment, a phenomenon once unique to civil servants.

As the Belgian study indicated, all the demands relating to stability of employment now being made in contract negotiations in behalf of workers in private employment can be traced in large part to the employment advantages long conceded to public employees, such as no discharge except for grave reason, very infrequent layoffs, sick pay and disability pensions.

A third factor which has had considerable impact on employment status has been the intervention of the State on a more active scale in matters of social and economic organization. It was especially during the two world wars and the intervening period of depression that public measures were enacted for the economy. In a number of countries where the State continues to have a controlling influence over economic life certain manifestations from this highly active period of government intervention still remain. Since employment constitutes one of the basic concerns of economic policy, the State has not been in a position to ignore the consequences of changes in the current status of the labor contract.

Another consideration relating to greater State intervention is the wider concept given now to the meaning of social order. In the nineteenth century a business firm was regarded as a purely private institution. However, today there is a tendency, even by corporation presidents themselves, to consider a private company as charged in an important degree with social responsibility since private firms are employers of manpower. An additional factor conducive to more State intervention in labor matters has been the demand for government protection by officials in militant trade union locals and by employee representatives on plant committees who may face greater risk in their employment than members of the rank and file.

Manifestations in the member countries of the modern concern for stability of employment is apparent in all phases of labor jurisprudence. It is found in social legislation, collective bargaining agreements, plant practice, court decisions and arbitration awards. The main thrust of this phenomenon is to prevent the cessation of the employment relationship. However, if the termination cannot be prevented, effort is then devoted to making reparation for the losses incurred from the breaking of the contract.[21]

It was the conclusion from the comparative study of labor law in the member countries by the research group appointed by the High Authority, that the instinctive drive for economic security is a dominant force in the domain of employment today. Old common law solutions to problems of employment have been discarded whenever they were found to be in conflict with this desire for security and new rules have been fashioned stressing the special character of labor law.

These developments, through modern labor law, have provided wage earners with unquestioned advantages, such as provisions against the breaking of the labor contract, the maintenance of wage income on certain occasions when work is interrupted and assurance of reinstatement upon its resumption. In the face of these transformations of the worker's status, Paul Durand, in his summary report, observes that in some countries there is a right over employment apparent, if not a right to employment. The point was noted that some authors of the French school speak of proprietorship over the job. In German parlance reference is now made to the juridical aspects of the job, as is also the case among even Italian authors.

A not surprising consequence of the numerous regulations designed to assure stability of employment has been the obvious complexity of modern labor law, with frequent additional legal controversies. Paradoxically, the observation is made that these complex regulations assume the existence of legal specialists in the labor field with an unusual competence enabling them to apply a simpler, speedier and less costly procedure than is found in other jurisdictions.

Moreover, in the face of the growing obligations which weigh on the employer because of legal safeguards to assure stability of employment, one conclusion made by the research group was that maintenance of wage income at a time of work cessation might better be made the main responsibility of social security institutions rather than remain a charge on the individual employer under rules imposed by labor legislation. In this fashion the economic burden would no longer weigh so heavily on a particular enterprise, but would be diffused over a broader social segment.

The study group also took note of other difficulties from the contemporary social policy encouraging stability of employment. It was found that the initiative of management tends to be restricted since authority to act during a crisis may be compromised. There was the finding that stability of employment tends to bring into economic life an aspect of rigidity capable of constraining the economy. Even workers themselves may feel the consequences of a too rigid policy of stable employment inasmuch as the restraint on management may dissuade it from concluding a pending labor contract. The research study disclosed that for some member countries an overly rigid policy of employment stability had actually increased the risk of economic insecurity for workers.

Nevertheless, the study group did not regard these difficulties as beyond solution and noted that such complexities are inherent in the structure of contemporary industrial society. Because of the accepted policy of stable employment, the need for new progress on juridical techniques was stressed so that a synthesis could be achieved between two contrary aspirations; economic stability and flexibility in adaptation.

With these reservations, the research group believed more advances toward stable employment will continue in the member countries. It was observed that in the laws of most of the Six a number of employment hazards have not yet been resolved by legislation, such as virtually depriving certain workers of paid vacations by using such periods to give advance notice of employment termination. Older workers still remain vulnerable to layoffs though they have great difficulty in finding new employment.

Among the different member countries an unequal development in the legislation governing contractual relations between workers and employers was observed. In Italy notice of termination is set in a framework of considerable technicality. In another country stress is placed on legal controls over the use of layoffs. Laws in some countries give special protection to temporary employment. It was suggested that by comparative study of legal experience in the various countries, mutual enrichment might result in the general area of legislation regarding employment security.[22]

In any event the collective bargaining agreement is regarded as a source of labor law throughout the Community. With the exception of Italy where this circumstance remains of no practical importance, other nations have tended to incorporate various provisions set forth earlier in labor contracts into general legislation[23]

Usually the collective agreement has two categories of provisions. The normative area deals with the regulations of working conditions in the companies under the agreement. The other section, frequently regarded as the source of obligations, sets forth the relations between the negotiating parties, defining their rights and duties. It aims to assure the enforcement of the contract. To this end the parties are to refrain during the life of the contract from seeking to modify its provisions or from precipitating a strike. They are pledged to respect the provisions mutually agreed to in the contract. This division of the collective contract applies generally in the member countries, except in Belgium where such agreements actually emerge from decisions of national commissions composed equally of employer and union representatives and which concern only regulations of working conditions.

In terms of sources of labor law, the rules set forth in these agreements on working conditions and wages tend very often to become the norm for general application to all the employees in a firm, even though not members of the unions covered by the collective agreement. Further, in all the member countries the same standards in the agreement tend to be applied to other employers affiliated with the employer association which signed the agreements. Accordingly, workers in firms associated with the organizations which signed the collective agreements likewise are eligible in some degree for the resulting benefits and also are bound by the obligations involved.

But at times the extension of benefits arising from collective agreements have been restricted for workers who are not members of the unions signing the contracts. In Germany and Italy these workers are not legally entitled to such benefits. In practice this legal barrier has not always been effective. In France, Luxembourg and The Netherlands the collective agreement applies, though there are technical differences, to all workers of the contracting companies, whether union members or not.[24]

The obligatory nature of the collective agreement may be extended over a wider area than the original contract by an act of government. Such an action is called "extension" in France and "declaration of general obligation" in Germany, Luxembourg and The Netherlands. In effect such a legal extension applies the standards of a collective agreement to a whole group of companies on the national or regional level. By the same token, government authority may refuse to grant such a requested extension and may also retract one already authorized.[25]

Collective agreements may be concluded directly between organizations of workers and employers, or through the intervention of a commission composed equally of employer and worker representatives. In Germany and Italy direct negotiation by the parties prevails. The same procedure holds true in France for routine agreements. However, in the case of contracts which are subject to extension of coverage by the State, they must be negotiated through the offices of a temporary commission, composed of employer, union and public representatives, appointed by the minister of labor.

In other countries there is also this recourse to outside commissions. For instance, in Belgium, by law, there has been set up a network of commissions made up of employer and union representatives for all types of industry and business. Their principal task is to negotiate collective agreements for the greater part of Belgian industry. Luxembourg also follows this procedure.

In The Netherlands all collective bargaining agreements must be submitted for approval to the College of State Conciliators. In turn for every issue of general significance the College of State Conciliators must take its guidance from the Foundation of Labor made up of employer and union representatives. Until recently, practically all collective agreements had to be submitted to the Foundation of Labor before being approved by the College of Conciliators.[26]

Resort has been made by the parties themselves to joint commissions representing employers and workers for the purpose of maintaining inspection over the application of collective agreements. At times the State has instituted such permanent bodies in order to prevent or resolve disputes arising over the application of a contract. If this recourse fails or is lacking, the judiciary normally resolves such issues.

Grievances may be filed concerning the application of the regulatory provisions on working conditions by any person eligible to benefit from such a contract and adversely affected from lack of its enforcement in his own job relationship.

For such an individual grievance, the union representing the worker is not permitted to act in behalf of the claimant, as in the United States, except in France and The Netherlands. Instead, a claim by an aggrieved employee seeks the enforcement of his own individual contract in accordance with the terms of the collective agreement, even by the awarding of damages if there has been a monetary loss. Should the matter not be resolved in the early stages, recourse ultimately may be had to a board of arbitration in France, Belgium and Luxembourg, or to a labor tribunal in Germany, or to the regular courts in Italy and The Netherlands.

With respect to grievances relating to obligations assumed directly by the negotiating parties to a union-management agreement, there even could be a request for dissolution of the agreement. In actuality, judicial sanctions against a signatory to a collective labor agreement have proved illusory. Statutory basis for bringing a case to court may be lacking. In practice, therefore, procedures of conciliation and arbitration have more significance than use of the courts when there is a dispute involving the principals in a collective agreement.[27]

COLLECTIVE CONFLICTS

From the special study sponsored by the European Coal and Steel Community on the legal aspects of the strike in the member countries, it is evident that governments since the nineteenth century have banned, then permitted, and finally regulated these acts of resistance by unions or workers. However, the research group found that the definition itself of the strike differs for various countries both in the legal measures once forbidding it and in the present laws recognizing its legality.

At times parallel treatment is given both the strike and the lockout in the legislation of the member countries. Yet the French Constitution of 1946 and the Italian Constitution both affirm the right to strike, but are silent in regard to the lockout. In effect, legal doctrine in both France and Italy makes a basic distinction between the concept of the strike and that of the lockout. In Germany there are also certain legal differences in the use of these two weapons of conflict.

In the relatively brief history of the right to strike, it is obvious that what was once prohibited by penal codes and other legislation over a century ago—especially collective action by workers—was rendered licit by abrogatory legislation in the second half of the nineteenth century. Nevertheless, it would be too precipitate to say that the mere abrogation of previous laws in itself established the legal right to strike, since the immediate result was only the removal of criminal sanctions. Not until later did constitutional amendments and special legislation actually establish the right to strike.

There is not much to be said on the lockout since legislation and court decisions seldom concern this alternative for the employer. It has been seldom used by management in the member countries of the Community.[28]

Upon examination of laws, the research group, comprised of legal authorities in each of the Six, found that in the early nineteenth century voluntary participation in a strike constituted a crime in every member country. During the first years of the twentieth century and later, the acts of a strike, regarded in themselves, ceased to be punishable by law. From then on the strike constituted a licit option which workers could elect at their own risk. In other words, they could be subject to damage suits, loss of employment or the hazard of losing some of their social security benefits. For the most part courts at that time regarded the voluntary participation in a strike as inconsistent with observance of a labor contract.

Actually it required a development of 30 to 40 years before the right to strike was recognized as a choice for workers, the normal exercise of which would not subject them to damage suits or to job discrimination. The result now intended is that the worker should sustain as little injury as possible as a consequence of voluntary participation in a strike.

Obviously he loses the right to wages during the period. The courts in France and Italy now interpret their constitutions to hold that under normal conditions a strike does not connote a violation of a contract; accordingly, the striker is no longer liable to suits for damages, nor does he break his labor contract and enable the employer to cancel the work relationship. However, in Luxembourg the legal innocence of the striker is secondary to the preliminary obligation of submitting the dispute to conciliation.[29]

Though the right to strike is not recognized formally in the Constitution of West Germany, it is generally admitted that such a right follows from the spirit of liberty and democracy inherent in the Federal Republic. Accordingly, in Germany the assumption of the right to strike has resulted in the same practical effects as in France and Italy. It must not be overlooked that security of employment for the strikers may be jeopardized by the recognition of the right of employers in Germany to declare a defensive lockout which in effect cancels individual labor contracts without indemnity.

The finding for Belgium by the research group of jurists indicates that from 1950 to 1960 the courts have been more disposed than formerly to acknowledge that a strike simply suspends the labor contract, but does not break it.

By contrast, in member countries where the right to strike is expressly recognized, this acknowledgement is supplemented by a rule of jurisprudence, including at times a limitation on the use of the strike or the methods involved. Thus the political strike is outside the category of licit acts.

Benefits due victims of industrial accidents or diseases generally are not reduced in the interval of a strike with respect to social security payments, family allowances and paid vacations. Note must be taken of the many legal rulings in Belgium during the 1950's designed to prevent strike periods from reducing the amount of these social benefits. Rulings of this nature scarcely are found in other member countries. Nevertheless, in France the right to family allowance is not weakened by the fact of a strike. The same is true in Germany, and in Italy for sickness and invalidity benefits.

Interestingly enough, in France and Italy the lockout, even of the defensive type, is regarded as an illicit breaking of the labor contract and is subject to damages.

In The Netherlands, strikes since World War II are so rare that there has been little need of legislative controls. Nevertheless, some authorities in industrial relations there urge the legal recognition of the right to strike and regulation of its exercise.

The research group of jurists found that in the member countries it is generally conceded that the strike has an ethical value because it postulates a hardship at times severe on workers—loss of wages in order to obtain an improvement in working conditions. It was the conclusion of the research study that in all the member countries the practical option of the strike actually existed, though with certain limitations.[30]

Examining the nature of the strike more closely in the member countries of the Community, two types of general issues have been discerned. One is called the juridical strike and the other the economic strike. The first relates to a conflict over a right and the second over an interest. The juridical dispute bears on the. application or interpretation of a right already existent in a provision of the collective contract. The economic dispute arises from an effort to establish provisions bearing on new rights not yet recognized in a labor contract.

Because the juridical dispute pertains to a right based on a contract, it lends itself to determination by judicial authority, such as a judge or arbitrator. However, the economic dispute does not rest on purely juridical factors, but on an uncertain complex of elements embracing economic, technical and sociological aspects. Accordingly, for a solution, equity requires a settlement based on compromise by some mutually acceptable procedure. It is true that at times there is even a mixture of both types of disputes in a particular conflict.

In any event, whatever the type of dispute and whatever the procedure best suited to resolve it, the efficacy of the approach is largely dependent on the good will shown by the parties involved. In the member nations it has been found that most ready acceptance has been given to voluntary procedures rather than to those imposed by the State, such as compulsory arbitration.[31]

Just as in the United States, the amicable procedures prevalent in the member countries of the Community for the settlement of industrial disputes are conciliation, mediation and voluntary arbitration. Conciliation means the parties themselves, frequently with a neutral party serving as chairman, seek to find a formula conducive to a compromise. No compulsory force is attached to acceptance of such a compromise.

Use of conciliation is optional in Germany for economic disputes and for juridical issues, providing that the parties refrain from use of the courts or arbitration. Voluntary concilation is also known in Belgium, Italy and The Netherlands. In the latter country its use is restricted because of controls over labor contracts exercised by government boards such as the Foundation of Labor. Compulsory conciliation is found in France and Luxembourg, but the parties are not bound to accept the compromise which may result.[32]

Mediation generally connotes exercise of initiative by a neutral third party in proposing solutions to the parties. In addition, he serves as an intermediary when the adversaries are separately convened. Legally established mediation has been very successful in France as a means of presenting recommendations to the parties for settlement of their disputes.[33] The legislature has not only given vast powers of investigation to the mediator, but the parties may be obliged to seek mediation at the request of the government where conciliation has failed. But the recommendation of the mediator is not binding unless the parties first agree to accept it.

As contrasted with compulsory arbitration, under voluntary arbitration the parties freely agree to entrust to an arbitrator of their choice the responsibility of resolving a dispute. Nevertheless, it is acknowledged in the member countries, as in the United States, that the decision of the arbitrator will be binding on the parties. Voluntary arbitration operates in Germany, France, Luxembourg and The Netherlands. It is virtually non-existent in Belgium and Italy.

Though in most member countries of the Community voluntary measures of some type are utilized exclusively for settling industrial disputes, Germany is the exception; the legislature has established the jurisdiction of labor courts to resolve labor disputes of a juridical nature, at least those which the parties have not agreed to submit to voluntary arbitration. The other member nations have avoided the institution of both labor courts and compulsory arbitration to interpret labor contracts.[34]

COLLABORATION ABOVE THE LEVEL OF THE FIRM

Wherever public authorities generally tend to intervene on matters of industrial relations there is usually found a union-management commission with official status from a particular industry or occupation. In Germany, France and Italy matters of industrial relations are almost exclusively the concern of employer and worker organizations; thus, no government-sponsored joint commissions exist in those countries. However, in Belgium a firmly established system functions at the occupational level composed of union-management commissions and concerns itself with questions of industrial relations or social issues. There are other occupational councils for strictly economic problems.

The joint commissions in Belgium are made up in equal numbers of management and worker representatives with a government official as chairman. These commissions have authority both to make decisions and present opinions in the social field. One of their important functions is to set down basic criteria for wage rates by actually negotiating collective agreements and by preventing or reconciling disputes between management and workers. Another function is to aid the government in drafting and enforcing social legislation relating to particular industries. About 80 such joint commissions extend over the greater part of the industrial, business and agricultural sectors of the Belgian economy.

The occupational councils for strictly economic issues exercise an exclusively consultative role. They are authorized to present government officials with all opinions or proposals bearing on economic problems from the occupation they represent. Four such councils in Belgium were functioning in 1962.

In Luxembourg the National Office of Conciliation exercises a role similar to that of the joint commissions in Belgium. It is likewise equally composed of representatives from employers and workers.

There are a number of different industries in The Netherlands where strictly private joint commissions of employer and worker representatives maintain collaboration for studying socio-economic problems. Besides such private conferences, there exist other worker-management organizations in The Netherlands which have public sponsorship. One category relates to industries and another to particular types of products. In the first group are joint organizations on a horizontal basis, that is, for firms carrying on the same type of activity. They may exercise regulatory power, especially on issues of wages and working conditions. The second group, based on a vertical structure, or including all the stages of production, has worker-management representation from firms producing the same type of product.

While such representative organizations have actually gained acceptance in agricultural and business sectors, they have made little headway in industrial areas because of the reluctance on the part of militant union and employer groups to submit to the regulatory power of such government sponsored organizations.[35]

Yet on the national economic level the only country in the Community which has no organization of a general character for worker-management collaboration is Germany. Certain states of the Federal Republic, however, have set up such joint commissions. German unions have favored the creation of a national body by legislative action. Management has been in opposition to the proposal. With the exception of The Netherlands, national organizations of this broad character have only consultative status.

In Belgium there is a distinct consultative body at the national level for social issues, the National Council of Labor. Another national organization deals with economic questions, the Central Council of the Economy. Both organizations are empowered either on their own initiative or upon request to present to a government agency or to the legislature an opinion or proposal which bears on particular issues of the social order or of the economy.

In Luxembourg there are similar organizations at the national level. For the economic sphere one finds the National Economic Council and for social problems there is the National Conference of Labor.

The official advisor for the French government on both types of problems is the Economic and Social Council. It is the duty of the French government to consult this body concerning legislative bills and proposals of an economic or social nature.

The corresponding body in Italy, the National Council of the Economy and of Labor, is also empowered to exercise the right of initiative in legislative matters. With certain reservations it may present drafts of bills to the Italian parliament on matters relating to the economy and to labor.

Of the countries of the Community it appears that The Netherlands alone has given its Economic and Social Council both consultative and regulatory status. For that country, consultation of the Council is obligatory for all significant government proposals of an economic and social character. Nevertheless, there is the provision that such consultation is unnecessary if the government believes it would not be in the public interest. The regulatory function of the Dutch Economic and Social Council pertains to its collaboration with the government in the enforcement of certain regulations by means of ordinances.[36]

Reviewing developments of the social situation for 1963, the EEC Commission has observed that joint examination and discussion of social demands by employer and worker representatives, with direct or indirect government participation, has tended to take on a somewhat organic character in the member countries. It noted that the Foundation of Labor in The Netherlands, concerned with collective bargaining contracts, has long been an established institution. The Commission found that in Belgium the Economic and Social Council, under a very supple arrangement, is taking part in efforts to bring about a new policy on social programs. A similar development is taking place in France for the social field. The Commission noted that even in Germany, in 1963, employers and workers have welcomed the federal establishment of a committee of experts to analyze general economic development.

It is the belief of the Commission that the creation and maturity of the Economic Community, and, in particular, the formation of a common program of policy for the Six has deepened the inclination of the parties in industrial relations to examine objectively their positions on what is needed for economic expansion and distribution of optimum income. Also the Commission has observed that the form and procedure for association of the two parties in formulating objective economic policy for the Economic Community has been a subject of study by the European Parliament and by the Economic and Social Committee.

Worker organizations have declared that the pursuit of objective policy by the Community would have ended in failure if participation by union representatives had not been assured at every step of the procedure.

Nevertheless, the EEC Commission cautions that it would be unwarranted to assume that this desire for objective joint discussion by the parties in industrial relations has brought about a basic change in employer-worker relationships. The winning of particular advantages by unions through collective bargaining, such as the check-off for union dues, or success in various claims for recognition, has not changed the economic system.

Despite national joint committees, employers and workers hold to their agreements to recognize and defend their own autonomy on collective bargaining. Under this principle they continue to establish wage rates and other working conditions in accordance with their relative bargaining strength as made known under free negotiation. The Commission does not overlook the serious labor strife which took place during 1963 in several major countries of the Community. Nevertheless, recent collective bargaining agreements have brought appreciable advantages to workers in spite of the higher cost of living.[37]

In the opinion of the Commission, Dutch experience has shown that discussion of issues within a general economic framework by the permanent organizations for collaboration among government, employer and worker representatives has not impaired the growth of responsibility and freedom of decisions in negotiations. It is interesting that The Netherlands in 1962 formally abandoned its previous regulatory policy on wage determination and modified its position anew in 1963. Here the objective has been to leave the negotiating parties broader powers so that they might have greater flexibility in adjusting to conditions in other member countries.

In the Community it appears that the industrial parties have endeavored to assume an adjustment in wage income which the differences in cost of living and working conditions would justify. Here the Commission ruefully notes, however, that one may argue on the global sphere that wage differences tend to push workers toward the most productive types of employment. Nevertheless the Commission finds that wage structures remain fairly rigid. While each wage category tends to improve its position, success in that endeavor may be only temporary, since other wage groups will then strive to reestablish their former parities.[38]

Recently the Free Trade Unions of the Community have published a Program for Joint Action on the part of European trade unions to advance a free and progressive Europe, with particular bearing on the economic and social development of the member countries. In the declaration were included concrete demands for action which aimed to gain an improved standard of living within each nation. Among the goals set forth is a policy of full employment and long-term planning to assure steady economic growth. Reference is made to "Democratization of the Economy" by participation of union representatives on a parity with management in the resolving of economic and socio-political issues. It is planned to seek acceptance of these goals both at the national and community levels.

Among the concrete demands made by the Trade Unions are reduction of the work week to a maximum of 40 hours and five days, increase of paid vacations to four weeks with supplementary vacation bonus, and a guaranteed income in the event of disability so as to maintain a reasonable standard of living.

According to the president of the executive committee of the Free Trade Unions, Ludwig Rosenberg, particular modes of procedure to achieve these common goals will be left to the discretion of the unions themselves. Rosenberg intimated at the time of the declaration that not all the demands it contained could be won immediately or simultaneously. The economic situation in a particular member country would determine relative priority.[39]

SOME RELEVANT AMERICAN ASPECTS

The wide development of worker representation plans in the Common Market recalls the history of the movement in the United States during the 1920's and early 1930's. It seems that the American model gave far less independent scope for action than the current programs in Europe. For the most part they were known in America as company unions and their primary purpose was to prevent independent outside unions from gaining members in a given plant. Company domination of these organizations was so widespread that under the National Labor Relations Act of 1935 it became an unfair practice for an employer to give support to this type of worker representation.[40] After 1935, in large numbers, they were supplanted or transformed into locals affiliated with a national union.

It is interesting to note that usually in the European worker representation plans members of national unions actually have considerable influence which is officially recognized. Nevertheless, it is obvious that the regular unions in Europe only appear to tolerate the worker representative plans and would prefer to replace them with union locals having national affiliation.

The desire to participate in management decisions on the part of worker organizations in Europe finds, it would seem, little accord with the view of American unions. In general, union policy here is to let management make its own economic decisions and then the unions negotiate vigorously for adjustments to meet the demands of their members.

From the comparative estimates on union membership in the member countries of the Community, the percentage of 22 per cent of the labor force as members of unions in the United States appears less than proportionate to the European ratio. It should be noted, however, that union membership for 1963 in relation to nonagricultural employment in the United States was 30 per cent.[41]

It is likely, however, that collective bargaining contracts are more significant in their application and content in the United States than in the Common Market. For many years the labor contract has been the principal means here for attaining better terms for workers. In 1961 it was estimated that 150,000 collective bargaining agreements were in force in the United States, covering over 16 million union members.[42] Since World War II, in Europe, the belief among union officials has been gaining strength that more dynamic gains can be won for workers through collective bargaining contracts than by slower, diverse and more cumbersome social legislation. For both the countries of the Common Market and the United States, union negotiations have in common the overall concern for stability of employment.

There is a close parallel between Europe and this country in the legal history of the strike. In the early nineteenth century the use of this extreme measure was regarded as a criminal conspiracy. Today recognition of its legality, under regulation, is given both in the United States and Europe. There seems to be more tolerance in Europe, however, toward allowing the use of a strike during an existing contract. It is accepted practice here for unions to regard the terms of a contract as binding until its expiration. Moreover, the express provision that there will be no strike during the life of the contract is often part of the terms of settlement.

Very likely the use of voluntary arbitration for resolving disputes arising over the interpretation of collective bargaining agreements is much more widespread in the United States than in the member countries. Over 90 per cent of the collective agreements in the basic industries of this country provide for voluntary arbitration as the ultimate point of the grievance process.[43]

It is beyond particular union-company relationships that a marked difference in industrial relations can be found between this country and the member nations of the Community. Use of joint union-management commissions on an official basis for consultative or regulatory purposes is seldom found in this country in time of peace. In time of war we have had such a body as the National War Labor Board with employer, union and public representation. Its purpose was to control increase of wage rates and other benefits and to settle disputes without work stoppages as much as possible. A similar agency, the National Wage Stabilization Board, was authorized for the period of the Korean conflict. Nevertheless, once the pressure of a war emergency is removed the negotiating parties in the United States prefer unrestricted collective bargaining, with some possible regard for guidelines suggested by Washington.

Little use has been made of joint union-management commissions for consultative purposes in the United States. For the most part there is the tendency by the parties in industry to exert their own pressures on government departments and legislatures directly. Moreover, the respective opinions by unions and management on national issues are often quite at variance with each other. Realistically, it might appear beneficial to the country for both employers and union groups to consider the possibility of establishing regular national and regional joint bodies as a consultative aid to government.

11.

Survey and Projection

IN TAKING FINAL NOTE HERE OF THE LABOR PROGRAMS WHICH are being promoted by the Common Market the point should be made that it was again emphasized by its Commission in 1965 that vocational training and upgrading are the most efficient methods for attaining an improved balance in the work force.[1] To this end the Commission observed that in 1964 the member states had made further advances toward revamping vocational training and upgrading to meet modern industrial requirements. As part of this approach, new teaching methods and new equipment are undergoing trials in the member countries. Retraining programs are now available for teachers. Financial outlays for vocational training have been constantly increasing in the Six, and there has been a greater tendency by some of the member governments to assume certain expenses for these programs which formerly were met by families or local organizations. One might cite here the provision of scholarships, travel expenses and even subsidies for private schools.[2] Unfortunately the Commission finds that despite these efforts to modernize, there is still no general agreement among the Six on legislation for technical training and apprenticeships.

A main factor which has shaped the conviction that vocational training is the nexus for economic expansion in the Community, centers on the growing demand by industry for a more highly qualified work force. Other factors include the unsteady supply of foreign manpower, mostly unskilled, and an expected older age for children leaving school in the near future.

With respect to Italy, a major handicap at present blocking the use of its excess manpower to meet critical shortages in other member states is the absence of sufficient vocational training. To counteract the shortage of some types of skilled workers, the Commission in 1964 proposed to the Council of Ministers that a joint high priority training program should be enacted.[3]

Deeply concerned over the critical shortage of manpower, the European Community noted that the very low rate of unemployment had declined again in 1964, except for Italy where the percentage rose to 4.2 per cent as against 3.9 per cent in 1963. This upturn in unemployment was the first such regression during recent years in the reabsorption of Italy's excess manpower. Elsewhere in the Community shortages in the labor market remained acute, particularly in Germany and the Benelux countries. A survey in 1965 indicated that in France the unemployment rate was two per cent and in Germany 0.6 of 1 per cent, where only 169,000 persons were officially listed as unemployed and where there were 700,000 job vacancies. Despite efforts to encourage free movement of workers among the Six and the relatively high unemployment of 4.2 per cent in Italy, the net outward movement of Italian manpower has stabilized at a low level while immigration from non-member countries is rising rapidly. In addition to a chronic lack of skills, the large percentage of workers who return to Italy also accounts for the small net outflow of manpower from Italy.[4]

It is still hoped, nevertheless, that through improvement in procedures for balancing supply with demand in the labor market and through greater cooperation by the labor departments in Italy and other countries, unemployment in Italy could be reduced and manpower shortages in other States of the Community could be eased. There is need generally for a more consistent employment policy at the Community level to encourage freer movement of workers within the Six and to lessen the growing competition for foreign workers by member countries.

With an overall population in the Community of 181.7 million at the end of 1964, the employed work force had only increased that year to 73.2 million, from 72.9 million in 1963. In terms of the total population the work force of somewhat over 41 per cent showed a slight decline as compared to 1963.[5]

During 1964, the member countries continued to put new regulations on industrial health and safety in effect which conformed to scientific and technological advances. Fortunately the special provisions in the laws of the individual member states, though adapted to the circumstances of the particular countries, generally followed standard trends and were in harmony with Community policy. Instances of such parallel action on safety regulations were evident in rulings on the handling of dangerous products and in the establishment of health and safety services in industrial plants.[6]

It was also found that monetary wages had risen considerably during 1964 but in terms of real wages these had been somewhat offset because of higher consumer prices. The effect on real wages varied to quite an extent among the different member countries. Nevertheless, there was a certain tendency toward harmonization of the wage pattern among the Six, since the greatest wage increases took place in the countries where wage rates were lowest. Furthermore, countries with the smallest family allowances received the most favorable adjustments for large families.[7]

Between the end of 1963 and the end of 1964, fixed hourly wage rates increased by approximately 8 per cent in Germany, 11 per cent in Belgium, but by 17 and 19 per cent respectively in such lower wage paying countries as Italy and The Netherlands. In France the gain in negotiated wage rates was less than attained in Belgium and Germany.

In terms of actual gross hourly earnings for industrial workers in 1964, the rate of increase was greater than for negotiated hourly wage rates. Between the fall of 1963 and the fall of 1964 gross hourly rates rose by 11 per cent in Germany and by 6.5 per cent in France. For Italy and The Netherlands, the increases in gross hourly earnings were 11 per cent and 16 per cent. For the high wage paying country of Luxembourg, the increase was only 5 per cent. Apart from increases in direct wage costs, total labor costs mounted still higher in about all member countries, due to greater employer contributions for social security, larger vacation allowances and longer vacation periods.[8]

Several of the member states in 1964 put new provisions for social security in effect, including some notable reforms requiring new legislation. In this direction, Belgium extended health insurance coverage to self-employed persons and in Luxembourg members of the professions were placed under the pension program the same as other

self-employed persons. New laws in Luxembourg and The Netherlands now assure a "social minimum" income, that is, more than
enough for sustenance, to all elderly persons. A draft for such a
minimum is under consideration in Italy.[9]

Satisfaction was expressed by the Commission on the practical
impact in 1964 of Community regulations on social security for migrant workers. For that year it was estimated that some two million people, including employed or pensioned migrant workers and
their dependents, received social security benefits because of special
Community regulations.[10]

In 1964 the Commission for the European Economic Community
found that lack of housing persisted as an obstacle to the prolonged
employment of workers outside their native countries. Frequently such
workers have returned home, and thus reduced the net total of emigration, because inadequate housing facilities prevented families from
joining wage earners working abroad.

Nevertheless, there was a notable increase in the number of homes
completed in the Community during 1964, estimated at 1,587,000 as
compared to 1,448,000 in 1963.[11] Record volume of construction
took place in Germany, France, Italy and The Netherlands. A complicating factor resulting from greater housing construction is the
growing difficulty in obtaining sufficient land areas to launch housing
projects of any magnitude near expanding urban regions. Municipal
ownership of such land is now being proposed. Another difficulty
experienced in 1964 was the unavailability of workers in the building
trades for new projects because of the great volume of housing construction. To a certain degree this problem has been met by greater
use of prefabricated materials.[12] During 1964 the rent index, maintained in four member countries, continued to advance and was
accompanied by an unappeased demand for minimum housing accommodations for low-income families.

Though Community legislation in effect bans any discrimination in
housing to the disadvantage of workers from another member country, it has not removed the problem of finding acceptable housing for
such workers and their families. Emphasis was given to this situation
by the Commission in its recommendation of July 7, 1965, to the
member states.[13]

Out of regard for harmonious development of regional labor programs, in 1964 the Commission saw the need for caution so as not
to encourage a heavy departure of manpower from a given area to
the extent that some regions may be left with an abnormally high per-

centage of senior citizens. Instances of such imbalances in age groups have led in some cases to the abandonment of entire villages and to industrial and urban density elsewhere.[14] To prevent such regional disharmony the Commission has recommended to the Council that more weight be put on coordination of assistance from the European Investment Bank and the Social Fund, in order to create new employment in depressed areas and thus reduce the differences in economic development between regions.[15]

In the field of industrial relations the EEC noted in 1964 that for some years advisory committees, composed of representatives from management and unions, have been established for such matters as the free movement of workers and vocational training. Moreover, study groups of a similar composition have been occupied with various labor problems mentioned in Article 118 of the Treaty of Rome, such as employment, labor legislation, working conditions, social security, industrial health and safety and collective bargaining.[16] In this connection the Commission has endeavored to encourage both management and workers to approach these problems on a European level and thus foster a more democratic structure throughout the Six. To achieve this objective, however, the Commission is aware that there must also be active cooperation by governments, employer associations, unions and various institutions of the Community itself such as the Council, the European Parliament and the Economic and Social Committee.[17] In this fashion the Commission hopes that exchange of ideas, expressed along clearly defined points of view, will serve to maintain a steady advance in the living and working conditions of the countries in the Six, the basic aim of Article 2.[18]

In 1964, the Commission saw continuation of the progress of recent years in keeping labor relations abreast of the objectives for the Community's overall economy. Furthermore there has been a growing awareness and response in the Six to industrial development in neighboring countries. The Commission noted that Italy has now drafted its first economic plan, in cooperation with labor and management. In Germany, where central planning has been opposed, there has been instituted a committee of experts who analyze general economic developments; the first annual report was favorably received by both management and unions.

For the most part negotiations in 1964 between management and unions served to establish or renew collective bargaining contracts incorporating benefits already conceded in previous years. In addition the terms of these agreements included the widening of certain provisions which notably advanced the economic status of wage earners: equal pay for equal work of women and men, longer vacation periods with larger vacation allowances, and recognition of certain rights for unions within the industrial enterprise.

With respect to work stoppages the number of days lost in 1964 because of strikes was considerably below that of 1963 in Germany and France, and moderately lower in The Netherlands. Belgium and Italy showed some increase.[19]

Speaking generally of the Community's labor programs, Levi Sandri, vice-president of the EEC Commission, advocated on November 24, 1965, a more extensive use of the Community's supranational powers to establish a comprehensive labor policy. In his address before the European Parliament on that occasion he declared that eight years of experience thus far had clearly shown the advantage of the supranational method over dependence on inter-governmental cooperation as a means of improving working and living conditions. From this procedure as set forth in the Treaty of Rome, Sandri found there had been much better results than when action was left to joint cooperation by governments which often was fraught with decided shortcomings and disappointing returns.

In his address to the European Parliament, Sandri acknowledged that the Commission lacked precise legal powers under the Treaty to implement social policies. Moreover, he noted that the social objectives set forth in the Treaty were not clearly defined and presented a difficulty in practical application. Further, Sandri recalled the almost complete lack of funds available to the Commission for promoting social legislation.

Despite these handicaps, Sandri declared that the European Community's labor programs have steadily developed over the years and significant advances have been obtained particularly where the Treaty had set down time limits and binding regulations. In this regard, attention was called to accomplishments concerning the free movement of workers, social security for migrant workers and use of the European Social Fund. In addition Sandri pointed out that progress had been made relating to coordinating legislative and administrative procedures for the improvement of living and working conditions in the Six.

In effect Sandri concluded that the Commission's social policy for workers in the Community was already in action, within the framework of the Treaty, and was in accordance with the time limits there set forth.[20]

MEDIUM-TERM POLICY (1966–1970)

In line with a decision of the Commission relating to the action program for the Community's Second Stage, beginning in 1963,[21] the draft for a medium-term economic policy (1966–1970) was approved by the Comission in 1963 and later presented to the Council.[22] Included in this medium-term policy is the objective of implementing the aims of Article 117 on the improvement of the standard of living for workers.[23] To this end it is desired that more coordination be obtained in decision-making between national authorities and Community institutions, each of course within their own spheres of authority.

Public investment is one instance where coordination will be needed, according to the Commission. Here it was pointed out that European living conditions in 1970 will in large part depend on decisions made earlier on public investments for infrastructures relating to hospital facilities, schools, highways and urban development. Present methods of research are ample, in the view of the Commission, to assure the foresight which will prevent the formation of a society able to meet immediate personal needs, but ill-equipped to cope with demands for education, health and social services.

With this objective in mind in 1963 the Commission urged that a conference be called of those in the member states directly concerned with economic policy for the purpose of drafting a medium-term economic program for the Six. It was considered that such a policy would serve as a background for the member states and the Community institutions when arriving at major decisions bearing on the years 1966–1970. In effect a committee on medium-term economic policy was proposed. Through the Economic and Social Committee workers and employers would cooperate in drafting the medium-term program.[24]

By April, 1965, this Committee on Medium-Term Economic Policy, which was established in December, 1964, had completed four conference sessions.[25] Among the points of emphasis in its deliberations have been the study of structural economic policy by region and sector within the Community. It is already acknowledged that the advance of economic integration within the Six has had its impact on demand for goods and their production.

Included in the list of objectives the Committee has set down for study in relation to medium-term policy are trends in the labor market, employment conditions, standards for vocational training, and regional development.[26] Extensive changes are expected by 1970 in labor market and employment policy. Accordingly the Committee intends to examine all measures which show promise of raising the quality and quantity of future manpower.

Of particular concern to the Committee is the provision for economic decisions during 1966–1970 which will provide for lasting full employment and a well-balanced expansion. However, there is no intention of setting production and employment goals for the different industries of the Community.[27]

In preparation for drafting this medium-term program, studies have also been made relating to the social implications of future trends in wage and non-wage incomes, revenue and disbursements relating to social security and low-cost housing developments. Improvement in this category of housing has become so critical a need that the Commission foresees governments giving it a prominent place in administrative policy for both medium and long-term planning.[28]

In regional labor programs for the period 1966–1970 the Commission intends to stress a more coordinated employment policy at the Community level. For this purpose, in 1965 the Commission submitted to the Council proposals that greater consideration be given to the impact of European integration in order to facilitate coordination of financial aid from the Social Fund and the European Investment Bank for regional policies.[29] Also in this connection the Medium-Term Economic Policy Committee has requested information on trends in budget aggregates for the Six from 1960 to 1970 with respect to regional investments in social infrastructures.[30]

For the medium-term the Commission has expressed its intention to continue its duty of consultation with management and union organizations on the basic problems involved in applying the provisions in the Treaty, particularly on labor problems and matters of social security referred to in Article 118.

The Commission found equal interest expressed by both management and labor in the decision of the Council on April 15, 1965, to establish the Medium-Term Economic Policy Committee. In accordance with Treaty requirements provision was made to submit the program, when completed, to the Economic and Social Committee before its adoption by the Council. To keep informed on medium-term planning, the Economic and Social Committee has set up a small study group which includes employer and worker representatives.[31]

Commenting on the Council's earlier decision to prepare a tentative medium-term program in order to coordinate general economic policies of the member States, vice-president Levi Sandri of the EEC Commission believed it may have a significant effect on future labor programs. He declared it would set up a general framework within which both governmental and Community action must fit in matters of vocational training, employment, hours of work, wages and social security.[32]

The political crisis besetting the Common Market in 1965 delayed the final draft of the medium-term program.[33] It also held back ratification of the merger treaty signed by the member states in 1965. With the resolving of this crisis in January, 1966, one may expect the eventual fusion of the two executive bodies now functioning separately for the European Economic Community and the European Coal and Steel Community. A more radical development which may come to pass is the fusion of the treaties of Paris and Rome which in fact now serve as the foundations for the two Communities. It is possible that under such an arrangement the revenue raising provision in the Treaty of Paris may be sacrificed as well as the power of the European Coal and Steel Community's High Authority to draft and execute its own policies without prior approval by the Council. Should these advantages be taken away, much of the originality and direct action in social programs contributed by the Coal and Steel Community would be lost by the Six.

Undaunted by these possibilities, Levi Sandri, responsible for labor affairs in the EEC, urged (before the European Parliament in November, 1965) that instead of removing the independent revenue raising power enjoyed by the European Coal and Steel Community, a similar treaty provision should be accorded to the European Economic Community as well, and thus free the Commission for the Common Market from its present dependence for funds on the will of the Council.[34] With the recent ending of the French boycott of the Commission on terms favorable to France, it does not appear that the Common Market will obtain this financial independence in the near future.[35]

NOTES

CHAPTER 1: THE ADVISORY ORGANS OF THE COMMUNITIES

1. European Economic Community, *Treaty Establishing the European Economic Community* (Rome, 1957), p. 151.
2. *Ibid.*
3. *Ibid.*, p. 50; *ibid.*, p. 77.
4. *Ibid.*, p. 95; *ibid.*, pp. 114, 115.
5. Ibid., p. 63.
6. Michael Shanks and John Lambert, *The Common Market Today—and Tomorrow* (New York: Frederick A. Praeger, Inc., 1962), p. 51.
7. *Treaty Establishing the European Community, op. cit.*, pp. 113–115.
8. *Ibid.*, p. 113.
9. European Coal and Steel Community, *Treaty Establishing the European Coal and Steel Community* (Paris, 1951), p. 20.
10. Bernard D. Nossiter, *The Myth Makers* (Boston: Houghton Mifflin Company, 1964), p. 5.

CHAPTER 2: THE EUROPEAN SOCIAL FUND

1. European Economic Community, *Treaty Establishing the European Economic Community* (Rome, 1957), p. 116.
2. Leo Crijns, "The Social Policy of the Common Market" (Brussels, 1963), p. 9. (Xeroxed)
3. Michael Shanks and John Lambert. *The Common Market Today—And Tomorrow* (New York, Frederick A. Praeger, 1962), p. 105.

4. European Economic Community. *Treaty Establishing the European Economic Community, op. cit.,* p. 157.

5. Lionello Levi Sandri, Director General, Social Affairs, European Economic Community, "Premier Bilan Du Fonds Social Européen" (Brussels, V/6043 /1963-F), p. 3. (Mimeographed)

6. Communauté Économique Européenne. *Règlement No. 9 Concernant Le Fonds Social Européen.* (Bruxelles, f/1960 gj), p. 16.

7. *Ibid.*

8. *Ibid.*

9. European Economic Community. *Sixth General Report of the Activities of the Community.* (Brussels, June, 1963), p. 179.

10. European Economic Community: *Treaty Establishing the European Economic Community, op. cit.,* p. 157.

11. European Economic Community. *Sixth General Report of the Activities of the Community, op. cit.,* p. 177.

12. *Ibid.,* p. 178

13. *Ibid.*

14. Lionello Levi Sandri, "Premier Bilan Du Fonds Social Européen," *op. cit.,* p. 1.

15. *Ibid.,* p. 2.

16. *Ibid.*

17. Treaty Establishing the European Economic Community, *op. cit.,* pp. 121–127.

18. Communauté Économique Européenne. "Le Fonds Social Européen," Bruxelles, le 21 Fevrier 1963, p. 3. (Mimeographed)

19. European Economic Community. *Sixth General Report of the Activities of the Community, op. cit.,* p. 179.

20. Communauté Économique Européenne. *Propositions De Reglements en Conseil Visant A Accroître L'Efficacité Des Interventions Du Fonds Social Européen* (Bruxelles, 27 Janvier, 1965), Annex I, p. 1. (Mimeographed)

21. *Ibid.,* Annex III, pp. 1–5.

22. Parlement Européen. *Rapport fait au nom de la Commission Sociale sur les Proposition de la Commission de la C.E.E. au Conseil* (Bruxelles, 14 Juin 1956), p. 1.

23. *Ibid.,* p. 2.

24. *Ibid.,* pp. 10, 11.

25. Lionello Levi Sandri "EEC Commission Proposes Widening Powers of Social Fund," *European Community* (Washington, March, 1965), p. 9.

CHAPTER 3: VOCATIONAL TRAINING AND RETRAINING

1. European Economic Community, Commission, *The First Stage of the Common Market*—Report on the Execution of the Treaty (January 1958–January 1962), (Brussels, 1962), p. 74.

2. Communaté Économique Européenne Commission, *Memorandum de la Commission sur le programme d'action de la Communauté pendant la deuxième étape* (Bruxelles, 1962), p. 54.

3. Communauté Économique Européenne, "Decision Du Conseil 2 Avril 1963

portant establissement des principes géneraux pour la mise en oeuvre d'une politique commune de formation professionnelle," p. 1. (Mimeographed)

4. European Economic Community. *Treaty Establishing the European Economic Community* (Rome, 1957), Article 128.

5. Communauté Économique Européenne Commission, *Exposé sur l'évolution de la situation sociale dans la Communauté en 1961* (Bruxelles, Juillet, 1962), p. 140.

6. Leo Crijns, "The Social Policy of the Common Market" (Brussels, 1963), p. 12. (Xeroxed)

7. Communauté Économique Européenne Commission. *Exposé sur l'évolution de la situation sociale dans la Communauté en 1961, op. cit.*, p. 155.

8. *Ibid.,* p. 145.

9. *Ibid.,* p. 149.

10. *Ibid.,* p. 141.

11. *Ibid.,* p. 140

12. European Coal and Steel Community. *Treaty Establishing the European Coal and Steel Community* (Paris, April 18, 1951), p. 11.

13. Communauté Européenne Du Charbon et de l'Acier, Haute Autorité, *Ile Rapport General sur l'activité de la Communauté* (Luxembourg, 1963), p. 486.

14. *Ibid.,* p. 479.

15. *Ibid.,* p. 484.

16. *Ibid.,* p. 488.

17. *Ibid.,* p. 493.

18. *Ibid.,* p. 491.

19. *Ibid.,* p. 496.

20. "Manpower Conservation Program Intensified As More Than Half of New York City Youth Found Unqualified for Military Service," Press Release from U. S. Department of Labor, May 17, 1964.

21. *Chicago Daily News,* Editorial, May 26, 1964.

22. *Ibid.*

23. Gunnar Myrdal, *Challenge to Affluence,* (New York: Random House, 1963), pp. 25–26.

24. *Ibid.,* p. 26.

25. *New York Times,* December 14, 1963, p. 24.

CHAPTER 4: CONDITIONS OF EMPLOYMENT

1. European Economic Community: *Treaty Establishing the European Economic Community* (Rome, 1957), p. 59.

2. *Ibid.,* p. 60.

3. European Economic Community. *Bulletin of the European Economic Community* (Brussels, June, 1961), p. 39.

4. European Community. *Bulletin from the European Community* (Washington, D.C., June, 1961), p. 5.

5. European Economic Community, *Bulletin of the European Economic Community* (Brussels, August, 1962), p. 33.

6. *Ibid.,* p. 61.

7. European Economic Community. *Bulletin of the EEC* (Brussels, December, 1962), p. 31.

8. Communauté Économique Européene. *Programme d'action de la Communauté pendant la deuxième Étape* (Bruxelles, 24 Octobre, 1962), pp. 20, 21.

9. European Economic Community. *Sixth General Report on the Activities of the Community* (Brussels, June, 1963), pp. 49–52.

10. European Economic Community. *Bulletin of the EEC* (Brussels, March, 1964), pp. 38, 39.

11. *Ibid.*, pp. 39, 40.

12. European Economic Community. *Bulletin of the EEC* (Brussels, May, 1964), p. 22.

13. "Community Worker Migration Follows Supply-Demand," *European Community* (Washington, D.C., July, 1964), p. 6.

14. European Economic Community. *Treaty Establishing the European Economic Community, op. cit.,* Article 118, p. 113.

15. *Ibid.*, p. 60.

16. European Community. *Bulletin from the European Community* (Washington, D.C., December, 1962), p. 6.

17. *European Community, op cit.* (Washington, D.C., October, 1963), p. 13.

18. *Bulletin from the European Community* (Washington, D.C., October-November, 1962), p. 8.

19. European Economic Community. *Seventh General Report* (Brussels, June, 1964), pp. 127, 128.

20. *European Community, op. cit.* (August, 1960), p. 8.

21. *Bulletin of the European Economic Community* (Brussels, September-October, 1961), p. 69.

22. European Economic Community. *Bulletin of the EEC* (Brussels, September, 1962), p. 54.

23. European Economic Community. *Seventh General Report, op. cit.* (Brussels, June, 1964), p. 246.

24. *Treaty Establishing the European Economic Community, op. cit.,* Article 117, p. 113.

25. Giuseppe Petrilli, "The Social Policy of the Commission," *Bulletin of the European Economic Community, op. cit.,* (May, 1959), pp. 5–9.

26. *Bulletin from the European Community, op. cit.* (December, 1961), p. 2.

27. European Economic Community. *The First Stage of the Common Market* (July, 1962), p. 75.

28. *Bulletin from the European Community, op. cit.* (December, 1961), p. 7.

29. "Report Shows Women's Status Improving in Community," *Bulletin from the European Community, op. cit.* (May, 1964), p. 10.

30. "Progress Toward 40-Hour Week," *Bulletin from the European Community* (Washington, D.C., December, 1961), p. 7.

31. *Treaty Establishing the European Economic Community, op. cit.,* pp. 113, 114.

32. *Bulletin of the European Economic Community, op. cit.* (January, 1962), pp. 86, 87.

33. *Bulletin of the European Community, op. cit.* (August, 1962), p. 60.

34. European Coal and Steel Community. *Treaty Establishing the European Coal and Steel Community* (Paris, 1951), pp. 47, 48.

35. Louis Lister. *Europe's Coal and Steel Community* (New York: Twentieth Century Fund, 1960), p. 396.

36. Communauté Européenne du Charbon et de l'Acier. *Bulletin de la Communauté Européenne du Charbon et de l'Acier* (Luxembourg, Fevrier, 1961), p. 48.

37. Communauté Européenne du Charbon et de l'Acier. *Neuvième Rapport General* (Luxembourg, 1961), p. 286.

38. European Coal and Steel Community. *12th General Report* (Luxembourg, March, 1964), p. 340.

39. *Ibid.,* p. 338.

40. Louis Lister, *Europe's Coal and Steel Community, op.cit.,* pp. 400, 401.

41. Communauté Européenne du Charbon et de l'Acier. *Obstacles a la Mobilite des Travailleurs et Problemes Sociaux de Readaptation* (Luxembourg, Fevrier, 1956), p. 16.

42. *Ibid.* pp. 38, 39.

43. *Ibid.,* p. 37.

44. *Ibid.,* pp. 40, 41.

45. *Ibid.,* p. 42.

46. *Ibid.,* pp. 45, 46.

47. *Ibid.,* p. 46.

48. *Ibid.,* p. 47.

49. *Ibid.,* pp. 19, 20.

50. Communauté Européenne du Charbon et de l'Acier. *11ᵉ Rapport General* (Luxembourg, Mai, 1963), pp. 465, 466.

51. *Ibid.,* p. 467.

52. *Ibid.,* p. 468.

53. Communauté Européenne du Charbon et de l'Acier. *Neuvième Rapport General* (Luxembourg, 1961), p. 254.

54. *Bulletin de la Communauté Européenne du Charbon et de l'Acier. Résumé Du Douzième Rapport General,* No. 49 (Luxembourg, 1964), p. 54.

55. Communauté Européenne du Charbon et de l'Acier. *Dixième Rapport General* (Luxembourg, 1962), p. 498.

56. Communauté Européenne du Charbon et de l'Acier. *11ᵉ Rapport General* (Luxembourg, Mai, 1963), p. 523.

57. "High Authority President Proposed New Talks on Miners' Code," *European Community* (Washington, D.C., August-September, 1964), p. 12.

58. Communauté Européenne du Charbon et de l'Acier. *Dixième Rapport General, op. cit.,* pp. 484, 485.

59. "Progress Toward 40-Hour Week," *Bulletin from the European Community* (Washington, D.C., December, 1961), p. 7.

60. *Dixième Rapport General, op. cit.,* pp. 485, 486.

61. European Coal and Steel Community, *12th General Report* (Luxembourg, 1964), pp. 348–353.

62. European Community (Washington, D.C., August-September, 1964), p. 11.

63. R. A. Gordon, "Some Comments on Employment Policy in Europe and the United States," *Lessons From Foreign Labor Market Policies,* U.S. Congress, Senate, Committee on Labor and Public Welfare, *Volume 4 of Selected*

Readings in Employment and Manpower, 88th Congress, 2d Session, 1964, p. 1586.

64. Eileen Shanahan, "Rate of Jobless Is Reduced to 4%, Lowest Since '57," *The New York Times,* Feb. 9, 1966.

65. "Selective Unemployment," Ed., *The New York Times,* January 31, 1966.

CHAPTER 5: INDUSTRIAL HEALTH AND SAFETY

1. European Economic Community. *Treaty Establishing the European Economic Community* (Rome, 1957), pp. 113, 114.

2. *Ibid.,* p. 138.

3. *Ibid.,* pp. 174, 175.

4. European Economic Community. *Sixth General Report on the Activities of the Community* (Brussels, June, 1963), p. 185.

5. European Economic Community. *Bulletin of the European Economic Community* (Brussels, July, 1962), p. 55.

6. European Economic Community. *Sixth General Report, op. cit.,* p. 185.

7. European Economic Community. *Bulletin of the European Economic Community* (Brussels, January, 1962), p. 87.

8. Communauté Économique Européenne. *Exposé sur l'évolution de la situation sociale dans la Communauté en 1962* (Bruxelles, Juillet, 1963), p. 217.

9. *Ibid.,* p. 219.

10. *Ibid.,* p. 217.

11. European Economic Community. *Sixth General Report, op. cit.,* p. 186.

12. *Bulletin of the European Economic Community* (Brussels, July, 1962), *op. cit.,* p. 55.

13. European Community. *Bulletin from the European Community* (Washington, D.C., June-July, 1962), p. 15.

14. *Bulletin of the European Economic Community* (Brussels, July, 1962), *op. cit.,* p. 66.

15. *Ibid.,* p. 65.

16. *Sixth General Report, op. cit.,* p. 187.

17. *Bulletin from the European Community* (Washington, D.C., June-July, 1962), *op. cit.,* p. 15.

18. European Coal and Steel Community. *Treaty Establishing the European Coal and Steel Community* (Paris, April 18, 1951), Article 49, pp. 32, 33.

19. *Ibid.,* Article 3, p. 12.

20. *Ibid.,* Article 46, p. 31.

21. *Ibid.,* Article 55, p. 35.

22. Communauté Européenne Du Charbon et de l'Acier. *Huitième Rapport General—1960* (Luxembourg, 1960), p. 343.

23. Communauté Européenne Du Charbon et de l'Acier. *Bulletin de la Communauté Européenne du Charbon et de l'Acier* (Luxembourg, Février, 1961), p. 51.

24. *Huitième Rapport General—1960, op. cit.,* p. 343.

25. *Ibid.,* p. 332.

26. Communauté Européenne Du Charbon et de l'Acier. *11e Rapport Général sur l'Activité de la Communauté* (Luxembourg, Mai, 1963), pp. 551–552.

27. European Coal and Steel Community. *Report on the Activities of the High Authority* (Luxembourg, November, 1955), p. III–6.

28. *11ᵉ Rapport General, op. cit.,* p. 544.

29. Communauté Européenne Du Charbon el de l'Acier, *Dixième Rapport Général Sur L'Activité De La Communauté* (Luxembourg, 1962), p. 517.

30. Communauté Européenne Du Charbon et de l'Acier, *Bulletin de la Communauté Européenne du Charbon Et De L'Acier.* (Luxembourg, Décembre, 1961), p. 44.

31. Communauté Européenne Du Charbon et de l'Acier. *Bulletin de la Communauté Du Charbon Et De l'Acier* (Luxembourg, 3ᵉ trimestre, 1962), p. 70.

32. *Ibid.*

33. Communauté Européenne Du Charbon et de l'Acier, *Dixième Rapport Général* (Luxembourg, 1962), p. 516.

34. *11ᵉ Rapport Général, op. cit.,* p. 548.

35. *Dixième Rapport Général, op. cit.,* pp. 515, 516.

36. *11ᵉ Rapport Général op. cit.,* p. 547.

37. *Dixième Rapport Général, op. cit.,* p. 520.

38. *Huitième Rapport Général, op. cit.,* p. 334.

39. Communauté Européenne Du Charbon et de l'Acier. *Bulletin de la Communauté Européenne du Charbon et de l'Acier* (Luxembourg, Avril, 1962), p. 41.

40. *Bulletin de la Communauté Européenne du Charbon et de L'Acier* (Décembre, 1961), *op. cit.,* p. 45.

41. *Dixième Rapport Général, op. cit.,* p. 513.

42. *11ᵉ Rapport Général, op. cit.,* p. 553.

43. Communauté Européenne. *Guide Des Communautés Européennes* (Bruxelles-Luxembourg, Avril, 1962), p. 101.

44. *11ᵉ Rapport Général, op. cit.,* p. 555.

45. Communauté Européenne Du Charbon et de l'Acier. *Bulletin de la Communauté Européenne du Charbon et de l'Acier* (Luxembourg, 2ᵉ trimestre, 1962), p. 68.

46. Communauté Européenne du Charbon et de l'Acier. *Bulletin de la Communauté Européenne du Charbon et de l'Acier* (Luxembourg, Avril, 1962), p. 41.

47. *11ᵉ Rapport Général, op. cit.,* p. 560.

48. *Ibid.,* p. 559.

49. *Huitième Rapport Général, op cit.,* pp. 342, 343.

50. *Ibid.,* p. 350.

51. *11ᵉ Rapport Général, op. cit.,* p. 550.

52. Communauté Européenne Du Charbon et de l'Acier. *Bulletin de la Communauté Européenne du Charbon et de l'Acier* (Luxembourg, Juin, 1960), p. 45.

53. *Huitième Rapport Général, op. cit.,* pp. 340, 341.

54. *Bulletin de la Communauté du Charbon et de l'Acier* (Février, 1961), *op. cit.,* p. 51.

55. *Dixième Rapport Général, op. cit.,* pp. 518, 519.

56. *11ᵉ Rapport Général, op. cit.,* p. 549.

57. *Dixième Rapport Général, op. cit.,* p. 522.

58. *Huitième Rapport Général, op. cit.,* p. 344.

59. *11ᵉ Rapport Général, op. cit.,* p. 543.

60. Euratom. *Treaty Establishing the European Atomic Energy Community* (Brussels, 1957), p. 38.

61. *Ibid.*

62. *Ibid.,* Article 219, p. 126.

63. *Ibid.,* Article 33, p. 39.

64. *Ibid.,* Article 81, p. 61.

65. Euratom. *First General Report on the Activities of the Community* (Brussels, September 21, 1958), pp. 70, 71.

66. Euratom. *Second General Report on the Activities of the Community* (Brussels, March 14, 1959), p. 75.

67. *Ibid.,* p. 76.

68. *Ibid.,* p. 78.

69. Euratom. *Sixth General Report on the Activities of the Community* (Brussels, March, 1963), p. 153.

70. Euratom. *Septième Rapport Général sur l'activité de la Communauté* (Bruxelles, Mars, 1964), p. 65.

71. Euratom. *Troisième Rapport Général sur l'activité de la Communautè* (Bruxelles, 12 Avril, 1960), pp. 84, 85.

72. Euratom. *Sixth General Report on the Activities of the Community* (Brussels, March, 1963), pp. 161, 162, 163.

73. *Ibid.,* p. 164.

CHAPTER 6: TRENDS IN WAGE STANDARDS

1. The European Economic Community. *Treaty Establishing the European Economic Community* (Rome, 1957), p. 113.

2. *Ibid.,* p. 167.

3. "Social Progress Gathers Momentum," *Bulletin from the European Community* (Washington, December, 1961), p. 6.

4. "Labor Costs in the EEC," *Bulletin from the European Community* (Washington, March–April, 1962), p. 7.

5. "Enquiry Into Industrial Wages in the European Economic Community," *Bulletin of the EEC* (Brussels, March, 1962), pp. 27–29.

6. "How Well Off are European Workers?" *European Community* (Washington, D. C., April–May, 1963), pp. 16, 17.

7. European Economic Community. *Seventh General Report* (Brussels, June, 1964), p. 251.

8. Communauté Économique Européenne. *Exposé sur l'evolution de la situation sociale dans la Communauté, en 1963* (Bruxelles, Juillet, 1964), pp. 97–103.

9. European Coal and Steel Community. *Treaty Establishing the European Coal and Steel Community* (Paris, April 13, 1951), Article 68, p. 46.

10. European Coal and Steel Community. *Report on the Activities of the High Authority* (Luxembourg, 1955), p. III, 4.

11. Communauté Européenne du Charbon et de l'Acier. *Etudes et Documents Comparaison Des Revenus Reels Des Travailleurs Des Industries De La Communauté* (Luxembourg, 1956), p. 14.

12. *Ibid.,* p. 15.
13. *Ibid.,* p. 143.
14. *Ibid.,* p. 144.
15. *Ibid.,* p. 145.
16. *European Community* (Washington, April, 1963), pp. 16, 17.
17. Office Statistique Des Communautés Européennes. *Informations Statistiques* (Bruxelles, Janvier, Février, 1960), p. 14.
18. *Ibid.,* p. 15.
19. *Ibid.*
20. *Ibid.,* p. 16.
21. *Ibid.*
22. *Ibid.,* p. 17.
23. *Ibid.,* p. 18.
24. *Ibid.*
25. *Ibid.,* p. 19.
26. *Ibid.,* p. 20.
27. *Ibid.,* pp. 22, 23.
28. *Communauté Européenne du Charbón et de l'Acier. Dixième Rapport Général* (Luxembourg, 1962), pp. 471–476.
29. U. S. President. *Economic Report of the President* (Washington, D.C., January, 1964), Table C-29, p. 242.
30. *Ibid.,* Table C-27, p. 240.
31. *Ibid.,* p. 58.
32. *Ibid.,* pp. 56, 57.
33. Gunnar Myrdal, *Challenge to Affluence* (New York: Pantheon Press, 1963), p. 34.
34. Michael Harrington, *The Other America* (New York: The MacMillan Company, 1962), p. 139.
35. *Ibid.,* p. 145.
36. *Ibid.,* p. 104.

CHAPTER 7: IMPROVING PATTERNS FOR SOCIAL SECURITY

1. European Economic Community. *Treaty Establishing the European Economic Community, op. cit.,* pp. 113, 114.
2. *Ibid.,* p. 61.
3. European Economic Community. "Regulation No. 3 of the European Economic Community Concerning Social Security for Migrant Workers" (Brussels, September 25, 1958). (Mimeographed)
4. European Economic Community. "Regulation No. 4 of the European Economic Community to determine the manner of the Regulation No. 3 concerning social security for migrant workers and to supplement the said provisions" (Brussels, December 3, 1958). (Mimeographed)
5. Regulation No. 3, *op. cit.,* p. 29.
6. European Economic Community. *Supplement to the Bulletin of the European Economic Community* (Brussels, December, 1961), p. 28.
7. *Ibid.,* p. 36.
8. European Economic Community. *Bulletin of the EEC* (Brussels, June, 1961), p. 44.

9. *Supplement to the Bulletin of the European Economic Community, op. cit.*, pp. 27–36.

10. *Bulletin of the EEC* (June, 1961), *op. cit.*, p. 44.

11. European Economic Community. *Bulletin of the EEC* (Brussels, September–October, 1963), p. 55.

12. *Bulletin of the European Economic Community* (Brussels, May, 1959), p. 11.

13. *Supplement to Bulletin of the European Economic Community* (December, 1961), *op. cit.*, p. 34.

14. *Bulletin of the European Economic Community* (July, 1962) *op. cit.*, p. 43.

15. *Bulletin of the EEC* (Brussels, March, 1962), p. 60.

16. European Economic Community. *Seventh General Report* (Brussels, June, 1964), p. 241.

17. "Regulation No. 3," *op. cit.*, p. 21.

18. *Bulletin of the EEC* (Brussels, January, 1961), pp. 57, 58.

19. *Ibid.*, April, 1961, p. 45.

20. *Ibid.*, September–October, 1961, pp. 71, 72.

21. *Ibid.*, September, 1962, p. 52.

22. *Ibid.* (February, 1964), pp. 35, 36.

23. *Ibid.* (January, 1962), p. 55.

24. *Bulletin of the EEC, op. cit.* (July–August, 1961), p. 70.

25. *Ibid.* (July, 1962), p. 43.

26. *Ibid.* (March, 1961), p. 40.

27. *Ibid.* (June, 1961), p. 46.

28. *Treaty Establishing the European Economic Community, op. cit.*, p. 113.

29. *Bulletin from the European Community, op. cit.* (December, 1961), p. 7.

30. *Bulletin of the EEC, op. cit.* (February, 1962), p. 70.

31. *Ibid.* (December, 1962), p. 30.

32. *Ibid.* (April, 1964), p. 27.

33. Communauté Économique Européenne, *Troisième Rapport Général* (Bruxelles, Mai, 1960), pp. 215, 216.

34. *Treaty Establishing the European Coal and Steel Community, op. cit.*, p. 48.

35. *Ibid.*, pp. 46, 47.

36. *Ibid.*, p. 12.

37. Communauté Européenne du Charbon et de l'Acier, *Dixième Rapport Général* (Luxembourg, 1962), pp. 470, 471.

38. *Bulletin de la Communauté Européenne du Charbon et de l'Acier* (Luxembourg, October, 1960), p. 50.

39. Communauté Européenne du Charbon et de l'Acier, *Dixième Rapport Général* (Luxembourg, 1962), pp. 493, 494.

40. *Ibid.*, p. 493.

41. *Ibid.*, pp. 481, 482.

42. *Ibid.*, p. 483.

43. *Ibid.*, pp. 482, 483.

44. *Ibid.*, pp. 483, 484.

45. Communauté Européenne du Charbon et de l'Acier. *Neuvième Rapport*

Général sur l'Activité de la Communauté (Luxembourg, 1961), p. 310.

46. Communauté Européenne du Charbon et de l'Acier. *Dixième Rapport Général* (Luxembourg, 1962), p. 492.

47. *Ibid.,* pp. 492–496.

48. *Treaty Establishing the European Coal and Steel Community, op. cit.,* Article 69, p. 48.

49. *Bulletin de la Communauté Européenne du Charbon et de l'Acier, op. cit.,* 2e Trimestre, 1962, pp. 62, 63.

50. Communauté Européenne du Charbon et de l'Acier. *11ᵉ Rapport Général, op. cit.,* pp. 515–517.

51. The European Economic Community. *Bulletin of the EEC* (Brussels, February, 1963), p. 53.

52. Communautés Européennes. Conference Européenne Sur La Sécurité Sociale. *Rapport, Theme 1: Extension Du Champ D'Application De La Sécurité Sociale* (Bruxelles, 1962), p. 144.

53. Communautés Européennes. *Rapport, Theme 3: Possibilitiés D'Harmonization Des Prestations De Sécurité Sociale* a) Prestations maladie—maternité, *op. cit.,* pp. 41–43.

54. *Prestation invalidité—viellesse—survivants, op. cit.,* p. 80.

55. *Prestations accidents du travail et maladié professionelles, op. cit.,* p. 102.

56. *Prestations familiales, op. cit.,* p. 80.

57. *Prestations chômage, op. cit.,* pp. 48, 49.

58. Communauté Économique Européenne. *Etude sur la physionomie actuelle de la sécurité sociale dans les pays de la CEE* (Bruxelles, 1962), p. 2.

59. *Ibid.,* pp. 126–129.

60. Dorothy McCammon and A. M. Skolnik, "Workmen's Compensations Measures of Accomplishment," *Social Security Bulletin,* XVII, No. 3 (March, 1954), p. 7.

61. Ellen J. Perkins, "Unmet Needs in Public Assistance," *Social Security Bulletin,* XXIII, No. 4 (April, 1960), p. 6.

62. "Johnson To Push Labor-Aid Plans," *New York Times,* January 8, 1965.

CHAPTER 8: HOUSING DEVELOPMENTS FOR WORKERS

1. The European Economic Community. *Treaty Establishing the European Community* (Rome, 1957), p. 113.

2. European Economic Community. *Bulletin of the EEC* (Brussels, April, 1961) p. 46.

3. *Ibid.,* December, 1961, p. 46.

4. Communauté Économique Européenne. *Synthese Des Rapports Etablis sur les Conditions De Logement des Travailleurs Migrants Dans Trois Pays De La CEE* (Bruxelles, 1961), p. 1.

5. *Ibid.,* pp. 30–36.

6. Communauté Économique Européenne Commission. *Programme d'Action de la Communauté Pendant la Deuxième Étape* (Bruxelles, 24 Octobre 1962), p. 57.

7. European Economic Community. *Bulletin of the EEC* (Brussels, December, 1963), p. 36.

8. *Bulletin of the EEC, op. cit.*, August, 1963, p. 33.

9. Communauté Économique Européenne. *Les Besoins En Logements—Les Methodes d'Evaluation* (Bruxelles, 16–19 Decembre 1963), pp. 62, 63.

10. Communauté Économique Européenne. *La Demande et sa Solvabilite— l'Analysis Des Facteurs* (Bruxelles, 16–19 Decembre, 1963), pp. 28, 29.

11. Communauté Économique Européenne. *Les Conditions d'Attribution Des Logements Sociaux Locatifs* (Bruxelles, 16–19 Decembre 1963), p. 1.

12. *Ibid.*, pp. 26–28.

13. Communauté Économique Européenne. *Exposé sur l'évolution de la situation sociale dans la Communauté en 1963* (Bruxelles, Juillet 1964), pp. 249–253.

14. European Coal and Steel Community. *Treaty Establishing the European Coal and Steel Community* (Paris, 1951), p. 12.

15. Communauté Européenne du Charbon et de l'Acier. *Obstacles a la Mobilite Des Travailleurs et Problemes Sociaux de Readaptation* (Luxembourg, 1956), p. 41.

16. *Ibid.*, p. 65.

17. Communauté Européenne du Charbon et de l'Acier. *Informations Statistiques* (Luxembourg, Mai, Juin, 1959), pp. 61–74.

18. Communauté Européenne du Charbon et de l'Acier. *Premiere Programme de Constructions Expérimentales* (Luxembourg, 1958), p. 9.

19. European Coal and Steel Community. *Report on the Activities of the High Authority* (Luxembourg, November, 1955), p. III-5.

20. Communauté Européenne du Charbon et de l'Acier. *Deuxième Programme de Constructions Expérimentales* (Luxembourg, 1962), p. 9.

21. Communauté Européenne du Charbon et de l'Acier. *Neuvième Rapport Général sur l'Activité de la Communauté* (Luxembourg, 1961), pp. 340, 341.

22. *European Community* (Washington, D. C., January, 1964), p. 11.

23. Communauté Européenne du Charbon et de l'Acier. *Résultats du Concours d'Architecture* (Luxembourg, 1960), p. 7.

24. Communauté Européenne du Charbon et de l'Acier. "Concours d'Architecture (Plans De Logements—Types)," *Huitième Rapport Général Sur l'Activité de la Communauté* (Luxembourg, 1960), pp. 324, 325.

25. European Coal and Steel Community. *Report on the Activities of the High Authority* (Luxembourg, November, 1955), *op cit.*, p. III, 6.

26. Communauté Européenne du Charbon et de l'Acier. *Dixième Rapport Général Sur l'Activité de la Communauté* (Luxembourg, 1962), pp. 501–506.

27. *Ibid.*, pp. 502–506.

28. Communauté Européenne du Charbon et de l'Acier. *Bulletin de la Communauté Européenne du Charbon et de l'Acier* (Luxembourg, 2e Trimestre, 1962), p. 65.

29. *European Community* (Washington, January, 1965), p. 4.

30. *Ibid.* (January, 1964), p. 11.

31. Communauté Européenne du Charbon et de l'Acier. *Bulletin de la Communauté Européenne du Charbon et de l'Acier* (Luxembourg, 1964), No. 50, p. 80.

32. Michael Harrington, *The Other America* (New York: The Macmillan Company, 1962), p. 139.

33. *Ibid.*, pp. 139, 140.

34. *Ibid.,* p. 148.

35. Gunnar Myrdal. *Challenge to Affluence,* (New York: Random House, 1963), p. 42.

36. "U. S. Study Finds Housing Gains for Families in Urban Renewal," *The New York Times,* March 19, 1965.

37. Michael Harrington. *The Other America, op. cit.,* p. 154.

38. "Excerpts from the President's Message on Housing," *The New York Times,* March 3, 1965, p. 30.

39. Lawrence O'Kane. "President's Message on Housing," *The New York Times,* March 4, 1965.

40. "The Cities: A Small Beginning," ed., *The New York Times,* March 3, 1965.

CHAPTER 9: ADVANCEMENT OF REGIONAL LABOR PROGRAMS

1. Walter Hallstein, "Inaugural Discours," *Conférence Sur les Économies Régionales,* Communauté Économique Européenne (Bruxelles, 6–8 Decembre, 1961), Vol. 1, p. 15.

2. European Economic Community. *Treaty Establishing the European Economic Community, op. cit.,* p. 17.

3. Walter Hallstein, *op. cit.,* p. 13.

4. *Ibid.,* pp. 14–18.

5. *Ibid.,* p. 9.

6. Robert Marjolin, "Rapport Introductif," *Conférence Sur les Économies Régionales, op. cit.,* pp. 21–33.

7. J. Milhau, "La Participation des Instituts Regionaux d'Études a l'Élaboration et à la Mise en Oeuvre de Programmes Régionaux" *Conferénce Sur les Économies Régionales, op. cit.,* p. 441.

8. G. Martinoli et Dr. G. De Rita, "Problèmes de la Main d'Oeuvre et de la Formation Professionelle dans le Midi de l'Italie." *Conférence Sur les Économies Régionales, op. cit.,* p. 107.

9. *Ibid.,* pp. 127, 128.

10. Sicco Mansholt, "Intervention," *Conférence Sur les Économies Régionales, op. cit.,* Vol. II, pp. 12, 13.

11. Hans Von der Groeben, "Intervention," *Ibid.,* p. 21.

12. *Ibid.,* p. 22.

13. M. B. Motte, "Intervention," *Ibid.,* p. 43.

14. M. J. Kulakowski, "Intervention," *Ibid.,* p. 45.

15. *Treaty Establishing the European Economic Community, op. cit.,* p. 118.

16. Robert Marjolin, "Rapport de Synthèse Final," *Conférence Sur Les Économies Régionales,* Vol. II, *op. cit.,* pp. 60–62.

17. European Economic Community, *Bulletin from the European Community* (Washington, D. C., December, 1961), p. 8.

18. *Ibid.*

19. *Ibid.* (October, 1963), p. 7.

20. Communauté Économique Européenne. *Objectifs et Methodes de la Politique Regionale dans la Communauté Européenne* (Bruxelles, 23, Mars 1964), p. 4.

21. *Ibid.,* p. 13.

22. *Ibid.,* pp. 17–19.

23. *Ibid.,* pp. 22–25.

24. Communauté Économique Européenne. *Moyens de la Politique Régionale dans les Etats Membres de la C.E.E.* (Bruxelles, 24 Mars 1964), p. 44.

25. *Ibid.,* pp. 142, 143.

26. Communauté Économique Européenne. *L'Adaptation des Régions d'Ancienne Industrialisation* (Bruxelles, 25 Mars 1964), pp. 17, 18.

27. *Ibid.,* pp. 19, 20.

28. *Ibid.,* pp. 61–64.

29. *Ibid.,* p. 87.

30. "EEC Commission Prepares Regional Policy Proposals," *European Community* (Washington, D. C., August–September, 1964), p. 6.

31. Communauté Économique Européenne, *Premiere Communication De La Commission Sur La Politique Regionale Dans La Communauté Économique Européenne* (Bruxelles, 11 Mai, 1965).

32. European Coal and Steel Community. *Treaty Establishing the European Coal and Steel Community, op. cit.,* p. 31.

33. Communauté Européenne du Charbon et de l'Acier. *Etudes et Documents. Obtacles a la Mobilite Des Travailleurs et Problemes Sociaux de Readaptation* (Luxembourg 1956), p. 22.

34. J. F. Gravier. *Auvergne-Aquitaine, Études Régionales d'Emploi* (Luxembourg: Communauté Européenne du Charbon et de l'Acier, 1957), pp. 5, 6.

35. *Ibid.,* p. 68.

36. *Treaty Establishing the European Coal and Steel Community, op. cit.,* p. 36.

37. Photostat of "Revision of Article 56 of the Treaty of Paris." (Approved by Court of Justice, March 4, 1960, and by the European Parliamentary Assembly, March 29, 1960).

38. "Discours de M. Piero Malvestiti, President de la Haute Autorité devant Assemblée Parlementaire Européenne a Strasbourg 27 Juin 1960" (Bruxelles, 1960), pp. 8, 9.

39. "Reconversion," *Bulletin de la Communauté Européenne du Charbon et de l'Acier* (Luxembourg, Octobre, 1960), p. 48.

40. *Ibid.*

41. "Reconversion," *Bulletin de la Communauté Européenne du Charbon et de l'Acier* (Luxembourg, Décembre, 1961), p. 42.

42. *Ibid.,* pp. 42, 43.

43. Communauté Européenne du Charbon et de l'Acier. *Huitième Rapport Général Sur l'Activité de la Communauté* (Luxembourg, 1960), p. 259.

44. *Ibid.,* p. 261.

45. Communauté Européenne du Charbon et de l'Acier. F. Vito, D. Mazzochi and L. Frey, *De La Situation Économique et de l'emploi Enterprises de l'Industrie Sidérurgique des Provinces de Brescia et Udine* (Luxembourg, 1961), p. 271.

46. *Ibid.,* p. 281.

47. *Ibid.,* p. 279.

48. "Reconversion," *Bulletin de la Communauté Européenne du Charbon et de l'Acier* (Luxembourg, Octobre, 1961), pp. 52, 53.

49. *Ibid.,* p. 52.

50. Communauté Européenne du Charbon et de l'Acier. *Dixième Rapport*

Général Sur l'Activité de la Communauté (Luxembourg, 1962), p. 465.

51. Communauté Européenne du Charbon et de l'Acier. *Etude du Dévelop-ment Économique des Régions de Charleroi, du Centre et du Borinage* (Luxembourg, 1962), pp. 7–10.

52. Communauté Européenne du Charbon et de l'Acier. *Bulletin de la Communauté Européenne du Charbon et de l'Acier* (Luxembourg 8 anne—No. 6, 1963), pp. 51, 52.

53. European Coal and Steel Community. *Arrangements to Facilitate the Establishment of New Economic Activities* (Luxembourg, 1962), p. D oo (1).

54. *Appalachia, A Report By the President's Appalachian Regional Commission, 1964* (Washington: U. S. Government Printing Office, 1964), p. XIX.

55. *Appalachia. Opportunity for Progress* (Washington: U.S. Department of Commerce, Area Redevelopment Administration, May, 1963), p. 5.

56. *Ibid.*, p. 15.

57. *Ibid.*, p. 26.

58. *Ibid.*, p. 15.

59. Rebecca R. Wise (ed.), *Rural Electric Fact Book* (Washington: National Rural Electric Cooperative Association, 1965), p. 131.

60. *Ibid.*, p. 47.

61. "Some ARA Accomplishments," *Redevelopment* (Washington: U. S. Department of Commerce—Area Redevelopment Administration, December, 1964), p. 5.

62. William L. Batt, Jr., "Economic Regions—How Big?", *Redevelopment, op. cit.*, p. 2.

63. *Ibid.*, p. 9.

64. "Johnson Asks 510 Million in New Regional Aid Plan," *The New York Times,* March 26, 1965.

65. "Appalachian Bill Becomes Law," *Redevelopment, op. cit.*, (March, 1965), pp. 1, 12.

66. *Industrial Development in the TVA Area During 1964* (Chattanooga, Tennessee: Tennessee Valley Authority, March, 1965), p. 2.

67. *TVA–1964* (Knoxville, Tennessee: Tennessee Valley Authority, 1965), p. 1.

68. Manufacturing Structure and Change in the Tennessee Valley Region, 1959–1963, (Knoxville, Tennessee: Tennessee Valley Authority, November, 1964), p. 5.

69. *Ibid.*, p. 11.

70. U. S. Department of Labor, *Manpower Report of the President* (March, 1965), p. 241.

71. *Manufacturing Structure and Change in the Tennessee Valley Region, 1959–1963, op. cit.*, p. 5.

72. *TVA–1964, op. cit.*, p. 9.

CHAPTER 10: INDUSTRIAL RELATIONS IN THE
EUROPEAN COMMUNITIES

1. European Economic Community. *Treaty Establishing the European Economic Community, op. cit.*, pp. 113, 114.

2. European Coal and Steel Community. *Treaty Establishing the European Coal and Steel Community, op. cit.,* p. 31.

3. Gerhard Boldt, *et al., Les Sources Du Droit Du Travail* (Paris: Dalloz et Sirey, 1962), pp. 5, 6.

4. Gerhard Boldt, "Rapport De Synthèse," *La Représentation des Travailleurs sur le Plan de l'Enterprise dans le Droit des Pays Membres de la C.E.C.A.,* G. Boldt *et al.* (Luxembourg: Communaute Europeenne du Charbon et de l'Acier, 1959), p. 82.

5. *Ibid.,* p. 83.

6. Jacques Piron. *Les Relations Collectives Du Travail Dans Les Pays De La C.E.E.* (Bruxelles: Federation des Industries Belges, 1962), p. 19.

7. *Ibid.,* p. 20.

8. Gerhard Boldt, "Rapport De Synthese," *op. cit.,* p. 84.

9. *Ibid.,* p. 85.

10. Jacques Piron, *Les Relations Collectives Du Travail Dans Les Pays De La C.E.E., op. cit.,* p. 20.

11. *Ibid.,* p. 21.

12. Gerhard Boldt, *op. cit.,* p. 86.

13. Jacques Piron, *op. cit.,* p. 21.

14. Gerhard Boldt, *op. cit.,* p. 86.

15. Jacques Piron, *op. cit.,* pp. 21–23.

16. Gerhard Boldt, *op. cit.,* pp. 86, 87.

17. Jacques Piron, *op. cit.,* p. 20.

18. Gerhard Boldt, *op. cit.,* p. 75.

19. Jacques Piron, *op. cit.,* pp. 3, 4.

20. Paul Durand, "Rapport De Synthèse," *La Stabilité de l'Emploi dans le Droit des Pays Membres de la C.E.C.A.,* G. Boldt *et al.* (Luxembourg: Communauté Européenne du Charbon et de l'Acier, 1958), p. 17.

21. *Ibid.,* pp. 18, 19.

22. *Ibid.,* pp. 52–54.

23. Armand Kayser, "Rapport De Synthèse," *Les Sources Du Droit Du Travail,* G. Boldt *et al., op. cit.,* p. 18.

24. *Ibid.,* pp. 19, 20.

25. *Ibid.,* p. 21.

26. Jacques Piron, *Les Relations Collectives Du Travail Dans Les Pays De La C.E.E., op. cit.,* pp. 6, 7.

27. *Ibid.,* pp. 10–13.

28. Paul Horion, "Rapport De Synthèse," *Grève Et Lock-Out,* G. Boldt *et al.* (Luxembourg: Communauté Européenne du Charbon et de l'Acier, 1961), pp. 13, 14.

29. *Ibid.,* pp. 77, 78.

30. *Ibid.,* p. 79.

31. Jacques Piron, *Les Relations Collectives Du Travail Dans Les Pays De La C.E.E., op. cit.,* pp. 13, 14.

32. *Ibid.,* pp. 15, 16.

33. *Ibid.,* p. 15.

34. *Ibid.,* pp. 15, 16.

35. *Ibid.,* pp. 23, 24.

36. *Ibid.,* pp. 25, 26.

37. Communauté Économique Européenne. *Exposé sur l'Évolution de la Situation Sociale dans la Communauté en 1963* (Bruxelles, Juillet, 1964), pp. 43, 44.

38. *Ibid.,* pp. 45, 46.

39. "The European Trade Unions Announce a Joint Action Program," *DGB News Letter* (Dusseldorf, May, 1965), p. 6.

40. Harry A. Millis and Emily Clark Brown. *From the Wagner Act to Taft-Hartley* (Chicago: University of Chicago Press, 1950), p. 104.

41. U.S. Bureau of Labor Statistics. *Bulletin No. 1395* (May, 1964), p. 48.

42. U.S. Bureau of Labor Statistics. *Monthly Labor Review,* Vol. 85 (1962), p. 1136.

43. Frank Elkouri and Edna Asper Elkouri. *How Arbitration Works* (Washington: BNA Incorporated, 1960), p. 6.

CHAPTER 11: SURVEY AND PROJECTION

1. European Economic Community. "Social Developments in the Community in 1964" (Brussels, August, 1965), p. 2. (Mimeographed)

2. *Ibid.,* p. 11.

3. *Ibid.,* p. 3.

4. *Ibid.,* p. 2.

5. *Ibid.,* p. 7.

6. *Ibid.,* p. 12.

7. *Ibid.,* p. 3.

8. *Ibid.,* p. 10.

9. *Ibid.,* p. 12.

10. *Ibid.*

11. *Ibid.,* p. 13.

12. *Ibid.*

13. *Ibid.*

14. *Ibid.,* p. 4.

15. *Treaty Establishing the European Economic Community, op. cit.,* pp. 116–121.

16. *Ibid.,* pp. 113, 114.

17. "Social Developments in the Community in 1964," *op. cit.,* p. 7.

18. *Treaty Establishing the European Economic Community, op. cit.,* p. 17.

19. "Social Developments in the Community in 1964," *op. cit.,* p. 9.

20. "Stronger Commission Powers Urged for Social Progress," *European Community* (Washington, January, 1966), p. 16.

21. Communauté Économique Européenne. *Programme d'action de la Communaute Pendant la Deuxième-Étape* (Bruxelles, 24 Octobre, 1962), p. 63.

22. European Economic Community. "The Community's Medium-Term Economic Policy" (Brussels, July 30, 1963), p. 1. (Mimeographed)

23. *Treaty Establishing the European Economic Community, op. cit.,* p. 113.

24. "The Community's Medium-Term Economic Policy," *op. cit.,* p. 2.

25. "EEC's Medium-Term Economic Policy Committee Complete Fourth Working Session" (Brussels, April 9, 1965). (Mimeographed)

26. European Economic Community. "Work of the Medium-Term Economic Policy Committee" (Brussels, April, 1965), p. 3. (Mimeographed)

27. "The Community's Medium-Term Economic Policy" *op. cit.*, p. 1.

28. "Social Developments in the Community in 1964," *op. cit.*, p. 13.

29. *Ibid.*, p. 4.

30. "Work of the Medium-Term Economic Policy Committee," *op. cit.*, p. 3.

31. "Social Developments in the Community in 1964," *op. cit.*, p. 9.

32. "Stronger Commission Powers Urged for Social Progress," *op. cit.*, p. 16.

33. "Market's Most Ambitious Undertaking Snagged," *New York Times,* January 21, 1966.

34. "Stronger Commission Powers Urged for Social Progress," *op. cit.*, p. 16.

35. "Trade Bloc Accord Cheered in France," *New York Times,* January 31, 1966.

INDEX